History Will Not Absolve Us

History Will Not Absolve Us

Orwellian Control, Public Denial, and the Murder of President Kennedy

E. Martin Schotz

Kurtz, Ulmer, & DeLucia Book Publishers
Brookline, Massachusetts
1996

ISBN 0-9653814-0-4 (cloth)
ISBN 0-9653814-1-2 (paper)

Library of Congress Catalog Card Number: 96-77807

To our children, all our children, the children of the world, who someday will want to know.

The Wayfarer

The wayfarer,
Perceiving the pathway to truth,
Was struck with astonishment.
It was thickly grown with weeds.
"Ha," he said,
"I see that no one has passed here
In a long time."
Later he saw that each weed was a singular knife.
"Well," he mumbled at last,
"Doubtless there are other roads."

Stephen Crane

On "Crimestop"

The first and simplest stage of discipline, which can be taught even to young children, is called in Newspeak, *Crimestop*. *Crimestop* means the faculty of stopping short, as though by instinct, at the threshold of any dangerous thought. It includes the power of not grasping analogies, of failing to perceive logical errors, of misunderstanding the simplest arguments if they are inimical to Ingsoc, and of being bored or repelled by any train of thought which is capable of leading in a heretical direction. *Crimestop*, in short, means protective stupidity.

George Orwell, *1984*

On Belief Versus Knowledge

It is so important to understand that one of the primary means of immobilizing the American people politically today is to hold them in a state of confusion in which anything can be believed but nothing can be known, nothing of significance that is.

And the American people are more than willing to be held in this state because to *know* the truth — as opposed to only *believe* the truth — is to face an awful terror and to be no longer able to evade responsibility. It is precisely in moving from belief to knowledge that the citizen moves from irresponsibility to responsibility, from helplessness and hopelessness to action, with the ultimate aim of being empowered and confident in one's rational powers.

Unpublished letter, E. Martin Schotz to Vincent J. Salandria, May 14, 1992

Today most Americans *believe* there was a conspiracy to kill President Kennedy, but they don't *know* it. They don't want to *know* it — and our government doesn't want to *know* it and our elected representatives don't want to *know* it, because *knowing* it would mean having to do something about it. That is an awesome thought.

Gaeton Fonzi, *The Last Investigation*

Contents

Acknowledgments

This book has been a long time in coming and, as the reader will readily see, is a collective work. As with most books, the list of those to whom one wishes to express thanks is too lengthy to recite. I can name only a few.

First of all I must thank my family: my parents, who questioned arbitrary authority and conducted Talmudic dinner table discussions on justice; and my sister and brother, for unstinting support and encouragement.

Of my many teachers I must thank three. My first "college professor" was Jack Foner, Emeritus Professor of History, Colby College. His loss of a job due to political persecution in the pre-McCarthy era was my incalculable gain. For several years during my youth, our home was one of the stops of this college professor turned itinerant lecturer. Jack, with brilliance and wit, taught us all how much truth is buried in the back pages of our press and how to read between the lines. The late Karl Niebyl, Professor of Economics at San Jose State University, a profound student of revolution, taught me the role of dialectics and partisanship in knowledge. Rudi Cardona, Emeritus University Professor, Boston University, is a man whose breadth and depth of knowledge of literature is exceeded only by his warmth, sensitivity, and capacity to encourage a student to develop his own ideas and projects.

I thank a quartet of citizens who have for years tirelessly pursued the truth of President Kennedy's assassination, and who, though little known throughout the land, are individuals to whom we all owe a tremendous debt: Gaeton Fonzi, Raymond Marcus, Vincent J. Salandria, and Christopher Sharrett. Gaeton Fonzi's *The Last Investigation*, which appeared in 1993, literally served as the point of departure for this book. His example and personal encouragement to me have been very important. Ray Marcus has amassed a monumental archive of documents and correspondence, and has generously allowed me to republish anything I wished from his remarkable *Addendum B.* I first encountered Vincent Salandria in the pages of *The Legal Intelligencer* and *Liberation*, and then met him twenty-five years ago at a demonstration against the War in Vietnam. What do you say about someone with whom you talk almost daily (and sometimes more often) for twenty-five years? Chris Sharrett, whom I had not known until Salandria introduced us four years ago, is one of the unsung heroes of this work, a defiant critic of our society, a scholar with an encyclopedic knowledge of the case, a researcher who assisted the House Select Committee on Assassinations in its initial phase, but was much too honest and insightful to be tolerated for long by our government. This book would not have been published were it not for the support, encouragement, and editorial assistance which Chris has so selflessly offered.

Finally, I wish to thank Rudi Cardona, Electra Cardona, and Elaine Bresnick for reading the manuscript and offering editorial suggestions, and Sid Gottlieb, whose skills as an editor and production supervisor are responsible for the professional quality of the volume.

Preface

It is customary to address the reader in a preface by some kind of epithet. "Gentle reader" is the one used by Cervantes in his introduction to the first volume of *Don Quixote.* I shall address you as curious and attentive reader, for attention and curiosity will be required of you to do justice to the book you now hold in your hands.

Post-structural literary criticism has taken the emphasis away from the author and placed it on the text. A work of literature is a system of signs and the intellectual job commended to the reader is to interpret them. The quality of the deciphered result will depend on the reader's aptitude to capture those signs and to understand their meaning. Never has the idea been more apt as in the present case.

The author/editor presents you with an anthology of documents that deal directly or indirectly with President John F. Kennedy's assassination in November of 1963. He introduces this anthology with a letter addressed to Vincent J. Salandria, one of the first, of many, who detected flaws in the versions, officially presented, of this magnicide and who later criticized the findings of the Warren Commission after examining carefully the twenty-six volumes of its proceedings.

But make no mistake. This is not one more book presenting a theory over the "mystery" of President Kennedy's assassination. There is no mystery involved. This book presents no new "theory." What Dr. Schotz does is something that you should do yourself: analyze carefully and logically the anthology of documents and put them together, for this book is what Julio Cortàzar would have called "A Model Kit." Cortàzar wrote a novel, which he called *62 Model Kit*; in it he presented the reader with snatches of narrative in no particular sequential order which the reader was supposed to assemble into a narrative. Here, of course, we are not dealing with fiction but with history. The documents presented are realities behind a national tragedy and lead to an inescapable conclusion. If we are shocked at what we find in the end, perhaps this shock will help to open our eyes to what really happened in Dallas on that fateful day and to its aftermath.

R. Cardona
Boston, MA

History Will Not Absolve Us

Introduction

My letter to attorney Vincent Salandria, dated April 5, 1995, which serves as the center of this book, belongs to a process of investigation, study, and thought which now spans more than three decades. Part of this discussion has been carried on of late by an informal committee of correspondents of which I have had the good fortune to be a member, and of which Mr. Salandria is the clerk.[1]

---

[1]The committee has amongst its principal members Vincent J. Salandria, Ray Marcus, Christopher Sharrett, Michael Morrissey, Gaeton Fonzi, and Robert C. Dean, but there have been others.

Vincent J. Salandria is a former high school history teacher and currently counsel with the Philadelphia Board of Education. On November 2, 1964, following the release of the Warren Report, but prior to the release of the twenty-six volumes of exhibits of the Warren Commission, there appeared in *The Legal Intelligencer* (the daily newspaper of the Philadelphia Bar Association, the oldest law journal in the United States) an article by Salandria entitled "*The Warren Report*: Analysis of Shots, Trajectories, and Wounds — A Lawyer's Dissenting View" (see Appendix III). This article was the first public challenge in writing to the Warren Report. Based on Salandria's analysis of evidence in the Report, combined with statements by Commission Counsel Arlen Spector, Salandria concluded that there had been a conspiracy to murder the President. Early the following year Salandria followed up this ground breaking work with two articles which appeared in the January and March, 1965 issues of *Liberation* (see Appendix III). The March article was based on the by then available 26 volumes of Commission exhibits.

Ray Marcus, a businessman, authored and self-published *The Bastard Bullet*, a minutely detailed analysis of all the Warren Commission

Though the members of this committee vary greatly in occupation, ethnic background, political ideology, manners, temperament, and attitude toward the government, nevertheless they have been united by a common desire to confront the truth of President Kennedy's murder. The group came long ago to the conclusion that President Kennedy was the victim of a high level CIA conspiracy.[2] Thus the central focus of the April 5th letter was not an examination of the immediate conspiracy which took President Kennedy's life. Instead, the letter was an attempt to examine just how it was possible, in a supposedly open society like our own, for the CIA to murder the President and for "no one to know about it."

---

evidence concerning Commission exhibit #399, the "magic bullet." Equivalent in its implications to the articles by Salandria, *The Bastard Bullet* also proved that there had been a conspiracy.

Christopher Sharrett, an Associate Professor of Communication at Seton Hall University, investigated the assassination during the 1970s and participated in early work of the House Select Committee on Assassinations. He has published on aspects of the assassination and the media.

Michael Morrissey, an expatriate American living and teaching in Germany since the Vietnam War, authored and self-published *Looking for the Enemy* (1993), a major portion of which deals with the assassination.

Gaeton Fonzi, a journalist and former editor for *Philadelphia* magazine, also worked as an investigator for the House Select Committee on Assassinations, and authored *The Last Investigation* (New York: Thunder's Mouth Press, 1993), in which he details his years of pursuit of President Kennedy's killers, a pursuit which ultimately led to the identification of certain CIA officials involved in the assassination plot.

Robert C. Dean is a businessman and entrepreneur, a combat veteran of the Vietnam war, and a supporter of the Committee on Political Assassinations.

[2]The term "CIA" as used here signifies the entire web of U.S. military intelligence agencies, including but not limited to the Central Intelligence Agency proper, the Office of Naval Intelligence, Army Intelligence, the National Security Agency, and so on.

A few words on the unusual form of this book are in order. The book is organized as a letter supplemented by extensive annotation and numerous appendices. This structure is deliberate and flows from my concept of knowledge and my purpose in writing/editing this book.

The book is an invitation to the interested citizen to participate in the conversation of this committee and to assimilate knowledge developed by the group.[3] On entering this conversation, the ordinary reader will not be familiar with many of the issues and documents that the committee has submitted to discussion; thus, the need for extensive annotations, references, and appendices in order to provide an adequate context for understanding what is being discussed and what the conclusions are based on.

Knowledge is not something which everyone wants. It is difficult to acquire, and in order to know, one must have a desire to know. In turn, one's desire to know depends on social attitudes and social activity. To acquire knowledge one must go through the laborious process of digesting the work of others and make it one's own. One can be helped to acquire knowledge and be guided in the process, but one cannot be given it directly. The process of acquiring knowledge has no true beginning. As with life one enters in the middle of the process and must attempt to go back and pick up what has been worked out historically while at the same time carrying the process forward. That the structure of this book may be difficult for some readers to confront is not a problem in and of itself, because it is written expressly for people motivated by a desire to inform themselves through study so as to be capable of discharging their responsibilities as citizens of a true social, economic, and political democracy.

In our efforts to confront the truth of the assassination of President Kennedy we are at a very different point today than we

---

[3]While I am indebted to various members of the committee for the discovery and development of much of the material presented in this book, the organization and the overall interpretation of this material are my own and do not necessarily have the complete agreement of every member of the committee.

were thirty years ago when the first critical analyses of the Warren Report were published. Dozens of books and thousands of magazine articles have been written about this case. Almost without exception, no matter what the author's view concerning who killed President Kennedy or why, these works have directly or indirectly contributed to the public's conviction that the murder of the President is a mystery. As a result, although a vast majority of our public believes that there was a conspiracy, most people do not know this as a fact and are convinced that they can never know for sure what happened.

On both points the public is mistaken. The murder of the President is not a mystery. The nature of the conspiracy that took President Kennedy's life was from the outset quite obvious to anyone who knew how to look and was willing to do so. The same holds true today. Any citizen who is willing to look can see clearly who killed President Kennedy and why.

The fact that "no one knows this" is an example of a subtle process of Orwellian mind control which has enveloped our society and which our public has been more than willing to have foisted upon it. The process has been orchestrated by the CIA in defense of itself and the "powers that be," but it has also been critically aided by the entire spectrum of our society's intellectual and political establishments, right, center, and left.

The assertion that I and other ordinary citizens know, *know for a fact*, that there was a conspiracy and that it was organized at the highest levels of the CIA — such an assertion is likely to strike most citizens as the ravings of a fanatic, a person whose mind is closed to civilized discourse. The ordinary citizen, on reading a simple, honest, and critical analysis of the facts (see Appendix III) will typically experience an automatic psychological reaction of recoil because of the vast national process of cover-up which an honest analysis of the facts implies. "Something is wrong here. It can't be this obvious," is the natural response. It is a measure of the Orwellian mind set that pervades America today that to assert what is obvious and known (as in the tale *The Emperor's New Clothes*) triggers such a psychological reaction. In reality it is the ordinary citizen's mind which has been closed to the vast process of denial and cover-up which has pervaded our society.

Thus, my starting point is to awaken the reader to how, in an "open society" like our own, the CIA could murder the President and see to it that the crime is "covered up." Once this befuddling matter is laid bare, the reader will be freed to go back and assimilate in an unobstructed manner what has long been quite obvious and known about who killed President Kennedy and why.

As I edited the April 5th letter for publication, it seemed logical to break the letter into two parts. The reason behind the division is the transition that occurs in the course of the letter, a transition in the underlying political ideological assumptions of the analysis. Part I is an analysis of the assassination for the light it throws on the Orwellian nature of our society. This section of the letter requires of the reader no particular ideological orientation other than a commitment to truth and logic, and a willingness to confront the dictates of logical analysis of facts wherever it leads. In other words, it requires a person whose mind is not bounded by the terms of American "Crimestop." The first section deals with how our public, government, and media approached the available facts on the assassination and what this implies about the nature of our democracy.

Part II is directed toward exploring a broader issue of history, how we as a people came to be in such a state of affairs. Here a certain political ideological orientation is required of the reader, or at least a willingness to be open to a certain political ideological orientation. In my view the way in which our society reacted to the murder of its President by the CIA is part of a seamless web of historical development which has now been occurring for more than a century, ever since the destruction of the "Reconstruction" movement following the American Civil War. An awareness of this overall historical context is important if we are to appreciate the true dimensions of the political problems we face as a people.

The thirteen appendices which follow the April 5th letter provide a variety of documentary evidence as well as additional analyses. The reader will find amongst these appendices important analyses of both the "external" record as well as the "internal" record on four significant points: the development of President Kennedy's thinking and activity with regard to the

Cold War, the immediate reaction of the government of the United States to the assassination of its President, the work of the Warren Commission, and the role of *The Nation* magazine and the left/liberal establishment in the cover-up of the assassination.

The appendices begin with the text of President Kennedy's June, 1963 speech at American University. This speech provides the context of the assassination and helps to clarify Castro's view of Kennedy, which appears in Appendix II. Appendix II, a speech by Fidel Castro, constitutes a highly sophisticated analysis of the external record of the immediate reaction of the United States government and its media sources. This can be correlated with Appendix IV, where one will find an analysis of important internal data on this question. Three articles by Vincent Salandria appear in Appendix III. These articles, taken together, show the progress of his analysis of the work of the Warren Commission. He at first used only the Warren Report as a basis (the external record), and subsequently used an "internal record" of the Commission's work, the twenty-six volumes of Commission exhibits which were released in early 1965. Appendix V provides data which identifies Lee Harvey Oswald as the CIA agent he was. Appendix VI presents a novel form of analysis which casts light on how the assassination of the President was covered up.

In Appendix VII the reader will find both an analysis of the "external record" of *The Nation*'s activity as well as a detailed memoir which represents an "internal record" of *The Nation*'s attitude toward the assassination. Finally, by correlating President Kennedy's June, 1963 speech at American University (Appendix I) with Nikita Khrushchev's January 31, 1963 letter to Fidel Castro (Appendix X), the McCloy-Zorin Agreement (Appendix IX), and Castro's speech (Appendix II), one is able to correlate external as well as internal data on the significance of President Kennedy's activity with regard to the Cold War as the motivating factor for his assassination. Appendix VIII, "The Work of Ray Marcus," provides additional external as well as internal data on many questions concerning the nature of our society and its response to the assassination.

Appendices XI and XII provide psycho-social and philosophical analyses of the society's response to the assassination.

Appendix XIII is a speech by Fidel Castro to a recent United Nations-sponsored meeting. It provides a context for the continuing significance of the President's assassination.

As citizens who have turned away for thirty years from the truth of the murder of our elected head of state, we should not be surprised that today we find our nation in intellectual, political, and moral chaos.[4] Confronting the truth of President Kennedy's assassination and its cover-up is but one small step on a long path out of that chaos and toward healing, a path along which we must confront the true nature of our democracy and the reality of what our nation has become for its own citizens and for people throughout the world. Such a process of healing is not pleasant. It is a difficult and painful path, but it is a necessary one. History will not absolve us.

---

[4]This is not to minimize the significance of the assassinations of others, Malcolm X, Martin Luther King, Jr., and Robert F. Kennedy, to mention only the most prominent. On the contrary, although these other murders are by no means the focus of this study, it nevertheless casts light on them as well.

Letter to Vincent J. Salandria
April 5, 1995

by E. Martin Schotz

Dear Vince,

Confronted with a crime so high and so great that all authority intuitively protects itself by turning away, we, citizens without authority, completely independent of the power structure, must see and utter the truth. This is the significance of our little committee. We can see who killed President Kennedy and why; and equally important, how and why the American people have failed to face the truth.

To those citizens who really want to know and for the generations to come who will need to, we have a responsibility. My idea is a book which would provide the essential documents and an analytical summary with notes and references. The analytical summary follows.

PART ONE

By now there is no doubt that the President's murder was organized at the highest echelons of the CIA. Indeed it is clear to us that immediately following the assassination this was obvious to any sophisticated observer, as Castro revealed the night after the assassination in his address to the Cuban people.[1]

Noting the instantaneous response of the U.S. government, which was not to pursue the truth but to follow the transparently phony scenario of Oswald as a deranged pro-Castro leftist, a truly sophisticated observer would have seen immediately the evidence of U.S. governmental involvement in the crime. The immediate release of critical information on Oswald's "possible motives" from CIA media assets and the immediate wedding of the government to Oswald as the lone assassin reveal its cooperation from the beginning with what was obviously a prearranged plan to shield the conspirators.[2]

Since we were not sophisticated observers at the time, we needed your early articles in *The Legal Intelligencer* (1964) and then *Liberation* (1965) to settle certain questions. You established, using the government's own evidence, that without a doubt there was a conspiracy, and that the Warren Commission was clearly and consciously cooperating with the cover-up. In other words, your articles proved much more than a conspiracy to kill Kennedy, for they demonstrated that across the entire spectrum of our governmental establishment there was a systematic involvement of the civilian authorities (either actively or through acquiescence) in covering for the murderers.

[1]On the evening of November 23rd, 1963 Cuban Prime Minister Fidel Castro delivered a speech, "Concerning The Facts and Consequences of the Tragic Death of President John F. Kennedy," on Cuban TV and radio. See Appendix II for an English translation of the speech, which was released by the Cuban Mission at the United Nations shortly after it was delivered.

[2]See Appendix IV, which includes internal memoranda by Nicholas Katzenbach, Assistant to the then-Attorney General Robert Kennedy, documenting the early marrying of the new Administration and even the President's own brother to the Oswald story. There were veiled hints of opposition, one from former President Harry Truman. See Appendix VIII. See also the Castro speech, Appendix II, for analysis of immediate response of the U.S. media.

The Pseudo-Debate

All of this brings us to the real cover-up over all these years, which was not "Oswald" *per se* but rather "the debate over Oswald."[3] In this process we see the CIA following the principles of intelligence agency assassination and cover-up as outlined by Isaac Don Levine, an associate of Allen Dulles, in his analysis of the assassination of Leon Trotsky by the Soviet Union's NKVD. As Levine revealed, the classic manner by which an intelligence agency attempts to cover itself is by the use of

---

[3]Because the work of Salandria, Marcus, and several others provided proof of a conspiracy that was simple and obvious, the media had to distort the work of these critics in order to rescue the government's good name. In this effort the media resorted to Orwellian use of the term "conspiracy theorists" in referring to all Warren Commission critics, including Salandria and Marcus. While there may be many conspiracy *theorists* among the critics of the Warren Report, Salandria and Marcus were not among them. Rather they were conspiracy *provers*. But by this use of language the media were able to take *proof* of conspiracy and turned it into *theory* of a conspiracy. With *proof* turned into *theory*, *knowledge* was turned into *belief*, and the government was able to retreat to the position that perhaps the Warren Commission was mistaken, but of course no one would be "so extreme" as to claim that Earl Warren and the other Commission members were anything but honorable men. Thus was launched the thirty-plus year debate over the Warren Report.

Since the Warren Report was an obvious fraud, so was the pseudo-debate over whether there was or wasn't a conspiracy, a debate over a question which had long ago been answered definitively. This thirty-year pseudo-debate over the validity of the Warren Report has occupied the efforts and attention of many honest citizens who were taken in by it. Unwittingly many honest citizens, tricked into participation, became part of the cover-up, because the debate gave legitimacy to the notion that there was doubt and uncertainty when there really was none.

While Salandria's and Marcus' proofs of conspiracy are detailed and conclusive, it turns out that there is a much simpler and more elegant proof of conspiracy which involves the bullet holes in the back of the President's shirt and jacket. See Appendix III.

confusion and mystery. The public is allowed to think anything it wants, but is not allowed to know, because the case is shrouded in supposed uncertainty and confusion. This was and is the big lie, that virtually no one is sure who really killed President Kennedy or why.[4]

Of course over the years the terms of the "debate" have been shifted as the public has learned more and more about the case. Thus initially the phony debate was organized around the question of whether the Warren Report was accurate or not. In other words, the public was supposed to debate whether there was or wasn't a conspiracy. As this position was gradually eroded and it became evident that more and more of the public did not believe in the lone assassin theory, another aspect of the debate was developed.

The first fallback position of the government was to acknowledge that *perhaps* or *more than likely* there was a conspiracy, but if there was, the chief suspects were Fidel Castro, the KGB, or the Mafia. And while these theories were pushed, it was argued that the Warren Commission, acting in haste, had perhaps erred in missing an assassin here or there. But all this was framed as honest error.

In order to bolster the government's credibility, the government always needed some writers who would argue that the Warren Report in fact had been true, that Oswald was the lone assassin after all. Thus the "debate" was broadened and complicated, but the honor of the members of the Warren Commission was never conceded by the government. It is important to understand that for the purposes of the government it was not necessary that anyone actually be convinced that these defenders of the Warren Report were correct. It was only necessary that people believe that their writings were debatable, i.e., that there was some substance to their arguments that Oswald was the lone assassin. If that point could be debated, then

---

[4]In 1959, Isaac Don Levine authored *The Mind of the Assassin* (New York: Farrar, Straus and Cudahy, 1959). See Appendix VI for insight that it throws on the assassination of President Kennedy.

the government was safe, because the criminal conspiracy of the government of the United States to shield the assassins after the fact was obscured.

With the emergence of Jim Garrison's efforts in New Orleans to pursue those parts of the assassination conspiracy over which he had jurisdiction as Orleans Parish District Attorney, and in the face of the fact that Garrison was unflinchingly pointing directly at the CIA as the source of the assassination conspiracy, a new phase of the pseudo-debate opened. Aside from obstructing and undoing Garrison's prosecution efforts and presenting him as a self-seeking and irresponsible person,[5] the CIA and the government had to be prepared to deal with the fact that significant portions of the public might believe that the CIA had killed the President. So at this point the debate was broadened again to "consider the possibility" of CIA involvement. But of course, if it were admitted that the CIA had been involved, it would have to be presented as the act of so-called "rogue elephants" within the Agency.[6]

Eventually we had the investigation by the House of Representatives Select Committee on Assassinations, which appears to have begun with some seriousness but was quashed, a process which Fonzi documents so brilliantly in his book.

The latest round of the "debate" is currently being organized around the question of whether President Kennedy would or would not have followed the course Johnson did in escalating the War in Vietnam. Two significant players in the process are John

---

[5]Repeatedly we see the Orwellian use of language (e.g., "black is white, peace is war") by the media as a form of mind control. The one public official in the entire country who courageously pursued the truth of the assassination of the President at enormous personal and professional cost was systematically labeled "irresponsible and self-seeking."

[6]That the conspirators were not "rogue elephants" in the CIA was proven by the promotion of certain officials after the assassination whom Fonzi identified as being directly involved in the plot. See Fonzi, *The Last Investigation*, p. 273.

Newman and L. Fletcher Prouty. Both of these individuals claim to have broken their earlier allegiances with military intelligence and the CIA. Both claim to be revealing the truth of the case, and yet both narrowly focus all "debate" around Vietnam, lending weight to the "rogue elephant" theory and obscuring the true motive for the assassination and the nature of the cover-up. Very interestingly, on the other side of this "debate," arguing that there is nothing of significance in all the talk about conspiracy, is Noam Chomsky.[7] This odd position for someone who is thought of as such a left-wing radical is worthy of exploration.

Of course, as part of this "debate" around Vietnam and JFK there is the requisite Warren Commission "defense" that Oswald was the lone assassin after all. This role, currently played by Gerald Posner with his *Case Closed*, is touted by the media as serious. And for those of a more literary bent, and to complete the circus atmosphere, we have Norman Mailer's foray into the archives of the KGB, *Oswald's Tale*.

The Role of the Establishment's Left/Liberal Wing in the Cover-up

Which brings us to another very interesting, important, and revealing aspect of this case: the defense of the Warren

---

[7]Well-known left-wing radical critic of U.S. foreign policy and MIT Professor of Linguistics, Noam Chomsky has pleaded "agnosticism" on the question of whether there was a plot to kill the President, but asserts that even if there was a plot, it would not be relevant, since it had no political significance. When confronted with Salandria's articles, Chomsky took the position that he was "unconvinced," without offering any explanation as to what aspect of the analysis left him unconvinced. In correspondence decades earlier with Marcus, Chomsky seemed quite clear that there had definitely been a conspiracy. See Appendix VIII. When pressed by Morrissey in recent correspondence, he merely retreated to saying that he refused to believe that his friends in the Academy of Arts and Sciences would lie (private correspondence).

Commission by the left/liberal establishment. I have in mind such individuals as Noam Chomsky, Alexander Cockburn,[8] the editors of *The Nation* magazine,[9] and, if everyone remembers, I.F. Stone[10] as well. I think the positions of these individuals are very important because in their surprising (to us) dishonesty and willingness to cooperate with the warfare state in covering up the crime, there is obviously something to be learned.

Here some principles and insights from my clinical work in child psychiatry are relevant. It is not uncommon for me to be told that a patient's actions are out of character. Excluding those instances of organic brain disease such as epilepsy, it is never the case that the patient's actions are truly out of character. Rather the patient's true character has not been previously adequately understood.

---

[8]Regular columnist for *The Nation*, and friend of Chomsky, Cockburn has defended the Warren Report and attacked critics of the Report. Recently he has been increasingly promoted by the establishment as a leftist critic of merit.

[9]Under former editor Carey McWilliams and most recently under retired editor Victor Navasky, *The Nation* has repeatedly published defenses of the Warren Commission. See Appendix VII.

[10]Legendary critic on the left through the McCarthy period, I.F. Stone for years published *I.F. Stone's Weekly* as well as other works, including *The Hidden History of the Korean War*. In order to appreciate I.F. Stone's credentials on the left one need only look at the title of a collection of his essays issued by Random House in 1967, *In a Time of Torment: Our Most Distinguished Independent Journalist on the most Urgent Issues and Key Personalities of our Time: LBJ, the War in Vietnam, Fulbright, the Negro Revolution, the Kennedys, Malcolm X, the Left, Right, and Where Do We Go from Here*. This is not an advertisement; this is the title of the book. And, interestingly, you will find in it an essay dated December 9, 1963 in which Stone argues that "Kennedy died just in time . . . to be remembered as he would like to be remembered" and that "in the tangled dramaturgy of events, this sudden assassination was for the author the only satisfactory way out." In 1967, with everything that was known about the case, I.F. Stone republished this essay letting such words stand. To appreciate I.F. Stone's and *The Nation*'s roles in the cover-up, see Appendices VII and VIII.

The positions of Chomsky, *The Nation*, I.F. Stone, et al., must be understood from this standpoint. They are disillusioning us and in the process indicating to us that we have not previously understood their true character.

Vince, the responses of I.F. Stone, Carey McWilliams, *The Nation*, and Chomsky et al., *form a pattern!* This is not merely the individual idiosyncrasy of an arrogant intellectual who cannot admit that he is wrong. Rather I suggest that it is symptomatic of the natural response of a section of our left/liberal intelligentsia which we have not properly understood. This pattern is something to ponder over in order to understand the nature of the assassination and our society more correctly.

I know there has been a lot of feeling in the "committee," amongst those of us on the left, about these left/liberal defenders of the government cover-up. Moral outrage, bewilderment, a feeling of alienation, and disgust are all appropriate and healthy responses. But necessary as these responses are, they are not sufficient to pursue a cure, i.e., if we wish to approach matters in a clinical fashion as healers. Here Galbraith's suggestion is valuable: that we are witnesses to a strange religious/ideological rite which is alien to us, and that we must try to observe it and describe it dispassionately as would the anthropologist.[11]

What is it that we are witnessing in this assassination and in the response which the left/liberal establishment has manifested to it? That is the question we must address.

For years I, like the rest of the members of our little committee, was captivated by the notion that the CIA's murder of the President was a grievous wound to our democracy in urgent need of being exposed so the society could heal. But if this is so, how could it be that people like Carey McWilliams and I.F. Stone, who were amongst the most ardent defenders of our democracy in some of its darkest days, how could it be that such people would oppose us — not only oppose us, but rail against us, manipulate so as to deflect before the public what we were

---

[11]John Kenneth Galbraith, *The Culture of Contentment* (New York: Houghton Mifflin Company, 1992), pp. 10-12.

saying?[12] There is something very big at stake here. And I think what we are confronted with is a profound flaw in our own thinking in regard to this case.

I suggest we consider that possibly the assassination of JFK was not a wound to American democracy. It was a wound against certain political forces in our democracy, but not to the democracy itself. In fact, I submit that the assassination was totally within the framework of how American democracy works, and that this was instantly the opinion of people who were knowledgeable, sophisticated, and leading participants in the so-called democratic politics of this society.

The notion that American democracy was not wounded by the assassination of its President is supported by the fact that virtually every segment of the establishment — right, left, and center — lined up to support the mystery cover-up and participate in the pseudo-debate. Not a single member of the Kennedy Administration resigned in protest over what had been done. Not a single member of Congress resigned in protest. Not a single judge in the entire country, not to mention a single justice of the Supreme Court, resigned in protest over the role of the Chief Justice of the United States in this case. The President's brother did not resign in protest, and the entire Kennedy family publicly accepted the Warren Report, albeit with their behind-the-scenes maneuvering and their delayed and lukewarm endorsements. Not a single editor of a major newspaper resigned over being forced to swallow this obviously phony story.

Jim Garrison, the only public official in the country who took his legal responsibility seriously as a district attorney, was

---

[12]Fred Cook has written a long memorandum recounting in detail how Carey McWilliams, then Editor of *The Nation*, frustrated, blocked, delayed, and ultimately sabotaged Cook's efforts to publish a challenge to the Warren Report. This is all the more significant since at the time Cook was a regular contributor to *The Nation*, and arguably the most significant and prominent investigative reporter in the country on the U.S. military industrial complex. See Appendix VII.

systematically attacked in the press and legally persecuted.[13] Notwithstanding the homage to him which Oliver Stone's *JFK* represented, toward the end of his life, Garrison expressed doubt about whether his efforts to reveal the truth of the assassination had been worth what it had cost him.[14] What a sad commentary on our society.

But how is it possible? How can you have a democracy in which there is a coup and literally no one, not a single person in power, protests by resigning? You could have this only if it is not really a coup. You could have this only if, no matter how distasteful it may be, all these people are prepared to find what had been done ultimately acceptable. The fact that for American democracy it was acceptable for the CIA to shoot Kennedy is proven by the fact that it was accepted virtually without protest.[15]

At first glance this idea may seem disorienting, shocking, even bizarre. Is it really conceivable that it is acceptable to the entire spectrum of the governmental establishment, the entire spectrum of the university establishment, the entire spectrum of our media establishment that the CIA can very obviously carry out the murder of a president? This seems crazy. But it is what happened. It was accepted, ergo it was acceptable.

Now I think the first thing the skeptical reader is likely to

---

[13]Garrison, as the District Attorney of New Orleans, was the only public official who openly took on the CIA over the assassination, trying Clay Shaw as a co-conspirator. Garrison tried to subpoena various federal officials to testify, but the federal authorities refused to cooperate in serving the subpoenas. Salandria played a key role in identifying one of Garrison's top aides as a CIA agent who had infiltrated his office. Subsequent to the Shaw trial, Garrison was framed on charges of having ties to organized crime. He was eventually exonerated and was ultimately elected a judge.

[14]*The JFK Assassination: The Garrison Tapes*, Blue Ridge Film Trust, Vestron Video, 1992, VHS videotape.

[15]This idea is not original with the author. Nobel Peace Laureate Conor Cruise O'Brien actually first broached it. See "Veto by Assassination?" in *The Minority of One*, December, 1967.

say in reading this is, "Well, wait a second. Maybe it wasn't all that obvious. Maybe all these people didn't know the CIA had done it." So let's allow this for argument's sake. Maybe they didn't know the CIA did it. But certainly they knew there was a conspiracy. Certainly no honest person could ever accept the "single bullet theory." So then we have a situation in which all these people basically know the Warren Report is a fraud. They know there has been a criminal conspiracy to kill the President and a conspiracy after the fact to obstruct justice in the murder of the President by the government. And they choose not to find out what happened. They look the other way. They are willing to live with the CIA's confusion and mystery story cover-up. Where does that leave us? Virtually the entire establishment knows that there was a conspiracy to kill the President but chooses not to find out who did it and why. What does that say? It says that a conspiracy to kill the President and its cover-up are acceptable. Not legal, mind you. Nor moral. Upsetting? Of course. But, in the end, acceptable. The government continues to function and everyone remains in place. This is American democracy.

Now I grant you, virtually none of these people are aware that it is acceptable to them for the CIA to kill the President. If you asked them, "Is it acceptable for the CIA to kill the President?" everyone would say, "No." And they would not be lying in any conventional sense. But here we must take another page from clinical psychiatry, because what we have here is a case of what is technically termed "denial." Only in this instance we have it on a mass scale.

Let me describe this phenomenon as it presents itself in the clinical situation. I am not infrequently confronted with a psychologically disturbed family which includes an anti-social teenager, a family in which the parents tell me that what the child is doing is "totally unacceptable." And then I start looking into the situation and I find that this isn't true. Much as the parents may not like what the teenager is doing, they are so wedded to the child and their need for the child, that they are unwilling to take the steps necessary to stop the process. So in reality what the teenager is doing is acceptable, and at the same time the parents maintain in their own minds the fiction about themselves that it isn't acceptable. This is "denial" in a technical sense, a part of the psychological illness, the ideological falsity, that can exist in a family system that is complicit with, if not actually fostering, anti-social conduct by a teenager.[16]

So I think we need to go back to the beginning and look at how this case unfolded all over again. I think we need to focus particular attention on Carey McWilliams and *The Nation*. Very early on *The Nation* published Harold Feldman's article which pulled together the available evidence pointing to Oswald as a U.S. intelligence agent, and explicitly identified the government as a possible suspect in the assassination. But at the same time that *The Nation* was publishing this article, what was their editorial policy in regard to the assassination and the government? Go back and look at that editorial process.[17]

Basically, *The Nation*'s position was one of tolerance and patience, urging their readers not to rush to judgment, that Feldman's material was important but that everyone should wait to see what the Warren Commission would come up with.

At first glance this position seems fair and open-minded. However, if we think about it, we see something else. There is a big problem in *The Nation*'s position which should have been obvious to us from the outset. If there was not U.S. governmental involvement in the murder, one would expect the government to be able to investigate the assassination; but what if there was? After all, Oswald certainly looked like a low-level CIA agent. Would it be reasonable to assume that the Warren Commission could actually entertain and honestly investigate the possibility that there had been a CIA conspiracy? Did such a question ever occur to Carey McWilliams and *The Nation*? It had to. And yet nowhere did they address this question to their readers. And this is critical.

---

[16]For further details and an analysis of how the typical reporter might fall into denial of a conspiracy when confronted with Salandria's early articles, see Appendix XI.

[17]See the review of *The Nation*'s editorial process in Appendix VII.

Perhaps the Warren Commission could be expected to assess honestly a non-governmental conspiracy, but it would certainly not be in a position to investigate a governmental conspiracy, since this would amount to the government investigating itself. At a very minimum, *The Nation* had the responsibility to ask the government what steps the Commission would take to ensure an honest investigation of the possibility of a conspiracy from within the U.S. government. In failing completely to address this point, *The Nation* was not being honest with its readers. Honesty would have compelled *The Nation* to say that that section of investigation which dealt with whether a U.S. government agency itself had been involved could not be carried out by the Warren Commission and would have to be handled by some institution or group of people independent of the U.S. government. And *The Nation* could have played this role. It could have assembled the same data which Castro, Salandria, and others assembled. It could have brought together a fearless group of individuals, its own Commission completely unbeholden to the U.S. government, and asked them to provide an analysis. And, of course, if this had been done, the group would have come to the inescapable conclusion that it was obvious that the CIA had killed the President.

Clearly *The Nation* did not wish to do this. From the outset its position was in reality that if there had been a government conspiracy, it would go unchallenged. Note again that they had in fact taken this position at the same time that they were publishing Harold Feldman's article. So we are left with the unavoidable conclusion that the staunchest liberal leaders of American democracy were prepared to accept a CIA assassination of President Kennedy and not object or protest; quite to the contrary, they were fully prepared to cooperate. And indeed *The Nation*'s editorial role in the cover-up has never wavered.

Think of it this way. Try to put yourself into the shoes of McWilliams, I.F. Stone, and Chomsky. You are leading participants in this process we call American democracy. You are opinion makers. You have access to the media and the media reports what you say to the public. You are leading figures in this "civilized" process of struggle we call our democracy. You represent certain forces and they struggle against other forces, but they must conduct themselves in a civilized manner. As leaders in the left/liberal establishment you may hate the military and the CIA and not give a damn what they think of you, but you cannot afford to be indifferent to what liberal, and more importantly, moderate members of Congress or the media think of you. You certainly would not want to wind up painting Earl Warren as an enemy in this civilized discourse. You are interested in building coalitions to effect change, and moderates are part of the process. Now if you go off and start calling Earl Warren an accessory after the fact in the murder of the President, where does that leave you? It leaves you totally outside.

Go back and look at Fred Cook's memoir about his efforts to get *The Nation* to publish his piece on the case.[18] McWilliams is just silent. He doesn't respond to Cook, because he can't. Cook is a reporter, but McWilliams is more than this; he is a player. And when you're playing a game, you don't go around trashing your opponent beyond a certain point, or there is no game any more.

And that was the situation in which the left/liberal establishment found itself with the assassination. "Do we or don't we blow the whistle on this game? Because if we level with the American people over what *has* happened, there is no telling what *would* happen. People might start asking questions. We might have wholesale unrest. Or maybe some kind of right-wing reaction, maybe a pogrom on the left. . . . Better leave well enough alone and go on with our struggle by continuing the game."[19]

---

[18]See Appendix VII.

[19]Raymond Marcus, *Addendum B: Addendum to the HSCA, The Zapruder Film, and the Single Bullet Theory*, self-published, July 1995, pp. 33-40. In these pages Marcus has preserved for us a tremendously revealing report of a debate between Mark Lane and a leading liberal spokesman, A.L. Wirin, which took place on the West Coast after the release of the Warren Report. In the debate Wirin attempts to defend the Warren Commission by citing I.F. Stone's endorsement of the

Look at what Chomsky tells us: "My friends in the National Academy of Sciences are not going to lie about this."[20] I.F. Stone did the same thing. He was apoplectic over the accusation that Warren was engaging in a fraud. But that tells us Stone is in an enormous bind or he wouldn't be driven to react in such an emotional fashion.

We are thus left with a conclusion that the President's murder by the CIA was accepted throughout the entire establishment. Indeed the liberal leadership ultimately confirmed that the murder of the President by the CIA and the military could go unpunished and unrevealed without disturbing our constitutional process. It is they who made the decision that the murder of the President by the CIA would be politically acceptable. And as a result, this murder did not cause the ripple of a single resignation. It was business as usual. This is not an ideological conclusion. This is a logical conclusion based on a factual analysis of the way our democracy reacted to the crime.

But why? Why did the CIA kill Kennedy and how did we get into this situation where the murder of the President by the CIA is acceptable? These are some of the questions to which I now want to turn.

PART TWO

Up to this point my analysis has not depended on any ideological orientation, just commitment to facts and logic. We must however go beyond this level of analysis if we want to see the assassination in the context of our society as it really is. We

---

Warren Report, and with the suggestion that those who question the Report should instead feel a sense of relief that the assassination has not led to a pogrom of the left. See Appendix VIII.

[20]Unpublished letter from Chomsky to Michael Morrissey. Here Chomsky is doing the same thing Wirin did thirty years earlier. Confronted with unassailable facts, he falls back on insisting that we maintain allegiance to the honor of his colleagues.

thus turn to an aspect which inevitably draws upon a certain ideological orientation to the world.

Ten years ago I wrote a scene in a play in which Allen Dulles and JFK confront each other in heaven and Dulles insists that he was the true upholder of American values and out of his patriotic duty had Kennedy killed. Eventually in the dialogue Kennedy is won over to Dulles' position and in the end JFK accepts the assassination.[21] Curiously when I wrote this scene, I did it as a way of simply exploring the logic of certain political positions. I did not fully understand what I was writing and the full truth of the ideas being expressed there. I say this because there is one critical point in the dialogue when Dulles says to JFK in heaven, "Look Jack, suppose you'd had a stroke and died in Dealey Plaza that afternoon. Would the history of the United States be any different? We didn't take over the government. We just shot *you*." And it turns out that from the standpoint of historical truth, this claim by the fictional Dulles is quite correct. Dulles and the CIA didn't take over the government, because they didn't have to. The CIA reasoned quite correctly that basically the balance of forces would be on its side if Kennedy were removed.

Kennedy ran afoul of the CIA because he departed from the Cold War script in his dealings with the U.S.S.R., and on the critical issue of peaceful coexistence with socialism. Kennedy's movement on the peace question, his rapprochement with Khrushchev facilitated behind the scenes by Pope John XXIII, his "secret" efforts in the U.N. to move toward normalization of relations with Cuba, all of this following the Cuban Missile Crisis, was the critical point at which Kennedy "stepped over the line."

For ideological reasons, liberal opinion, which remains steeped in anti-communism and the mentality of the Cold War,

---

[21]The play, entitled *How Ronald Reagan Finally Saved the World, or As You Like It So Long As You Finally Save the World*, is a closet drama which explores the logic of the Cold War and an alternative logic which people might use as a basis for building peace. See Appendix XII.

cannot acknowledge the significance of the moral challenge that the Cuban Revolution represents to the United States. Mike Morrissey has recently pointed out that Chomsky has publicly declared that in spite of everything, he (Chomsky) still considers the United States to be the freest country in the world. Such a statement reflects a narrow notion of freedom, which is characteristic of liberalism and perhaps explains why for all of Chomsky's radical critique of American foreign policy he is still so welcome in the halls of the establishment.[22]

Failing to note the critical significance of the Cuban Revolution, the left/liberal intellectuals will not be able to take account of the full significance of Kennedy's rapprochement with Khrushchev and Castro. They will note it of course, and support it, but they will not be aware of the critical departure that these actions represented on Kennedy's part. And consequently they will not be able to make sense of the reasons the CIA felt compelled to do away with Kennedy. They will not correctly assess the significance of the split in socialism as well as within capitalism that was represented by the Sino-Soviet split and the split of Kennedy from the CIA. I have detailed the importance of all this in earlier correspondence in a discussion of the "radical" nature of Kennedy's shift at the Cuban Missile Crisis.[23] Similarly the question of the significance of the break in capitalism and socialism is discussed in the analysis of Khrushchev's very important January 31, 1963 letter to Castro.[24]

---

[22]See Appendix XI for an analysis of the ideological reasons Chomsky would have to be blind to the significance of the assassination.

[23]Unpublished letter to Salandria on the significance for peaceful coexistence of Kennedy's willingness to negotiate the removal of Soviet missiles from Cuba rather than removing them by ultimatum and eventually war. See Appendix XI.

[24]"Premier Khrushchev's Letter to Castro Reviewing the Crisis, January 31, 1963," *The Cuban Missile Crisis, 1962: A National Security Archive Documents Reader*, ed. C. Chang and P. Kornbluh (New York: The New Press, 1992), pp. 319-29. On January 31, 1964 Soviet Premier Khrushchev wrote a very long letter to Castro in which he describes

All of this will be of little or no interest to people who do not include social and economic democracy within their concept of freedom. And unfortunately that probably characterizes the majority of Americans at this point.

I would argue that the lack of interest in social and economic democracy which Americans manifest today, the failure of American society to address the problems of social and economic democracy, is ultimately related to the vulnerability of American society to the Kennedy assassination. Again, how, after all, did we come to a point as a society in which this conspiracy to murder the President would be acceptable? This is a critical question. In order to answer it we have to go back and look at this democracy we call America, the real one, as it is day in and day out.

Let us turn to what Michael Parenti reminds us of — the murder and suppression of the radical leadership that emerged in the sixties.[25] Think about "Jim Crow" and the lynchings in the South, where African Americans were subjected to systematic terror for asserting basic democratic rights, while in the North legal forms of discrimination, an American form of apartheid, served and serves similar purposes. This was the America which accepted the murder of President Kennedy, the America which was prepared to accept the systematic terror of African Americans.

Indeed, President Kennedy as President was prepared to accept this.[26] Shortly after coming into office, he had a meeting

---

his view that politically the world has suffered a fracture with the Chinese and right wing Americans on one side, and on the other side moderate elements within the socialist camp including the Soviet Union and Cuba. This document is critical for anyone who wishes to understand the balance of forces in the world on the question of peace that existed in 1963, and the likely impact of Kennedy's removal on this balance. See Appendix X.

[25]Michael Parenti, "State Power and the JFK Assassination," *Prevailing Wind*, issue #1 (1995), pp. 31-39.

[26]Richard Reeves, *President Kennedy: Profile of Power* (New York: Simon and Schuster, 1993), pp. 54-62.

with a number of African American leaders who urged him to take action on the problem of systematic racist terror in the South and his response was to tell them not to rock the boat, that the Democrats had won a narrow victory over the Republicans, that he was not in a political position to take a stand on this question. Of course, he didn't say and didn't have to say that he owed his election in part to Lyndon Johnson and the racist southern power structure.

We are talking about an American democracy that found McCarthyism acceptable as a means of ridding our labor movement, the entertainment industry, and our educational institutions of "communists," people who refused to accept the legitimacy of the Cold War and insisted that the United States should reach accommodation with the Soviet Union, people who insisted that the arms race was a rip-off of the American people and the world. The systematic persecution of these people was acceptable within American democracy. The murder of the Rosenbergs was acceptable. The repression and persecution of Robeson and DuBois and all the others was acceptable. All of it was acceptable to America and her democracy. Indeed, McCarthy was only brought down when he lost his wits altogether and began to attack the military itself. And of course here Robert Kennedy can be found playing a role as a McCarthyite witch-hunter.

As steeped in this Cold War tradition as President Kennedy was, he nevertheless was capable of moving beyond the confines of Cold War thought. He was a person with a certain independence of mind. He was sensitive to the erosion of civilian control of the military. He was appalled at the glib approach the Pentagon could take to the idea of millions and millions of casualties in a nuclear war. He was, as Castro has pointed out, a person of a certain kind of "moral authority" in his connection with the American people. And thus when roused by them as he was in the crisis over civil rights, he was capable of providing a definite moral leadership. And roused by his own sense of disquiet over the direction and implications of the Cold War domestically as well as internationally, Kennedy set about trying to work out some alternative. But in this case, unlike the case of the civil rights issue, there was no mass movement to propel

Kennedy and to provide the social momentum necessary for ending the arms race and the Cold War. In this case Kennedy took the lead, hoping eventually to galvanize sufficient support.[27] He backed off on Cuba and started negotiating recognition.[28] He refused to support the junta in the Dominican Republic. He was dragging his feet in Vietnam. He began working with the Pope and Khrushchev on the nuclear arms race (a portion of Kennedy's correspondence with Khrushchev is still hidden from the American people[29]). And in doing all this he was moving in a direction which communists had been advocating for decades. Castro tells us that the Cuban government had come to recognize that it was possible to talk with Kennedy, that he was someone who could be dealt with, and that there was, with him in office, the possibility of accommodation.[30]

---

[27]Norman Cousins, *The Improbable Triumvirate: John F. Kennedy, Pope John, Nikita Khrushchev* (New York: W. W. Norton, 1972). In this memoir Mr. Cousins details his role as an intermediary between Pope John XXIII, President Kennedy, and Premier Khrushchev in the process of achieving a ban on atmospheric testing of nuclear weapons.

[28]William Attwood, *The Reds and the Blacks: A Personal Adventure* (New York: Harper & Row, 1967). Atwood, a former editor of *Look Magazine*, was given the secret assignment of discussing normalization of relations with Cuban representatives in the U.N.

[29]Reeves, p. 698n: "Khrushchev's letters [to President Kennedy] were long and often rambling, and ranged over a wide variety of topics. Many were unmistakably personally dictated . . . Kennedy based his replies on the sections . . . most palatable to American interests and often closed by sending greetings from his family and his hopes for better relations between the superpowers. . . . In January 1992, a series of Kennedy-Khrushchev letters relating to the aftermath of the Cuban missile crisis was released, and it proved highly revealing. These letters were obtained through a Freedom of Information Act lawsuit by the National Security Archive and are now available at that institution and at the Kennedy Library. But despite the passage of almost thirty years and the pleas of nearly every top living member of the Kennedy Administration for the release of the rest of the letters, the U.S. State Department has kept much of the remaining correspondence secret."

[30]See Castro speech, Appendix II.

Look at Kennedy's American University speech in which he tried to indicate to the American people the direction our nation needed to go in securing world peace.[31] Interestingly he could not bring himself to tell the American people about the dangerous conflict that had erupted in Washington over the direction he was taking, even though at the time his brother, the Attorney General, was sending messages to Khrushchev to cool it, because they were worried about the possibility of assassination.[32]

This American University speech is so important. As I go back and reread it, I realize how advanced Kennedy's position was at that time, much more advanced than anything we have coming from our government today. In that speech there is an understanding very close to the position George Kennan articulates in the later essays in *The Nuclear Delusion*.[33]

What I am referring to is an understanding that there was something of value to the powers that be in the United States, as well as to the people of the United States, in the existence of the Soviet Union: namely that there was an organized force on "the other side" that was also interested in disarmament. When I go back and read Mikhail Gorbachev's *Perestroika*[34] today I think of where Kennedy and Khrushchev were in 1963 and the opportunity that was beginning to emerge and that was destroyed.

I know that no one seems to be interested in the McCloy-Zorin agreement.[35] Hardly anyone even knows about it any

---

[31]President John F. Kennedy, at American University, Washington, D.C., June 10, 1963. See Appendix I.

[32]Reeves, pp. 347, 364.

[33]George F. Kennan, *The Nuclear Delusion: Soviet-American Relations in the Atomic Age* (New York: Pantheon Books, 1982). A collection of essays from 1950-82.

[34]Mikhail Gorbachev, *Perestroika: New Thinking for Our Country and the World* (New York: Harper & Row, 1987).

[35]In 1961, continuing a process begun by President Eisenhower, John J. McCloy at the direction of President Kennedy held a series of meetings with Valerian A. Zorin, representing the U.S.S.R., and on

longer. And I really don't understand why. Maybe they were just words as far as Kennedy was concerned in 1961 when it was signed. But as events developed, particularly after the Cuban Missile Crisis, I think the McCloy-Zorin agreement began to take on real significance. Because if you go back and look at that American University speech, I think Kennedy is talking about the McCloy-Zorin agreement without mentioning it by name. Khrushchev and Kennedy were talking about worldwide disarmament, *conventional* as well as nuclear. That is really radical. That is what Gorbachev was talking about, that you can't settle problems with military means any longer. And the "powers that be" in this country didn't want Gorbachev. And even the liberals were ecstatic when the Soviet Union collapsed and Yeltsin replaced Gorbachev. You read the American University speech by Kennedy and George Kennan's later writing and you read Castro, Gorbachev, and Nelson Mandela[36] and you realize how foolishly narrow the political mind set that dominates this country is.

People are always asking how would our history be different if President Kennedy hadn't been assassinated. For me this isn't the question to ask. Rather ask how would history have been different if President F.W. de Klerk had been assassinated in the midst of South Africa's transition to majority rule and the ending of apartheid. It seems to me that South Africa would still have gone through the changes it has accomplished because that society had the organized social momentum to move in that direction.

This is why I see Kennedy as a "de Klerk without an ANC." He saw the handwriting on the wall in our situation, the way de Klerk did in his. But Kennedy didn't have an "ANC," an

---

September 20, 1961 they signed the Joint Statement of Agreed Principles for Disarmament Negotiations, known as the McCloy-Zorin Agreement. The agreement was submitted to the United Nations General Assembly, which on December 13, 1961 adopted it as the foundation for future negotiations towards general disarmament. See Appendix IX.

[36]Nelson Mandela, *Long Walk to Freedom* (Boston: Little, Brown & Co., 1994).

organized social movement for peaceful coexistence that could compel the society to move in that direction. So he was in a very vulnerable position.

And as in South Africa before the ascendancy of Nelson Mandela and the ANC to the government, we too in America are confronted by a "third force" which is shadowy and operates behind the scenes. You will recall that this "third force" in South African society turned out to have the clandestine backing of the government.

It seems to me that at the moment of the assassination the Kennedy forces had a choice. They could openly acknowledge to the American people what had happened. To do this might have meant to release a popular disillusionment with the military and the CIA. You understand that in such a situation these liberal leaders as well as the conservatives might lose control of the situation to popular forces. Or they could decide not to run that risk; they could accept the assassination as a brutal, heinous wound to their side, but nevertheless keep going with the people in the dark. Obviously this was the decision that was made. And in so doing they decided (perhaps unconsciously like the "innocent" parents of the anti-social teenager) that the CIA murder of the President was acceptable to American democracy. The fact that our press and universities fell into line is an indication that they too accepted American democracy as delimited by this liberal-conservative establishment.

Are the American people really any different? Do they really want to know what happened and take responsibility, as opposed to indulging themselves in endless speculation?

Warren Commission member John J. McCloy is quoted by Edward J. Epstein in *Inquest* as saying that the paramount importance of the Commission was to "show the world that America is not a banana republic where a government can be changed by conspiracy."[37] Nowhere has the primary concern of the establishment been more honestly acknowledged in this case.

---

[37]Edward J. Epstein, *Inquest: The Warren Commission and the Establishment of Truth* (New York: Viking Press, 1966), p. 33.

Anyone with any real access to the public, any person of importance who dared to speak the truth that would threaten the purposes of the government would be immediately suspended. Note if you will the case of Malcolm X, who instinctively read the situation correctly and said publicly, "the chickens have come home to roost." He was immediately censured by Elijah Muhammad and the Black Muslim leadership for being insensitive to the American people.

As far as I am concerned, in confronting the murder of JFK we are not confronted with the task of repairing something that has been injured. We are confronted with the task of addressing a society that in 1963 was already profoundly ill, and if anything has become sicker in the intervening years. At the core of this illness is that mentality which pursues anti-communism and the Cold War above all else, a mentality which will subordinate any crime, including the threat to annihilate mankind, in pursuit of defeating this supposed enemy. I reiterate, what did Kennedy in was his effort to depart from this insanity. And on this score, in deciding to handle the assassination as they did, the left/liberal establishment revealed that when push came to shove, when they had to make a choice, this left/liberal establishment was more addicted to the military and the CIA than to the Constitution. And by and large the American people are part and parcel of this addiction.

Of course this is not to say that you or anyone else must accept this liberal/conservative definition of American democracy. But in practical terms, the quality of American democracy is ultimately up to the American people to determine. And the people for now are dominated by the "powers that be" and their press. For American democracy to return to being governed by the Constitution, instead of by the mentality of the Cold War, will mean confronting truly vast forces that will stand in opposition. Such a process can only proceed on the basis of a broad social movement which is prepared to challenge the political assumptions of our society at its roots. Along the way such a movement will inevitably want to know everything it can about the illness it must overcome.

I believe that as people become part of such a movement they will want to know, they will *need* to know, who killed President

Kennedy and why and how the murder was covered up. They will need to know because they will be struggling to overcome the Orwellian forces that today dominate our nation and the world. And this case is a window on those forces. So no matter if our work is ignored today, it will have something to offer people eventually.

From my point of view, the Kennedy assassination is a strand in the fabric of a society suffering from an illness which is the outgrowth of more than a century, an illness which has been growing since shortly after the American Civil War, when the reconstruction process was short-circuited. From that point on, the "powers that be" in the United States from a moral standpoint have more often than not been on the wrong side of history, frustrating change, opposing human freedom, exploiting the majority in the interest of the privileged few. For most of this century anti-communism and the Cold War formed the rationale for this American policy.

The only exception is the period in which Hitler went too far and had to be called back, at which point the United States joined with the Soviet Union. And the minute Hitler was out of the picture, U.S. policy reverted. Our military intelligence began working with the Nazis, helping them find their way to South America, coordinating repression in Latin America with fascist military regimes, embarking on domestic witch hunts in order to cancel the cultural and political progress which the American people had achieved through the struggles of the Depression and World War II.

The real reason for the Cold War was that the Soviet Union, with all its problems and deviations, remained throughout an obstacle to the U.S. policy of dominance in the Third World. The minute Communist China abandoned the anti-colonialist stance, it was able to normalize relations with the United States. The reason the United States will not normalize relations with Cuba is because of Cuba's determined, principled anti-colonialist foreign policy and the fact that its development as a Third World country independent of U.S. control stands as a glaring alternative to the results in those third world countries which submit to United States domination.

Look at the points where Malcolm X and Martin Luther King, Jr. were assassinated. These are also political assassinations in which there is evidence of involvement by the federal government. Malcolm was killed when he had joined the struggle of African Americans in the United States with the anti-colonialist movement internationally. King was killed at the point he was joining our civil rights movement to our anti-war movement, again with the possibility of our domestic movement being linked with a worldwide movement against colonialism.

As an example of the timeliness of these issues I am enclosing an article which appeared in the March 22nd issue of *Granma International*,[38] remarks that Fidel Castro recently made in Europe at the U.N.-sponsored conference on social development.

So this is where we are today. The assassination of President Kennedy is a window onto the reality of American democracy, a militarist political democracy lacking in social and economic democracy and justice, a system that is apparently threatened by a small island of a few million people ninety miles off its shore who for thirty-five years have refused to allow the United States to define for them their notion of freedom, democracy, and justice. And make no mistake about it. Although the powers that be are trying to convince everyone that the Cold War has ended, the refusal by the U.S. to recognize Cuba and to peacefully coexist with this nation, the continuing attempt to embargo this nation — all this is proof that the Cold War is *not* over. Virtually every month brings a new exposé on the role of the CIA in horrors committed in El Salvador, Guatemala, Nicaragua, Chile, and so on. But the struggle continues.

Since peace is the order which flows from social justice, so long as there is an absence of social justice in any society, that society will find itself at war. This is a law of human life. It is true for our society, and it is true for the world. The struggles for social and economic justice in the United States are connected with the struggles against colonialism and for social and economic development throughout the world, and these struggles are

---

[38]See Appendix XIII.

connected with the struggle for peace and the transformation of mankind's relationship to nature.

I leave you with the following quotation from Chinghiz Aitmatov, the great Kirghiz writer:

> The movement for peace . . . is an irreversible process of the social awakening of the masses, a spiritual birth. . . . Mankind is proposing liberation from a universal humiliating terror, from feelings of isolation, indifference, and cruelty — from everything that impudently inspires and provokes one through propaganda to serve insanity. . . . In the movement for peace, as in no other, concretely and not abstractly, the contemporary thought of mankind in all its fullness is reflected, tests itself, and is realized.[39]

---

[39]Chinghiz Aitmatov, "Humanism — The General Language of Mankind," *Sputnik*, September 1983, p. 11. Translated from the Russian edition.

Appendices

Appendix I

Speech at American University June 10, 1963

by John F. Kennedy

The following speech was delivered by President Kennedy in the Spring of 1963. It reflects the significant change in his thinking which followed the Cuban Missile Crisis and was part of the successful campaign for an agreement between the U.S. and the U.S.S.R. banning atmospheric testing of nuclear weapons.

Speech at American University
June 10, 1963

by John F. Kennedy

Professor Woodrow Wilson once said that every man sent out from a university should be a man of his nation as well as a man of his time, and I am confident that the men and women who carry the honor of graduating from this institution will continue to give from their lives, from their talents, a high measure of public service and public support.

"There are few earthly things more beautiful than a university," wrote John Masefield in his tribute to English universities — and his words are equally true today. He did not refer to spires and towers, to campus greens and ivied walls. He admired the splendid beauty of the university, he said, because it was "a place where those who hate ignorance may strive to know, where those who perceive truth may strive to make others see."

I have therefore chosen this time and this place to discuss a topic on which ignorance too often abounds and the truth is too rarely perceived — yet it is the most important topic on earth: world peace.

What kind of peace do I mean? What kind of peace do we seek? Not a Pax Americana enforced on the world by American weapons of war. Not the peace of the grave or the security of the slave. I am talking about genuine peace, the kind of peace that makes life on earth worth living, the kind that enables men and nations to grow and to hope and to build a better life for their children — not merely peace for Americans but peace for all men and women — not merely peace in our time but peace for all time.

I speak of peace because of the new face of war. Total war makes no sense in an age when great powers can maintain large and relatively invulnerable nuclear forces and refuse to surrender without resort to those forces. It makes no sense in an age when a single nuclear weapon contains almost ten times the explosive force delivered by all of the allied air forces in the Second World War. It makes no sense in an age when the deadly poisons produced by a nuclear exchange would be carried by wind and water and soil and seed to the far corners of the globe and to generations yet unborn.

Today the expenditure of billions of dollars every year on weapons acquired for the purpose of making sure we never need to use them is essential to keeping the peace. But surely the acquisition of such idle stockpiles — which can only destroy and never create — is not the only, much less the most efficient, means of assuring peace.

I speak of peace, therefore, as the necessary rational end of rational men. I realize that the pursuit of peace is not as dramatic as the pursuit of war — and frequently the words of the pursuer fall on deaf ears. But we have no more urgent task.

Some say that it is useless to speak of world peace or world law or world disarmament — and that it will be useless until the leaders of the Soviet Union adopt a more enlightened attitude. I hope they do. I believe we can help them do it. But I also believe that we must reexamine our own attitude — as individuals and as a nation — for our attitude is as essential as theirs. And every graduate of this school, every thoughtful citizen who despairs of war and wishes to bring peace, should begin by looking inward — by examining his own attitude toward the possibilities of peace, toward the Soviet Union, toward the course of the Cold War, and toward freedom and peace here at home.

First: Let us examine our attitude toward peace itself. Too many of us think it is impossible. Too many think it unreal. But that is a dangerous, defeatist belief. It leads to the conclusion that war is inevitable — that mankind is doomed — that we are gripped by forces we cannot control.

We need not accept that view. Our problems are man-made — therefore, they can be solved by man. And man can be as big as he wants. No problem of human destiny is beyond human beings. Man's reason and spirit have often solved the seemingly unsolvable — and we believe they can do it again.

I am not referring to the absolute, infinite concept of universal peace and goodwill of which some fantasies and fanatics dream. I do not deny the value of hopes and dreams but we merely invite discouragement and incredulity by making that our only and immediate goal.

Let us focus instead on a more practical, more attainable peace — based not on a sudden revolution in human nature but on a gradual evolution in human institutions — on a series of concrete actions and effective agreements which are in the interest of all concerned. There is no single, simple key to this peace — no grand or magic formula to be adopted by one or two powers. Genuine peace must be the product of many nations, the sum of many acts. It must be dynamic, not static, changing to meet the challenge of each new generation. For peace is a process — a way of solving problems.

With such a peace, there will still be quarrels and conflicting interests, as there are within families and nations. World peace, like community peace, does not require that each man love his neighbor — it requires only that they live together in mutual tolerance, submitting their disputes to a just and peaceful settlement. And history teaches us that enmities between nations, as between individuals, do not last forever. However fixed our likes and dislikes may seem, the tide of time and events will often bring surprising changes in the relations between nations and neighbors.

So let us persevere. Peace need not be impracticable, and war need not be inevitable. By defining our goal more clearly, by making it seem more manageable and less remote, we can help all peoples to see it, to draw hope from it, and to move irresistibly toward it.

Second: Let us reexamine our attitude toward the Soviet Union. It is discouraging to think that their leaders may actually believe what their propagandists write. It is discouraging to read a recent authoritative Soviet text on military strategy and find, on page after page, wholly baseless and incredible claims — such as the allegation that "American imperialist circles are preparing to unleash different types of wars . . . that there is a very real threat of a preventive war being unleashed by American imperialists against the Soviet Union [and that] the political aims of the American imperialists are to enslave economically and politically the European and other capitalist countries [and] to achieve world domination . . . by means of aggressive wars."

Truly, as it was written long ago: "The wicked flee when no man pursueth." Yet it is sad to read these Soviet statements — to realize the extent of the gulf between us. But it is also a warning — a warning to the American people not to fall into the same trap as the Soviets, not to see only a distorted and desperate view of the other side, not to see conflict as inevitable, accommodation as impossible, and communication as nothing more than an exchange of threats.

No government or social system is so evil that its people must be considered as lacking in virtue. As Americans, we find communism profoundly repugnant as a negation of personal freedom and dignity. But we can still hail the Russian people for their many achievements — in science and space, in economic and industrial growth, in culture and in acts of courage.

Among the many traits the peoples of our two countries have in common, none is stronger than our mutual abhorrence of war. Almost unique among the major world powers, we have never been at war with each other. And no nation in the history of battle ever suffered more than the Soviet Union suffered in the course of the Second World War. At least twenty million lost their lives. Countless millions of homes and farms were burned or sacked. A third of the nation's territory, including nearly two thirds of its industrial base, was turned into a wasteland — a loss equivalent to the devastation of this country, east of Chicago.

Today, should total war ever break out again — no matter how — our two countries would become the primary targets. It is an ironic but accurate fact that the two strongest powers are the two in the most danger of devastation. All we have built, all we have worked for, would be destroyed in the first twenty-four hours. And even in the Cold War, which brings burdens and dangers to so many countries, including this nation's closest allies — our two countries bear the heaviest burdens. For we are both devoting massive sums of money to weapons that could be better devoted to combating ignorance, poverty, and disease. We are both caught up in a vicious and dangerous cycle in which suspicion on one side breeds suspicion on the other, and new weapons beget counterweapons.

In short, both the United States and its allies, and the Soviet Union and its allies, have a mutually deep interest in a just and genuine peace and in halting the arms race. Agreements to this end are in the interests of the Soviet Union as well as ours — and even the most hostile nations can be relied upon to accept and keep those treaty obligations, and only those treaty obligations, which are in their own interest.

So, let us not be blind to our differences — but let us also direct attention to our common interests and to the means by which those differences can be resolved. And if we cannot end now our differences, at least we can help make the world safe for diversity. For in the final analysis, our most basic common link is that we all inhabit this small planet. We all breathe the same air. We all cherish our children's future. And we are all mortal.

Third: Let us reexamine our attitude toward the Cold War, remembering that we are not engaged in a debate, seeking to pile up debating points. We are not here distributing blame or pointing the finger of judgment. We must deal with the world as it is, and not as it might have been had the history of the last eighteen years been different.

We must therefore persevere in the search for peace in the hope that constructive changes within the Communist bloc might bring within reach solutions which now seem beyond us. We must conduct our affairs in such a way that it becomes in the Communists' interest to agree on a genuine peace. Above all, while defending our own vital interests, nuclear powers must avert those confrontations which bring an adversary to a choice of either a humiliating retreat or a nuclear war. To adopt that kind of course in the nuclear age would be evidence only of the bankruptcy of our policy — or of a collective death-wish for the world.

To secure these ends, America's weapons are nonprovocative, carefully controlled, designed to deter, and capable of selective use. Our military forces are committed to peace and disciplined in self-restraint. Our diplomats are instructed to avoid unnecessary irritants and purely rhetorical hostility.

For we can seek a relaxation of tensions without relaxing our guard. And for our part we do not need to use threats to prove that we are resolute. We do not need to jam foreign broadcasts out of fear our faith will be eroded. We are unwilling to impose our system on any unwilling people — but we are willing and able to engage in peaceful competition with any people on earth.

Meanwhile, we seek to strengthen the United Nations, to help solve its financial problems, to make it a more effective instrument for peace, to develop it into a genuine world security system — a system capable of resolving disputes on the basis of law, of insuring the security of the large and the small, and of creating conditions under which arms can finally be abolished.

At the same time we seek to keep peace inside the non-Communist world, where many nations, all of them our friends, are divided over issues which weaken Western unity, which invite Communist intervention or which threaten to erupt into war. Our efforts in West New Guinea, in the Congo, in the Middle East, and in the Indian subcontinent, have been persistent and patient, despite criticism from both sides. We have also tried to set an example for others — by seeking to adjust small but significant differences with our own closest neighbors in Mexico and in Canada. Speaking of other nations, I wish to make one point clear. We are bound to many nations by alliances. Those alliances exist because our concern and theirs substantially overlap. Our commitment to defend Western Europe and West Berlin, for example, stands undiminished because of the identity of our vital interests. The United States will make no deal with the Soviet Union at the expense of other nations and other peoples, not merely because they are our partners, but also because their interests and ours converge.

Our interests converge, however, not only in defending the frontiers of freedom, but in pursuing the paths of peace. It is our hope — and the purpose of allied policies — to convince the

Soviet Union that she, too, should let each nation choose its own future, so long as that choice does not interfere with the choices of others. The Communist drive to impose their political and economic system on others is the primary cause of world tension today. For there can be no doubt that, if all nations could refrain from interfering in the self-determination of others, the peace would be much more assured.

This will require a new effort to achieve world law — a new context for world discussions. It will require increased understanding between the Soviets and ourselves. And increased understanding will require increased contact and communication. One step in this direction is the proposed arrangement for a direct line between Moscow and Washington, to avoid on each side the dangerous delays, misunderstandings, and misreadings of the other's actions which might occur at a time of crisis.

We have also been talking in Geneva about other first-step measures of arms control, designed to limit the intensity of the arms race and to reduce the risks of accidental war. Our primary long-range interest in Geneva, however, is general and complete disarmament — designed to take place by stages, permitting parallel political developments to build the new institutions of peace which would take the place of arms. The pursuit of disarmament has been an effort of this government since the 1920s. It has been urgently sought by the past three administrations. And however dim the prospects may be today, we intend to continue this effort — to continue it in order that all countries, including our own, can better grasp what the problems and possibilities of disarmament are.

The one major area of these negotiations where the end is in sight, yet where a fresh start is badly needed, is in a treaty to outlaw nuclear tests. The conclusion of such a treaty, so near and yet so far, would check the spiraling arms race in one of its most dangerous areas. It would place the nuclear powers in a position to deal more effectively with one of the greatest hazards which man faces in 1963, the further spread of nuclear arms. It would increase our security — it would decrease the prospects of war. Surely this goal is sufficiently important to require our steady pursuit, yielding to neither the temptation to give up the whole effort nor the temptation to give up our insistence on vital and responsible safeguards.

I am taking this opportunity, therefore, to announce two important decisions in this regard.

First: Chairman Khrushchev, Prime Minister Macmillan, and I have agreed that high-level discussions will shortly begin in Moscow looking toward early agreement on a comprehensive test-ban treaty. Our hopes must be tempered with the caution of history — but with our hopes go the hopes of all mankind.

Second: To make clear our good faith and solemn convictions on the matter, I now declare that the United States does not propose to conduct nuclear tests in the atmosphere so long as other states do not do so. We will not be the first to resume. Such a declaration is no substitute for a formal binding treaty, but I hope it will help us achieve one. Nor would such a treaty be a substitute for disarmament, but I hope it will help us achieve it.

Finally, my fellow Americans, let us examine our attitude toward peace and freedom here at home. The quality and spirit of our own society must justify and support our efforts abroad. We must show it in the dedication of our own lives — and many of you who are graduating today will have a unique opportunity to do so, by serving without pay in the Peace Corps abroad or in the proposed National Service Corps here at home.

But wherever we are, we must all, in our daily lives, live up to the age-old faith that peace and freedom walk together. In too many of our cities today, the peace is not secure because freedom is incomplete.

It is the responsibility of the executive branch at all levels of government — local, state, and national — to provide and protect that freedom for all of our citizens by all means within their authority. It is the responsibility of the legislative branch at all levels, wherever that authority is not now adequate, to make it adequate. And it is the responsibility of all citizens in all sections of this country to respect the rights of all others and to respect the law of the land.

All this is not unrelated to world peace. "When a man's ways please the Lord," the Scriptures tell us, "he maketh even his enemies to be at peace with him." And is not peace, in the last analysis, basically a matter of human rights — the right to live out our lives without fear of devastation — the right to breathe air as nature provided it — the right of future generations to a healthy existence?

While we proceed to safeguard our national interests, let us also safeguard human interests. And the elimination of war and arms is clearly in the interest of both. No treaty, however much it may be to the advantage of all, however tightly it may be worded, can provide absolute security against the risks of deception and evasion. But it can — if it is sufficiently effective in its enforcement and if it is sufficiently in the interests of its signers — offer far more security and far fewer risks than an unabated, uncontrolled, unpredictable arms race.

The United States, as the world knows, will never start a war. We do not want a war. We do not now expect a war. This generation of Americans has already had enough — more than enough — of war and hate and oppression. We shall be prepared if others wish it. We shall be alert to try to stop it. But we shall also do our part to build a world of peace where the weak are safe and the strong are just. We are not helpless before that task or hopeless of its success. Confident and unafraid, we labor on — not toward a strategy of annihilation but toward a strategy of peace.

Appendix II

Concerning the Facts and Consequences of the Tragic Death of President John F. Kennedy November 23rd, 1963

by Fidel Castro

The following is the text of a speech/commentary delivered by Fidel Castro on Cuban radio and TV, Saturday evening, November 23, 1963, one day after the assassination of President Kennedy. The speech gives the reader insight into the immediate analysis of the assassination which a political expert such as Castro was able to make.

This English translation of the speech was released by the Cuban delegation to the United Nations in 1963. It is here reproduced with minor editing of grammar and punctuation.

Concerning the Facts and Consequences of the Tragic Death of President John F. Kennedy November 23rd, 1963

by Fidel Castro

Always, when something very important has happened, national or international, we have thought it desirable to speak to the people, to express our opinions. And in every such case to express the orientation of the Government, the orientation of our Party, so that each one of us all know the attitude we should adopt in each one of these situations.

It is true that we are somewhat accustomed to various types of unexpected events, important, serious events, because since the victory of the Revolution our country has had to face a series of problems, a series of situations that have prepared the people to carry forward their victorious revolution.

Therefore, because of the events of yesterday in the United States in which the President was murdered, because of the repercussion these events can have, because of the role that the United States plays in the problems of international policy, because of this, we believe that we should make a specially objective and calm analysis of these events and of their possible consequences.

The government of the United States, the former administration of Eisenhower and the Kennedy administration, did not practice precisely a policy of friendship toward us. The policy of both administrations was characterized by its aggressive, hostile, and implacable spirit toward our country.

Our country was the victim of economic aggressions intended to cause the ruin of our economy and the starvation of our people; it was the victim of all kinds of attacks that caused bloodshed; hundreds of our compatriots have lost their lives, defending themselves from attacks of U.S. imperialism, and not only this. The hostility and the aggressiveness of U.S. imperialism toward our country took us to the brink of war which was fortunately avoided, took the world to the brink of thermo-nuclear war.

And even when we were not facing a situation like the crisis of October, and the time of the invasion of Giron [Bay of Pigs], we were all perfectly aware that if the plots they were planning against our country had been carried through, that is to say, if imperialism had been able to establish a beachhead on our shores, that struggle would have cost our people tens of thousands, and perhaps even hundreds of thousands of lives.

We have been victims of the constant hostility of the United States. And among the rulers and the leading men of the United States, there falls on Kennedy an important responsibility in these events.

Nevertheless, the news of the murder of the President of the United States is serious news and bad news. We should analyze it thoroughly in order to understand it; above all, analyze it serenely and dispassionately, as revolutionaries should analyze these things.

I say it is bad news, leaving aside the human question, in that the sensitivity of man, any man, is affected by an act of this nature, by a crime, by a murder. I say that leaving these questions aside, I always react and I am sure that this is the reaction of the immense majority of human beings — we always react with repulsion toward murder and toward crime.

We cannot consider this to be a correct weapon of struggle — no, we cannot consider that. Above all under the conditions in which it happened, because — like all these things — it is always necessary to consider the atmosphere, the things, the circumstances.

In other settings, under other circumstances, whatever they may be in a normal situation, in a peaceful situation, a deed of this nature is never justifiable. Especially in the middle of a crowd, in the presence of women, all these things, which above all — I say — are the circumstances that lead us to take a condemnatory attitude toward something, even though some deeds of a political nature, some crimes of a political nature, may or may not be justified.

In the circumstances that surrounded the assassination of President Kennedy, we believe it has no justification.

But analyzing the question from the political, objective point of view, I also said it was serious news, bad news.

And some will ask why? Why precisely the Cubans, who have received so many aggressions on the part of the United States, from the Kennedy Administration itself, why can they say that it is bad news, why can they take an attitude of this kind in the face of this news? But in the first place we Cubans must react as revolutionaries. In the second place, we Cubans, as conscious revolutionaries, should not confuse men with systems. And we have to begin by considering that we do not hate men, we hate systems.

We hate the imperialist system, we hate the capitalist system, but this does not mean that we hate men as such, as individuals, part of a machine, a more or less important part of a system.

So we should not confuse hatred of a system with the sentiment we should harbor toward men, which is a different sentiment; it is not a sentiment of hatred, and much less a sentiment of hatred which in a case like this would be despicable.

As Marxist-Leninists, we know that the role of man is a relative role in each historical epoch, in each society, at each given moment, and we should know the role that man plays in each society. And above all it is a question of elemental principle: we do not hate men, we hate systems.

We would be happy at the death of a system; the disappearance of a system would always make us happy. The victory of a revolution always makes us happy.

The death of a man, even though this man may be our enemy, does not make us happy. In the first place, this should be our attitude as a matter of principle.

And further it is very characteristic of us Cubans, of Latins, of Spanish-Americans — who are a mixture of races with certain characteristics — that death always ends our animosity. We always bow with respect in the face of death, even though it may be the death of an enemy.

But then, I said that the deed itself could have very negative repercussions on the interests of our country. But it is not the interests of our country in this case but the interests of the whole world that are involved. We must know how to place the interests of mankind above the interests of our country. I consider it a negative event for the interests of mankind. And I am going to explain why.

Because in certain international political situations, at a given moment, there can be bad situations or worse situations. The death of President Kennedy has all the perspectives involved in going from a bad situation to a worse situation: the possibility exists that from a determined situation, another situation could unfold and develop that could be highly damaging to the interests of peace, to the interests of mankind.

Why? Do we perhaps think that the United States holds a defensible political position in the international field? No, the international policy of the United States cannot be defended. Its policy of aggression, policy of violating the rights of other nations, of interference in the internal affairs of other countries, of domination, of repression, of bloodshed, of alliance with the most reactionary sectors of the world, of participation in bloody wars against the people who struggle for their liberation — as in the case of South Vietnam — its attitude towards the people of Latin America, its attitude towards us, and finally its international position, is in no way defensible from the moral point of view.

However, within American society and within the policy of the United States, there are supporters of a much more reactionary policy, of a policy much more aggressive, much more warlike.

And the whole condition of the internal policy of the United States, the internal struggle for power in the United States, the currents that struggle within the United States, the assassination of President Kennedy, tend to convert the present policy of the

United States into a worse policy and to aggravate the evils of U.S. policy.

That is to say that there are elements in the United States who defend a more reactionary policy in every field, in international and internal policy, and these are the sole elements who can benefit from the events that occurred yesterday in the United States.

Why? Because in the United States a number of forces, a number of very powerful bodies within U.S. society, very much influenced by big interests in the United States, have been developing, and there is no doubt that a U.S. President possessing the highest authority implies a situation less serious than a President without the highest authority, in such a situation.

A President is a political man, who should take into account many factors, advice, opinions, and influences, who is eminently political, who without doubt, behaves differently in general than those who we might say are not professional politicians, who have other professions, other interests, and those political reactions are always the worst reactions.

In the United States there are a number of powerful forces: economic, political, military. Many of these forces have a fixed policy and more than once we have spoken of this problem. Take the clash, for instance, between the political currents of the State Department and the military currents of the Pentagon. We have often seen the manifestations of this struggle in Latin America, how there are currents in the United States, above all military currents that support the policy of military coups, and there are political currents that defend another type of policy — not that it is a good policy, but clothed in a civilian government, even pseudo-liberal.

Unquestionably when [there] is a recognized, accepted, strong authority in the United States, the dangers that arise from the struggle of a whole series of reactionary currents within the powerful organizations of the United States are much less than when this authority does not exist. And without any shadow of doubt, Kennedy had this authority in the United States.

Now, suddenly a new situation is created, where a President who, because of circumstances in which he holds power, that in being Vice President, and then because of an unexpected circumstance becoming President of the Republic, independent of what his character may be, because here it is not a question of the character of the person or his personality, but [because] of the circumstances, does not come to power with the same personal authority as President Kennedy had. And therefore a question begins to arise in respect to the influence within all those forces, of the new authority who assumes power, of the new President who takes over the reins of Government.

In the United States there are very reactionary currents, racist currents, that is to say opposed to the demand for the civil and social rights of the Negro population, Klu Klux Klan people, who lynch, who kill and use dogs, who bitterly hate all Negro citizens in the United States, who nurture a brutal hatred. Those naturally are the ultra-reactionary.

In the United States there are economic forces, powerful economic interests, just as ultra-reactionary, who have a completely reactionary position on all international problems. In the United States there are forces that support an increased intervention by the United States [in] international questions, a greater use of the U.S. military in international questions. There are, for example, currents in the United States that are intransigent supporters of the direct invasion of our country.

In the United States there are partisans of the application of drastic measures against any government that adopts the smallest measure of a nationalist character, of an economic character that benefits its country.

And finally, there are a number of groups that can all be included in one concept: the ultra-right in the United States, the ultra-reaction in the United States, and this ultra-reaction in each and every one of the internal and external problems of the United States is an advocate of the worst procedure, of the most aggressive and most dangerous and most reckless policy against peace.

In the United States there are also liberal currents, some more liberal, some more advanced, other less advanced. There are some men on the right who are more radical, and other more moderate. There are certain intellectual sectors that are not constantly thinking in terms of force, but are thinking along lines of diplomacy, instead of force, who have a less aggressive policy — a more moderate policy.

That is to say, in the United States there is a whole range of political thinking that runs from men of the extreme right to men of the extreme left, men who are more to the left in their political thinking.

And in this situation there is a variety of opinion, of more or less moderate attitudes. There are liberals, intellectual sectors of the United States who understand the errors in the policy of the United States, who are not in agreement with many of the things that the United States has done in international policy.

And what happened yesterday can only benefit those ultra-rightist and ultra-reactionary sectors, among which President Kennedy or some of the men who worked with him cannot be included. They could not be placed in the extreme reaction — in the extreme right.

And even within the situation in the United States, within the policy of the United States, which as a whole is indefensible, Kennedy was strongly attacked by the most reactionary, most aggressive, and most war-like circles.

You will recall that on the eve of the October crisis of last year, there was a whole campaign, with great pressure, including laws and resolutions in Congress, pushing Kennedy [and] the Administration towards war, trying to create a situation of imperative action.

Everybody will recall that on other occasions, we have stated that one of the political errors of Kennedy in respect to Cuba was to have played the game of his enemies. For example, to have continued the invasion plans against Cuba that the Republican administration had organized.

And out of all this arose the possibility in the United States for a policy of blackmail on the part of the Republicans. That is, Kennedy presented the Republicans with the weapon of Cuba. How? He continued the aggressive policy of the Republicans, and they used it as a political weapon against him.

But at times very strong campaigns, powerful movements within the United States Congress pressed the Administration for a more aggressive policy against us. All those factors and all these forces on the extreme right in the United States fought Kennedy very hard precisely on those points in which he did not agree with the extreme aggressive policy called for by these sectors.

There are a number of issues that gave rise to constant criticism by these ultra-right sectors. For instance, the Cuban problem, the agreement reached at the time of the October Crisis not to invade Cuba, one of the points in Kennedy's policy most consistently attacked by the ultra-reactionary sectors. The agreement on the ending of nuclear tests was another point very much debated within the United States, and it had the most resolute and fierce opposition of the most ultra-reactionary.

Elements in the United States were against agreements of this type.

Everyone knows what our position was on this problem. Everyone also knows the reason for our position, regardless of the fact that we consider that this was a step forward that could mark the beginning of a policy of lasting peace, in favor of true disarmament, but a policy that was never applied in our case. Because while the nuclear test ban treaty was being signed, the policy of aggression against Cuba was accentuated.

But we are not now analyzing the problem in relation to what happened in our case, but in relation to what was happening in the world, and above all in relation to what some were doing and others thinking in the United States.

That is to say, there were many sectors in the United States, many ultra-reactionary elements that carried out a fierce campaign against the nuclear test ban treaty.

There are other elements in the United States that violently opposed the legislation of civil rights proposed by Kennedy regarding the Negro problem in the United States.

We are not dealing with the case of a revolutionary law or of a great effort, because this great effort in favor of equality and civil rights, especially in favor of the rights of the U.S. Negroes, has not been made in the United States. But be that as it may it was legislation that contained a series of measures that, from a legal point of view, tended to protect the rights of the Negro population. This legislation was blocked and held back by the strong opposition of the most reactionary sectors in the United States, of those sectors in favor of racial discrimination.

And thus, on a whole series of issues of international policy, there are in the United States elements that support a preventive nuclear war, who are in favor of launching a surprise nuclear war, because they stubbornly think that this should be the policy of the United States. Reactionary and neo-fascist elements without any consideration whatsoever for the most elementary rights of nations or the interests of mankind.

And it is a strictly objective fact that there are such types of capitalists, such types of reactionaries. And there is no doubt that the worst type of capitalism is nazism; the worst type of imperialism was nazism. And the most criminal mentality was the mentality of imperialism in its nazi form. And so there is a whole series of degrees in these questions.

So analyzing the question objectively, whenever a strong accepted personal authority is lacking in the situation, ways and conditions in which U.S. policy is carried out, all these reactionary forces find a magnificent opportunity, and in fact are finding a magnificent opportunity, to unleash their unbridled and ultra-reactionary policy.

And these are the sectors, the currents, the only ones that could benefit by an event such as the one that occurred yesterday in the United States.

This is analyzing the automatic result of this event. Independent of another aspect of the question: What is behind the assassination of Kennedy? What were the real motives for the assassination of Kennedy? What forces, factors, circumstances were at work behind this sudden and unexpected event that occurred yesterday?

News that took everyone by surprise, something that possibly no one had even imagined.

Even up to this moment, the events that led to the murder of the President of the United States continue to be confused, obscure, and unclear.

And there are some things which are clear symptoms of what I have been saying: that the most reactionary forces in the United States are at large.

For instance, the worst symptom is the advantage they are taking of the event to unleash within the United States a state of anti-Soviet hysteria and of anti-Cuban hysteria; this, in the first place. It means that the new administration that is taking over may find itself facing a situation of hysteria, unleashed in the United States, precisely by the most reactionary sector of the country, by the most reactionary press, with the great resources that powerful political currents have within the United States.

That is to say that already they are combining to create a frame of mind in the U.S. public opinion, and its worst characteristic is that they are waging a campaign in the worst McCarthyite spirit, in the worst anti-communist spirit.

At the time of President Kennedy's murder, it ran through the minds of most people . . . and surely it ran through the minds of the large majority of U.S. citizens, and this was only logical — that President Kennedy's assassination was the work of some elements who disagreed with his international policy; that is to say, with his nuclear treaty, with his policy with respect to Cuba — which they did not consider aggressive enough, and which they considered weak — with his policy with respect to internal civil problems of the United States. Not many days ago, the U.S. Ambassador to the U.N. Adlai Stevenson was attacked in the same city of Dallas by ultra-conservative elements of the John Birch Society and counter-revolutionary elements in league with them. This event drew the attention of us all.

I even thought, what degree of reaction will those people reach, when they consider that Stevenson deserves attack for his international policy?

In spite of how reactionary U.S. international policy has been, there are elements who physically assault Stevenson, because they consider that U.S. policy is a weak policy, a bad policy, that it is not a sufficiently reactionary policy.

This ran through everybody's mind. Did it run through the mind of anyone that it might be a leftist? No, that did not occur to anyone. Why? Because the controversy within the United States today, the fierce controversy was taking place between the most ultra-reactionary elements, the ultra-right elements, and the more moderate elements of U.S. politics.

The internal controversy was not characterized by a struggle of the communists of the United States with the Government of the United States; it was not characterized by a struggle of leftist elements or liberal elements. This does not mean that the leftist elements supported Kennedy's policy; but the struggle, the battle waged without quarter was taking place within the United States between the extreme right, the extreme reaction, and the more moderate elements, in Congress, in the press, on the streets, everywhere.

International tension had even diminished considerably in recent months. These months were not months like the October crisis, not like the months following the October crisis. . . . The United States was not living through one of those stages of McCarthyism characterized by unbridled persecution of the most progressive elements of the United States. No, there have been other stages in which the struggle is between reaction and the progressives. The main task of reaction was to persecute the progressive elements, and in such circumstances one might think that a progressive, persecuted by blood and fierce, a fanatic haunted by his ideas, might be capable of reacting in such a way. No, the United States was not living through such a period. It was not living through a period of unbridled McCarthyism. It was living through a period of fierce controversy between the more moderate sectors — among which can be found many of Kennedy's collaborators — and the ultra-reactionary sector of American society.

Therefore, it was neither logical, nor reasonable, that anyone could think that it could be a leftist fanatic; in any case it would be a rightist fanatic, if it was a fanatic at all.

But naturally it was very difficult in the face of an event of this nature for such unscrupulous people — like many U.S. politicians — such immoral people, such dishonest and shameless people as are many of those elements who represent the reactionary cynical sectors of the United States, warmongers, irreconcilable enemies of Cuba, supporters of an invasion of Cuba — although this might be at the cost of thermonuclear war — it was very difficult for them not to try to take advantage of this circumstance to turn all their hatred, all their propaganda and all their campaign against Cuba.

This did not surprise us. I have already said that we were somewhat used to these things. The struggle, life, have made our people into a people with iron nerves, a serene people. We have just lived through the hurricane, and we faced the test with dignity and honor, we have faced many tests with dignity and honor. We foresaw that from these incidents there could be a new trap, an ambush, a Machiavellian plot against our country; that on the very blood of their assassinated President there might be unscrupulous people who would begin to work out immediately an aggressive policy against Cuba, if the aggressive policy had not been linked beforehand to the assassination, if it was not linked, because it might or might not have been. But there is no doubt that this policy is being built on the still warm blood and the unburied body of their own tragically assassinated President.

They are people who do not have an iota of morality; they are people who do not have an iota of scruples; they are people who do not have an iota of shame; who perhaps may believe that in the shadow of the tragedy they can take us off guard, demoralized, weak, the kind of beliefs into which the imperialists always so mistakenly fall. And sure enough, yesterday at 2 P.M. the first cable: November 22, UPI . . . because we should note this; that of the news agencies, one has been more moderate, more objective — the AP — and there is another that has been excessively and unrestrainedly untruthful, a shameless promoter of a policy and a campaign of slander against Cuba, that is UPI. But that is not all, because there is a previous series of very interesting UPI reports, and even a series of UPI campaigns against President Kennedy himself, which links the news agency with the ultra-right groups, which are interested in taking advantage of the situation for their adventurous and warlike policy, or because these circles are connected with the assassination of President Kennedy.

And we can see this clearly through the cables: "Dallas, November 22, UPI — today the police arrested Lee H. Oswald, identified as the chairman of the Fair Play for Cuba Committees, as the main suspect in the assassination of President John F. Kennedy." Right away Cuba and right away the Soviet Union.

And so they dedicated themselves to carrying out a fierce anti-Soviet and anti-Cuban campaign.

Cable: "The U.S. Embassy today confirmed that Lee H. Oswald was in the Soviet Union. An Embassy official stated that Oswald visited the Embassy in November of 1959 and according to available information he left the Soviet Union in 1962. He added that it was not known when the man suspected of killing President John F. Kennedy had traveled to the Soviet Union, what the purpose of his trip had been and how long he had stayed in the Soviet Union. There were unconfirmed reports that Oswald asked for Soviet citizenship and that he could not get it."

Thus, from the very first cables there is an attempt to suggest the responsibility of the Soviet Union and the responsibility of Cuba, as if anyone could believe — anyone who is not a half-wit — and has a little common sense — that any Government, the Soviet government or the Cuban Government . . . and if they don't want to believe us, they don't have to believe us; that is unimportant. Perhaps they will think that we are hot-headed; perhaps they feel that they have carried out too many aggressions against us, but to suggest that the Soviet Union could have any responsibility in this incident . . . can anyone believe that to suggest that we could have had any responsibility . . . can anyone believe that? Anyone who is not a half-wit, who has a little common sense, who knows when men are working for a cause and who know which roads lead a cause to victory?

Yet, nevertheless, this was the first thing they tried to suggest. Listen to this cable "that they did not know the purpose of his trip and how long he stayed in the Soviet Union." That was the first insinuation. And that was what made all this seem suspicious, because it so happened that the most unexpected thing — as unexpected as the assassination itself — was that immediately a suspect appeared who — by a coincidence — had been in Russia, and — what a coincidence — he is related to a Fair Play for Cuba Committee. That is what they began to say. And so, immediately a guilty person appeared: a suspect who had been in the Soviet Union and who sympathized with Cuba.

Of course, although it is extraordinarily difficult to manufacture a frame-up of this nature, it is possible that at this moment they are not pursuing such an objective. They are pursuing another objective, because they cannot invent just any kind of responsibility.

They are trying to organize a campaign of hysteria, to excite the minds of the people and unleash hysteria within the United States; an anti-communist, anti-progressive, anti-liberal, anti-Soviet, anti-Cuban warmongering hysteria within the United States. If they had the slightest sense of responsibility, of seriousness, or of good faith, they would not unleash a campaign of this nature, as they have done, as can be seen in all the cables.

Let us read this one: "November 22, UPI — The assassin of President Kennedy is an admitted Marxist who spent three years in Russia trying to renounce his U.S. citizenship, but later changed his mind and got a return trip to the United States paid for by the United States Government." That is already a suggestion of blame to the Soviet Union. He was identified as Lee H. Oswald, 24 years old, ex-U.S. marine and chairman of the Fair Play for Cuba Committee.

So, right after that, the insinuation against Cuba. And this is how they have begun all cables, all UPI cables, all reports, Through the reports they have twenty times repeated the same idea and the same thing, using a well-known technique at which they are masters — to insinuate what they want to insinuate, to sow the suspicion that they want to sow over this affair, to slander the Cuban Revolution, to slander the Soviet Union, to create hysteria against our countries.

It says: "Oswald was captured after a shooting fray when he hid in a movie house" . . . Thousands of reports came in on this, many of them contradictory.

" . . . The police say that Oswald worked in a school textbook warehouse in Texas . . . after the crime the police found a Mauser rifle in the building," etc. . . . It says where he was born, it says that on October the 30th he turned up at the U.S. Embassy in Moscow, on October 30th of 1959, and told the officials that he wanted to give up his American citizenship.

"According to reports, he told the Embassy officials: 'I am a Marxist.' The Federal Bureau of Investigations confirmed that Oswald went to Russia and requested Soviet citizenship.

"Oswald told the Embassy officials that he intended to disclose to the Soviet authorities everything he knew from the three years he had been in the Marine Corps."

Listen to that: "Oswald told the Embassy officials that he intended to disclose to the Soviet authorities everything he knew from three years he had been in the U.S. Marine Corps. The Embassy officials said that Russia never granted Oswald the citizenship he requested."

Already they have in their hands a guilty person — true or false? They have already produced someone who is guilty. They have him. And now look: you will see the whole course followed by this campaign.

". . . He told the officials that he intended to disclose all the secrets he knew." Well, later I will refer to that again.

In February, 1962 Oswald apparently changed his mind and returned to the United States. He had in the meantime married a Russian, Marina, had a child. This man, who is charged with something more than desertion, with being a spy, with confessing that he is going to disclose military secrets, simply returned peacefully to the United States — according to them.

It says: "The Embassy officials went over the case and since he had not been granted Soviet citizenship, they decided to give him a passport for the United States . . ."

Can anyone who has said that he will disclose military secrets return to the United Sates without being arrested, tried, without being sent to jail?

It says: "Government records show that he left Moscow with 485 dollars for expenses, which the United States Government gave to him.

"This year Oswald requested another passport. He told the State Department that he wanted to visit England, France, Germany, the Netherlands, Finland, Italy, and the Soviet Union; he said he planned to make a trip in October or December 1963, or in January of 1964. The passport was issued in New Orleans on June 25th; however, it is not known whether Oswald returned the money that was loaned to him for the first return trip to the United States.

"If he did not pay, the new passport should not have been issued," they say. We will use their own reports:

"Dallas, November 22 — another cable — the President of the United States, John F. Kennedy, was shot to death today. The police arrested, as the main suspect of the murder, a pro-Castro American" . . .

Now we find that the man who murdered Kennedy is pro-Castro. We know there are very few pro-Castros — what they call "pro-Castros" in the United States.

They call them "pro-Castro." They label as "pro-Castro" anyone it suits them to according to their propaganda and the business at issue.

Now we find that the man who was yesterday in the Fair Play Committee — in the first cable — was then a "pro-Castro" American who had once tried to become a Soviet citizen. That is how all the cables go, you will see.

Another cable, "Dallas, November 22, UPI — Police arrested Lee H. Oswald today, a Marxist supporter of the Cuban Prime Minister Fidel Castro."

There is not a single cable in which they do not connect the action, the name of the individual whom they assure is guilty, with the Cuban Revolution, with the Soviet Union, with Fidel Castro, pro-Castro, supporter of the Prime Minister, admirer of the Cuban Prime Minister.

It says: "A supporter of the Cuban Prime Minister, Fidel Castro, who tried to obtain citizenship in the Soviet Union, where he lived for several years, denied any knowledge of the criminal action. Oswald killed a policeman. . . ." etc.

And later on, in the same cable: ". . . although Oswald, who heads the Fair Play for Cuba Committee, a pro-Castro entity in this city, admitted ownership of the gun with which the policeman . . ." They keep repeating this all the time.

This one comes later. The most noticeable item here is the lie that this gentleman headed a Fair Play Committee. A lie. We started putting together all the information and statements that have appeared, to see whether there was a Fair Play for Cuba Committee in that area of Texas or in New Orleans. They said that this man . . . where did they get that? . . . They said that he presented himself as secretary of a sectional unit of the Fair Play for Cuba Committee in New Orleans or in Dallas. Some cables say that it was in the month of August, other cables say it was last week. That is what they say.

That is the reason for calling this man "pro-Castro." And that he had defended the Cuban Revolution in a broadcast there.

All this is very queer. We had no news of any such statement. But we looked for reports: Cities where there were Fair Play for Cuba Committees of which we had knowledge — New York, Los Angeles, Cleveland, Baltimore, Chicago, Tampa, Youngstown, Washington, San Francisco, Minneapolis, Philadelphia, Detroit — but nowhere is there a Fair Play for Cuba Committee in Dallas or in New Orleans.

Strange because within their Organization they are super-infiltrated by U.S. citizens, and F.B.I. and CIA agents. Isn't that so? Because everything that the CIA and the FBI do there has been proved. Later they said other things.

Here it says also: "The Chairman of the National Committee declared that the Fair Play for Cuba Committee has never authorized the establishment of a chapter in any city of Texas or Louisiana. 'I can say that Lee Harvey Oswald was never Secretary or Chairman of any Fair Play for Cuba Committee in any city of the United States.' "

But you see, throughout the world, they began to spread the poison from the first moments, that a Fair Play for Cuba Committee was involved. Other things appear later on. Later we will try to analyze who this true or false culprit could be. And we must stick to what they say, we must base ourselves on what they themselves say. All right. That was the 22nd . . .

"November 23, Dallas UPI — Pro-communist Lee Harvey Oswald was charged today with the assassination of President Kennedy. Police said that the paraffin test on Oswald's hands gave positive results that traces of gun-powder were found" etc. . . .

Dallas, November 23rd, UPI — The result of the tests made on Oswald's face is still unknown. Such traces could only exist if the suspect had fired a gun."

So, in the first paragraph they start by saying, "pro-communist," in the second paragraph they speak of something else. Third paragraph — Oswald, a Marxist and sympathizer of the communist regime in Cuba had oatmeal for breakfast . . . In other words, in order to say what he had for breakfast, they repeat that he was a Marxist and sympathizer of the communist regime of Fidel Castro in Cuba. Get it? It is clear enough. We know these people quite well; we have become almost experts in knowing these shameless characters.

They say: "He had oatmeal, apricots, bread, and coffee for breakfast, and sat down comfortably to wait for the authorities to continue questioning him."

"Dallas, November 23rd, UPI — The local police have proof that President John F. Kennedy was assassinated by Castro-Communist Lee Harvey Oswald, according to an official announcement today." So he was murdered by a Castro-communist? Now this man is no longer an American, he is no longer a Marine, this man whom they taught to shoot and kill in the Marine Corps, now this man whom they made an expert shot and sent to all U.S. imperialist bases throughout the world is no longer a Marine. No, he was no longer an American, he was a Castro-Communist, even though we never in our life heard of the existence of this person.

You see how all this propaganda works. An American, a real American, born there, educated by American society and American schools, seeing American films, in the American armed forces, American in every way. All of a sudden he is no longer this; there is nothing of this in the cables. Now we read: 'By the Castro-communist."

All right, Captain Will Fritz said they were certain of this, etc. This was yesterday; now this was today in the afternoon: "Jesse Curry, Dallas Chief of Police, said today that Lee Harvey Oswald admitted being a communist. And now he admitted it today; yesterday he admitted nothing. Today it appears that he admitted being a communist. "Curry added that Oswald admitted to police officers questioning him last night that he was a member of the Communist Party." Now the man has turned out to be a member of the Communist Party. As time passes they discover more titles for this man. The true man or supposed man, this they do not know. Who can . . . ?

All right. One thing is clear: among all the things connected with the assassination is the unleashing of a campaign of slander against the Soviet Union and against Cuba, and a series of perfidious insinuations that have no other object than to repeat a thousands times their intrigue and sheer infamy to create an anti-Soviet and anti-Cuban hysteria among the U.S. people and in public opinion.

So these gentlemen are playing a very strange role in a very strange play, and no one knows what sinister plans may be behind all this.

All right. On the other hand, there is an official statement by the State Department, issued today, which declares: "State Department authorities said today that they had no evidence to indicate that the Soviet Union or any other power is involved in the assassination of President Kennedy.

"Lee Harvey Oswald, a former Marine who lived three years in Russia, has been charged with the crime. When 24 years old Oswald went to Russia; he announced his intention of giving up his U.S. citizenship. After changing his mind and returning to the United States last year, Oswald became a sympathizer of the Cuban prime Minister, Fidel Castro." So they repeat themselves even in the cables where they say they deny they lie. . . . The cable goes on: "State Department officials say that they have no evidence that Cuba is involved in what Oswald did."

Naturally, there is no need for anyone to make excuses for Cuba. There is no need for anyone to apologize for Cuba. Cuba is not asking anyone to excuse her, or pardon her, because even the very idea that we should have to defend ourselves from such an infamy is repugnant in itself. Repugnant in itself.

So we have no need for anyone to defend us or apologize on our behalf. Why does the State Department have to come out today with such a statement? What does this show? It shows that the U.S. authorities themselves, some people in the United States, have become aware of the danger of the anti-Soviet and anti-Cuban campaign unleashed by the most reactionary and warlike circles in the United States.

In other words, the State Department itself understands the danger of such a policy, the very dangerous dead end into which such a campaign of slander and hysteria can lead the United States.

So this shows that there are people in the United States who have understood the need to get out of this situation. This does not mean that the danger is over, because we do not know what is behind the assassination of Kennedy. What is behind the assassination of Kennedy is not known at the moment.

The statement does not eliminate the danger of some frame-up that could be concocted there, but indicates that there are already people in the United States who have understood the danger and risk in such a campaign and indicates that, possibly, there are people in the United States who do not agree with such an adventure, with such madness, with such nonsense that is being carried out in such a criminal and irresponsible way.

All right. The State Department has felt the need to counteract this policy, because who knows where this policy, this campaign, may lead.

Later other things have appeared, because all this is very mysterious. Another cable, this time by Associated Press, says: "A 1961 letter . . ." Of course the United Press International has said nothing on this because its campaign has been one-sided, in one direction only, but not just the UPI. We were listening yesterday to broadcasts of U.S. stations and the very same campaign was being carried on the radio. The name of Castro was mentioned almost more often than the name of the man whom they charge with the murder, incessantly repeated over the radio in the United States.

See how these people act and how much they hate the Revolution. Why should we not suspect that these people could be capable of anything, from the murder of Kennedy up to what they are doing now? People moved by such hatred, people who act with such absolute lack of scruples . . .

The AP cable reads: "A letter dated 1961 found in Pentagon files raises doubts whether Texas governor, John Connally, and not President Kennedy, was the main target of the assassin who shot both yesterday in Dallas.

"The letter, dated January 31st, 1961, was written by hand in Minsk, Soviet Union, by Lee Harvey Oswald, a former Marine, charged with murdering Kennedy and wounding Connally.

"Oswald returned a year ago after spending three years in the Soviet Union.

"The letter was addressed to Connally, then Secretary of the Navy, asking that the dishonorable discharge of Oswald be canceled. The request was denied, and if it is shown that he is the man who fired at Kennedy and Connally, the question might be raised of whom he had more motive to want to kill.

"A copy of Oswald's letter was sent to Connally, who had left his post as Secretary of the Navy on December 20th 1961. Connally briefly replied to Oswald on February 23, 1962, that he was no longer in the Navy and that he had referred his letter to the new Secretary of the Navy.

"A copy of Connally's letter was sent to the new official, Fred Korth, who referred it to the Marine Corps. The Marine Corps referred it to a court of appeals which confirmed Oswald's dishonorable discharge. Oswald's letter maintained that his discharge was a gross error or an injustice."

There are some other cables here in which they speak about a threat, cables that say that in the letter Oswald threatened the then-Secretary of the Navy, that he would take any means to avenge himself for that injustice. And that very same Secretary of the Navy was accompanying Kennedy.

So they themselves have now brought up another possible version.

We have here a report which reads: "District Attorney Henry Wade declared today that he expects to be able to secure a death sentence for Lee Harvey Oswald, former Marine, who has been formally accused of the murder of President John F. Kennedy, according to reports issued by U.S. new agencies.

The report adds that Wade has been District Attorney in twenty-four murder cases and secured twenty-three death penalties. It seems that this District Attorney is a hangman — a life sentence in the other case.

"Wade added that he is in possession of material evidence against Oswald, but refused to say what this evidence was. He said that it has not yet been established whether the Mauser that was found is the murder weapon.

"In all the questioning Oswald has denied that he took any part in the murder.

"Captain Will Fritz, Chief of the Homicide Squad of the

Dallas Police, said that in his opinion, Oswald killed President Kennedy and that for him the case is closed."

Later we have to try to look at some of the facts on who this accused man can be, but we want to speak of the campaign carried on by United Press International.

It just so happens that these events occurred precisely at a moment when Kennedy was being severely attacked by those who considered his Cuban policy too weak.

It could not be us, but only the enemies of the Revolution and the enemies, in general, of a more moderate policy, a less warlike policy, the enemies of a policy like this who might be interested in the death of President Kennedy, the only ones who perhaps could have received the news of the death of Kennedy with satisfaction.

A few days ago an incident drew my attention. This was while the Inter-American Press Association Conference was taking place. It was a scandal, because several governments were strongly attacked, crudely attacked like the government of Brazil, by a certain Mexquita, who said horrible things about the President of Brazil, who even talked about and called for a coup in Brazil; where statements were also made against other presidents, against other Latin American countries, there in the United States, and they made long tirades publishing a whole series of opinions against the speech delivered by Kennedy in Florida, because the speech delivered by Kennedy in Florida was disappointing for a number of persons who favor a more aggressive policy against Cuba. It was a disappointment for the counter-revolutionary elements and it was a disappointment for the warmongering elements in the United States.

And so, a series of cables. Here "Miami, Florida — The Cuban exiles waited tonight in vain for a firm promise from President Kennedy to take energetic measures against the communist regime of Fidel Castro."

It says: "They waited tonight in vain for a firm promise" . . . Many met in the offices of the revolutionary organizations and in their homes, to listen to President Kennedy over the radio. The Spanish translation broadcast over the radio station of the exiles. They listened when the President said: "We in the hemisphere should use all the means at our disposal to prevent the establishment of another Cuba in the hemisphere." That is, they did not accept the fact he said "to prevent the establishment of another Cuba in the hemisphere," because they thought that it carried with it the idea of accepting one Cuba. Many exiles had hopes of more vigorous statements to liberate Cuba from communism, but nevertheless, some felt that the U.S. government was waging a secret war of infiltration against Castro that could not be disclosed. It says that thousands of exiles attended an open air rally in view of Kennedy's arrival, and they heard criticism because of what they described as a weak U.S. policy toward Cuba.

Jose Ignacio Rivero, Editor-in-exile of the *Diario de la Marina*, the oldest Havana newspaper (he will stay there all his life), and Emilio Nuñez Portuondo, former President of the United Nations Security council, called for more positive action by the United States.

Rivero, a member of the Inter-American Press Association, where Kennedy spoke, expressed his doubts over a sinister intrigue among international politicians. That is an "intrigue" because they want to co-exist with us.

It says: He also said in the meeting that "the weak U.S. policy towards Cuba and other American nations is an international shame." This was said by Ignacio Rivero, this one from *Diario de la Marina*, who you know is an ultra-ultra and who has to be linked to the ultra-ultra elements in the United States.

So these elements openly state there that "the weak U.S. policy toward Cuban and other American Nations is an international shame. . . .

"Miami Beach: Latin American newspaper publishers and editors in response to the speech delivered by President Kennedy tonight . . . said that he had not taken a strong enough position against the communist regime of Fidel Castro." That is, that there, where the most reactionary representatives of the press within and without the United States met, according to UPI and AP cables, many of them said that he had not taken a strong enough position against the communist regime of Fidel Castro . . .

Augustin Navarre of *El Espejo* of Mexico, felt that the speech was extremely weak and that his observations on Cuba were not sufficient. . . . He added that "it was necessary to rescue Cuba under Fidel Castro from Communism and not to maintain the status quo." They are speaking against any coexistence. Other Cuban newspaper owners in exile made similar statements.

A series of cables began to arrive. Here: "The president of the Cuban Medical Association in exile, Enrique Huerta, stated that the speech did not clarify any of the fundamental questions related to the Cuba problem . . . He wanted a unanimous attack, a unanimous attack of Kennedy.

The newspaper added that the weak policy followed by the Kennedy Government in respect to Castro, as a result of the policy followed by his predecessor Eisenhower, made it possible for Castro and Khrushchev to cement Cuba into a police state, where the people have practically no hope of successfully rebelling without large-scale outside help.

The newspaper continued: "Kennedy now refuses to allow Cuban exiles to launch attacks against Cuba from U.S. territory."

What is the difference between that way of thinking and taking advantage of the assassination of their President to carry out that policy? See what some of those reactionary circles thought about Kennedy. It says: "Kennedy now refuses to allow Cuban exiles to launch attacks against Cuba from U.S. territory, and in fact uses U.S. air and naval power to maintain Castro in power." That is to say, they accuse Kennedy of using naval and air power to maintain Castro in power.

"There is a considerable difference," says the newspaper, "between this attitude and the daring words about Cuba said by Kennedy during the 1960 Presidential campaign. We doubt that many voters have been disoriented by the President's remarks in relation to Cuba the day before yesterday." It says "And many voters will not have been disoriented."

So there was observed a current of unanimous criticism against what the ultra-reactionary sectors considered a weak policy toward Cuba. And that is how these people think.

And there are cables and more cables and more cables, because they never wrote so many cables. It is obvious, how the news agencies made a tremendous propaganda of all the criticisms made of Kennedy because of his Cuban policy. The UPI overflowed with information as it had never done before, picking up all the criticisms of Kennedy because of his Cuban policy. . . .

Julio Mexquita Ciro, an utterly shameless reactionary who went there to speak against the President of Brazil to carry on a campaign against Brazil and to promote a reactionary, fascist coup against Brazil — see what he says: "Julio Mexquita Ciro, . . . who yesterday moved the editors of the IAPA meeting with his analysis of the economic and political situation in his country, said it was an error on the part of the United states not to have realized the danger that the presence of Cuba meant for the whole continent. Mexquita was in favor of collective action, armed collective action by the hemisphere against Cuba, because 'I am a defender of free determination of nations,' he said."

Mexquita, Mosquito, Mezquino, all means the same thing; just see how reactionary he is. The cable adds; ". . . the Brazilian editor described as primitive President Kennedy's way of looking at the agrarian problem of the hemisphere, and he said that the agrarian problem cannot be measured with the same yardstick for all the nations of the hemisphere." Why did he say this? Because he represents the oligarchy, the big landholders in Brazil, and as I was talking precisely about different shades of policy. Kennedy's policy prompted a type of agrarian reform which is not revolutionary, of course, which is not revolutionary but which clashed with the interest of the oligarchs. And it is very strange that in these days, on the eve of the assassination of Kennedy, a coincidence as never before had been noted. In the opinion of the ultra-reactionary sectors within and without the United States. . . .

And this individual talks here about Kennedy's primitive way of looking at the agrarian problem. And then finally there is something very interesting — really very interesting . . .

It says the third editor to express his opinion, Carbo, who is director of the Executive Council of the Inter-American Press Association — which is a very important job in the intellectual sectors of reaction and the oligarchy — emphasized that there were not strong statements in favor of the liberation of Cuba like the statements that had been made in previous speeches by President Kennedy, especially in the one he made after the heroic battle of Playa Giron — that "heroic battle" where every one of them ended defeated and imprisoned — forecasting the crisis of the communist regime of Cuba. He claims in "Cuba the situation of the government verges on the insoluble, economically, politically and internationally since Castro is no longer reliable, not even to Russia."

But most important of all is how the statement made by this gentleman who holds an important post in reactionary intellectual circles in the United States and abroad as Director of the Executive Council of the Inter-American Press Association, how his statement ends — and this is what drew my attention. The editor of the confiscated Havana newspaper ended by saying: "I believe a coming serious event will oblige Washington to change its policy of peaceful co-existence." What does this mean? What did this gentleman mean when he said this three days before the assassination of Kennedy? What did this gentleman who holds an utmost post in the ultra-reactionary intellectual circles in and outside of the United States, the Director of the Executive Council of the Inter-American Press Association, mean in a cable that is not from *Prensa Latina*, but from Associated Press, dated November 19th — AP Num, 254, AP November 19th, Miami Beach — when he said: "I believe that a coming serious event will oblige Washington to change its policy of peaceful co-existence?"

What does this mean, three days before the murder of President Kennedy? Because when I read this cable it caught my attention, it intrigued me, it seemed strange to me. Was there perhaps some sort of understanding? Was there perhaps some sort of thought about this? Was there perhaps some kind of plot? Was there perhaps in those reactionary circles where the so-called weak policy of Kennedy toward Cuba was under attack, where the policy of ending nuclear threat was under attack, where the policy of civil rights was under attack. . . . Was there perhaps in certain civilian and military ultra-reactionary circles in the United States, a plot against President Kennedy's life?

How strange it is really that the assassination of President Kennedy should take place at a time when there was unanimous agreement of opinion against certain aspects of his policy, a furious criticism of his policy. How strange all this is.

And this man who appears as the guilty person, who was he? Who is he? Is he really guilty? Or is he only an instrument? Is he a psychopath, sick? He could be one or the other. Or is he by any means an instrument of the most reactionary circles in the United States. Who is this man?

Here we have a report of the *New York Times* on Oswald that says, "Last July he tried to enter the Cuban Student Directory, to take part in the plans to overthrow the revolutionary regime of Fidel Castro." It was no longer a Castro-plot. According to the *New York Times* he was trying to enter a counterrevolutionary organization to overthrow the Cuban Revolution. The paper names Cuban refugee sources as the basis for this information.

Oswald was able to return to the United States thanks to a loan of 435 dollars and 71 cents granted to him by the U.S. Government. He succeeded in getting money after an appeal to Senator John G. Tower, Republican, Texas, and he returns from the Soviet Union on U.S. Government money through the intervention of a Republican Senator from Texas.

Oswald has at present a U.S. passport which he obtained as a photographer who wanted to travel abroad during the months of October, November, and December of this year and visit the Soviet Union, Great Britain, the Netherlands, France, and Italy. How strange it is. Since he was arrested yesterday in Dallas, as a suspect, the U.S. radio and television have been stressing that Oswald is the chairman of the Dallas chapter of the Fair Play for Cuba Committee.

"Questioned in New York on this point the Executive Secretary of the Fair Play for Cuba Committee denied that Oswald held such a post, and added that there is no chapter of this organization in Texas."

The *New York Times*, in explaining the contact established between Oswald and the Cuban counter-revolutionaries, says that Jose Antonio Denuza, spokesman of the so-called Cuban Student Directory, had declared in Miami that Oswald met with the delegates of that anti-Castro group in New Orleans last July.

Denuza — The *New York Times* added — said that Oswald said he wanted to aid the Cubans in the fight against communism, and offered 10 dollars contribution and his help in military training of an invasion.

Carlos Bringuier, delegate of the counterrevolutionary organization referred to, said to the *New York Times* that "at first I suspected Oswald. I frankly thought that he might be an FBI or CIA agent trying to find out what we were doing." So Cuban counter-revolutionaries are saying that when Oswald tried to enter their organization he was not accepted because they believed he was from the CIA or FBI, and that he was trying to find out what they were up to.

How curious! And this is not what they publish but they say that he is a Castroite, a communist, an admirer of Fidel Castro. And now it appears that he tried to enter the organization and was not admitted because they thought he belonged to the FBI or CIA. They must know pretty well the kind of agents the FBI and CIA have since they deal with them a lot.

But for the time being, without affirming anything, because we cannot affirm anything, since Oswald could be guilty or innocent, we can't tell; or he could be a CIA or FBI agent, as those people suspected, or an instrument of the most reactionary sectors that may have been planning a sinister plot, who may have planned the assassination of Kennedy because of disagreement with his international policy; or he could be a sick man now being used by U.S. reactionary sectors.

However, there is a series of strange things about this man who is presented to be guilty, who tried to enter counterrevolutionary organizations and yet later they say turned up distributing pro-Castro propaganda — that is what they say — who later appeared on TV. That is strange . . . because he was not a personality, and American television and radio stations do not call just anyone off the street and present him; much less do they go around calling the people of Fair Play for Cuba to carry out campaigns for Cuba. No! They close the newspaper doors to them, they close the radio and television doors to them. How strange that this Oswald — who was first trying to join a counterrevolutionary organization — should turn up now, resorting to television to defend us. How strange! How strange that this former marine should go to the Soviet Union and try to become a Soviet citizen, and that the Soviets should not accept him, that he should say at the American Embassy that he intended to disclose to the Soviet Union the secrets of everything he learned while he was in the U.S. service and that in spite of this statement, his passage is paid by the U.S. Government on the backing of a Texas Republican Senator who is considered to be, as it says here: Texas is considered by them to be . . . Well, I cannot find the paper, but there is a cable around here where they themselves say that Texas is the bulwark of reactionary spirit. And then we find that this man, who says in the Embassy . . . who makes a statement in the Embassy that he is going to disclose the secrets he knows to the Soviet Union, later returns with money given on recommendation of a Republican Senator from Texas. He goes back to Texas and finds a job. This is all so strange!

He is not tried, he is not sentenced, he is given money to return, supported by a Senator from Texas and then, again they give him a passport to travel. This is all so strange! What is there behind all this? What sinister maneuver are they scheming behind all this? Who are those guilty for the murder of Kennedy? Who will benefit from this murder, who could be the only ones to benefit from this murder? The supporters of the invasion of Cuba, the supporters of brink of war policy, and the supporters of war; enemies of peace, the enemies of disarmament, the worst enemies of Negro rights in the United States, the worst enemies of progressive elements and of liberal thought in the United States.

Who can benefit from this, from this action, from this murder, if not the worst reaction, the worst elements of U.S. society? Who could be the only ones interested in this murder? Could it be a real leftist, a leftist fanatic, at a moment when tensions had lessened, at a moment when McCarthyism was being left behind, or was at least more moderate, at a moment when a nuclear test ban treaty is signed, at a moment when speeches are described as weak with respect to Cuba were being made?

It says here — now more things are beginning to come out: "Dallas, Texas, November 23rd, AP — All his life Lee Harvey Oswald has been a solitary, an introverted type with communist ideas, but he was not regarded as a troublemaker. Deep down, his introverted personality was imbued at an early age by an alien ideology enunciated a century ago by Karl Marx."

Dallas police chief Jesse Curry has said that Oswald readily admitted being a communist. How strange, what contradictions. He does not confess to committing the crime. It is supposed that if a fanatic commits a crime of this kind he says so or as someone said: fanatics fire their revolvers in front of everybody, they run out with a revolver as the car passes. The strange case of a fanatic who denies committing a murder, but on the other hand, readily confesses to being a communist — according to the cables.

" 'Apparently he feels proud of being a communist,' Curry added. 'He does not try to conceal it.' "

All these are new stories which did not appear yesterday. They are of today. "Although accused of the assassination of the President, Lee Harvey Oswald has resisted all efforts by the authorities to make him confess; Oswald has told newsmen: 'I did not kill President Kennedy. I did not kill anyone.' "

What sort of person was Oswald before his arrest? He was born in New Orleans on the 18th of October, 1939. "My father died before I was born," Oswald said. "His widowed mother brought the family to Fort Worth. A Fort Worth police officer, who asked that his name not be revealed said he has known Oswald since both were in fifth grade, until he entered high school at Fort Worth. This police officer, Oswald's former classmate, recalled the following: he always opposed any sort of discipline. He seemed to hold something against people there, against any authority; he was never like the rest of the kids. He rarely associated with them, but he never was a troublemaker.

"At high school he talked a lot about how things should be. Oswald — he added — began to be interested in communism when he was 15 years old, when a Marxist pamphlet came to his hands. Later, he read Karl Marx's *Capital*, the bible of communism. At 17, Oswald left school only 23 days after the high school term started, and soon joined the Marine Corps.

"His military career was a failure. On two occasions he was court martialed for violating regulations. His specialty was as an operator of electronics equipment. He served in Japan but never got farther than private first class.

"Oswald's career in the Marines concluded on September 11th, 1959, when he was given leave to support his mother. He was transferred to inactive reserve but later on was dishonorably discharged.

"One month later, Oswald arrived in Moscow. On October 26th, 1959, he visited the American Embassy and announced his intention of giving up his citizenship. He told Embassy officials: 'I am a Marxist.'

"In February 1962, after a study of his case, the conclusion was reached that Oswald had not acquired Soviet citizenship and therefore at his request they gave him a U.S. passport and granted him a loan in order to return to the country.

"Back in the United States, Oswald went to his native New Orleans. Last June, he requested a new passport to return to the Soviet Union. In the meantime he was involved in a dispute with an anti-Castro Cuban, Carlos Bringuier, who said: 'I suspected him from the beginning. Frankly I thought he could be an agent of the FBI or CIA who tried to infiltrate us and see what we were doing.' "

The rest is similar to what we already have read here. but there are new ingredients. In fact a whole series, a whole propaganda chain, distributed in doses.

First that he is a member of the Fair Play for Cuba Committee which was false. Later a man who lived in the Soviet Union. Afterwards, a whole series of insinuations in several cables. Today, he is not only all that, he is also a communist and a very willing communist at that, he admits it. In fact all this is really very strange.

Their description is not that of a fanatic. But that of an individual with a number of characteristics that really fit what U.S. reaction wants like a ring on a finger, that fit the worst policy of the United States; a person who seems to have been expressly made for this purpose, expressly made for specific ends: to create hysteria, to unleash an anti-Soviet, anti-Cuban, anti-communist, anti-progressive, anti-liberal campaign in the United States; to eliminate a President whose policy collided head on with the policy promoted by the most reactionary circles in the country after the nuclear test ban treaty, after several speeches which were unanimously attacked for being weak toward Cuba.

What can have been the motives for the assassination of President Kennedy? What can there be behind all this? We cannot affirm anything because we do not have other elements for judgment: both the personality of the individual and the propaganda being carried out are suspicious, everything is suspicious.

We cannot categorically affirm what is behind all this, but we do affirm that it is suspicious; that we must be careful, that we must be vigilant, that we must be alert. Because this man may be innocent, a cat's paw, in a plan very well prepared by people who knew how to prepare these plans; or he may be a sick man and if so, the only honest thing is to hand him over for a medical examination and not to be starting a campaign extremely dangerous to world peace; or he may be an instrument very well chosen and very well trained by the ultra-right, by ultra-conservative reaction of the United States with the deliberate aim of eliminating a President who, according to them, did not carry out the policy he should have — more warlike, more aggressive, more adventuresome policy. And it is necessary for all people of the United States themselves to demand that what is behind the Kennedy assassination be clarified.

It is in the interest of the U.S. people and of the people of the world, that this be made known, that they demand to know what is really behind the assassination of Kennedy, that the facts be made clear: whether the man involved is innocent, sick or an instrument of the reactionaries, an agent of a macabre plan to carry forward a policy of war and aggression, to place the Government of the United States at the mercy of the most aggressive circles of monopoly, of militarism and of the worst agencies of the United States. It is in our interest, in the interest of all people and of the U.S. people that we demand this.

We believe that intellectuals, lovers of peace, should understand the seriousness of a policy of this nature, a campaign of this type. They should understand the trend of the events and the danger that maneuvers of this kind could mean to world peace, and what a conspiracy of this type, what a Machiavellian policy of this nature could lead to.

This is the analysis we wanted to make and the things we wanted to take into consideration; to express our opinion, the opinion of our Party and of our Government; to make known the strong antagonisms between the governments of the United States and ourselves, to make known the more moderate side of their policy, that least warlike; the policy that is less aggressive than the policy advocated by the others, or by the other U.S. sectors. So that we, as revolutionaries, as conscious men and women, may know how to analyze problems of this nature, difficult problems, delicate problems, complex problems; because policy in a country like the United States is very complex. A countless number of factors are taken into consideration in the policy making of this country. Very often they are contradictory factors. But undoubtedly, these things that we have been pointing out about the campaign are some of the means — certainly the most immoral — by which policy is worked out.

What are these right-wing circles trying to do? To impose on the new administration? What is the plan of these circles? To place the new administration in a *de facto* situation facing an inflamed public opinion, exacerbated by propaganda, by the campaign; a public opinion moved by profound hatred toward the Soviet Union, toward Cuba, toward progressive ideas, even towards liberal ideas. That is, this campaign tends to place the United States in the worst international position, in the most reactionary international position. And that surely is a serious threat to peace.

We are not worried about ourselves. We are worried about the interests of mankind.

We know that the fate of our country depends also on the fate of mankind; we do not fear for ourselves; we are and always will be calm. We are concerned about peace and about calling attention to all these events.

We are concerned to give warning of the dangers of these events. We want the people to be informed and calm, as they have always been, as staunch and as willing as always, to defend the Revolution. That they be ready always to defend the fatherland, with a morale as high as ever, as high as the Turquino mountain — as Camilo used to say: that they be ready, alert, and vigilant as always, facing intrigues and dangers, whatever they may be!

However contemptible, however infamous, however criminal these campaigns may be, let the enemies of our country know that they will always find us unwavering, that they will always find us alert, with our head held high, ready to fulfill our slogan, Homeland or Death! We will win!

Appendix III

Analyses of the Warren Commissions's Evidence and Conclusions by Vincent J. Salandria

The following Appendix includes three articles by Vincent J. Salandria. They originally appeared between November, 1964 and March, 1965 and analyze the Warren Report. With each succeeding article Salandria was able to deepen his analysis, and in the third article, which appeared in the March, 1965 issue of Liberation, *he was able to bring to bear evidence from the then available 26 volumes of Warren Commission exhibits. A careful reading of this March article is critical for the reader to see that the Warren Report was not the work of a commission that "rushed to judgment," but was rather a conscientiously prepared fabrication. As such this article stands as an indictment of the Commission members as accessories after the fact in helping to conceal the assassination conspiracy.*

Following Salandria's articles is a brief essay on the bullet holes in the back of the President's jacket and shirt.

The Warren Report Analysis of Shots, Trajectories, and Wounds: A Lawyer's Dissenting View

by Vincent J. Salandria

Arlen Specter, Esq., Assistant Counsel of the President's Commission on the Assassination of President Kennedy, was quoted by *The Philadelphia Evening Bulletin* of October 23, 1964, page 4, as follows: "The people are going to have to rely on the conclusions (that have been drawn) and the stature of the men on the Commission."

We know that Mr. Specter did not mean by the above statement that the Warren Commission was ever meant to be construed as a "ministry of truth." Nor would the members of the Commission, as public servants in a democracy, ever consider that their "stature" insulated their interpretations and findings from public criticism. Since we are all agreed on this score, we can now proceed to disagree.

Let us then, as lawyers, address ourselves to the evidence and findings of the Commission, limiting ourselves for the present to Mr. Specter's area of particular interest relating to the shots, their number, source or sources and trajectories. We will also look briefly into the subject of the wounds inflicted. Then we will scrutinize the Commission's conclusions that their evidence supports the propositions that three shots were fired by Lee Harvey Oswald alone from a bolt-action 6.5mm. Carcano rifle

Originally published in *The Philadelphia Legal Intelligencer*, November 2, 1964.

while he was stationed at a window on the sixth floor of the Texas School Book Depository Building. The Commission further concluded that the three shots caused all the damage at the assassination site and that the time span between the first and last shot which struck President Kennedy and Governor Connally was 4.5 to 5.6 seconds. These conclusions I commend to your scrutiny and urge that you relate them to the evidence of the Commission.

First, with reference to the source of the shots, it is not central to my thesis that the Warren Commission erred in determining that three shots came from the Book Depository Building. On the contrary, I am willing to concede for the purposes of this presentation that three shots did come from the Book Depository Building. But I will endeavor to prove that all the evidence of the Commission's Report points up that another shot or shots came from a source other than the Depository Building.

The following witnesses reported evidence indicating a source other than the Book Depository Building: Austin L. Miller on the railroad bridge thought the shots came from the Presidential limousine itself.[1] Frank E. Reilly, an electrician on the same bridge, heard three shots that seemed to come from the trees "on the north side of Elm Street at the corner up there" (W-70). S.M. Holland heard "four shots which sounded as though they came from the trees on the north side of Elm Street where he saw a puff of smoke" (W-76). Thomas J. Murphy said the two shots he heard "came from a spot just west of the Depository" (W-76). L.E. Bowers, Jr. said they came "either from the Depository Building or near the mouth of the Triple Underpass" (W-76).

Arlen Specter, Esq., stated that Senator Ralph W. Yarborough said he smelled gunpowder at the assassination site. Mr. Specter dismissed this as the function of "an overly active olfactory

---

[1]*Report of the President's Commission on the Assassination of President Kennedy*. United States Printing Office, Washington, D.C. 1964, p. 70. References to this Report are designated by "W," followed by a page number.

sense." He admitted that a Dallas police officer was reported to have smelled gunpowder 350 to 400 feet from the Depository Building immediately following the assassination shots. Mr. Specter did not comment on this.[2] If the smell of gunpowder was detectable at street level immediately after the assassination, then this would indicate a source of shots other than the sixth floor of the Book Depository Building.

So, the Commission ignored all of the above in so far as the evidence reveals auditory, visual, and olfactory stimuli reception incompatible with the source of shots exclusively from the Book Depository Building. Needless to say, this aforementioned evidence does not rule out additional shots having been fired from the building in question. But it certainly supports the conclusion that one or more shots originated from the tree and fence area north of Elm Street.

Further support for the inference that at least one shot emanated from a source other than the Book Depository Building is the fact that James T. Tague was hit in the cheek by a bullet, or part of a bullet, which impact evidently was the result of a ricochet from the "south curb of Main Street." Tague "got out of his car to watch the motorcade from a position between Commerce and Main Streets" (W-116). Please take careful note that Tague was not on Elm Street, not on Main Street, but between Main and Commerce Streets "near the Triple Underpass" (W-116). From my view of the pictures, maps and exhibits of the Commission Report (let us except my personal inspection of the situs in Dallas) I conclude that the South curb of Main Street near the Triple Underpass was not in the line of fire with the presidential limousine traveling on Elm Street. Tague was about 1½ blocks from the building in question. But he was directly across from the tree and fence area on the north side of Elm Street from which so many witnesses reported the shots came. The Commission finds "The mark on the curb could have originated from the lead core of a bullet but the absence of

---

[2]Arlen Specter, Esq., Bar Association Meeting, October 22, 1964, Room 653, City Hall, Philadelphia, Pennsylvania.

copper precluded the possibility that the mark on the curbing section was made by an unmutilated military full metal-jacketed bullet such as the bullet from Governor Connally's stretcher" (W-116). The obvious deduction that this was a bullet fired from the north side of Elm Street and that it came from a rifle which was different from the Carcano that the Commission described as the assassination weapon, is scrupulously avoided. The bullet smear on the curbing did not reveal a trace of the metal jacket which coated the bullets allegedly fired from the Carcano. This fact cries for the inference that the bullet which hit Tague was of a different type, made of lead and antimony, and sans copper. If such was the case then more than one gun was firing on that fateful day, and more than one man was firing. My law school professors described such activity as pointing in the direction of a conspiracy. Such a conclusion is in accordance with the basic scientific law of parsimony which requires us to select as between two equally good explanations.

Next, let us consider the number of shots. The Commission states, "It is possible that the assassin carried an empty shell in the rifle and fired only two shots with the witnesses hearing multiple noises made by the same shot. Soon after the three empty cartridges were found, officials at the scene decided that three shots were fired . . ." (W-111). So, therefore the Commission concedes that since only three shells were found, no more than three shots could have been fired from the vantage point of the sixth floor of the Depository Building. It suggests that maybe less than three were fired if the assassin brought in a discharged shell. In that event he would have fired only two shots on that day from that point. The Commission speaks as if their problem is perhaps one of superfluous shots which are not required to explain the carnage of that dreadful site. Examination of the Commission's evidence, however, indicates the opposite to be true. This reader is not satisfied that only three shots could possibly have raked that lead-spewn site on November 22, 1963.

Let us presently read G.A. Bennett's testimony with reference to the number of shots fired. "Secret Service Agent Glen A. Bennett, stationed in the right rear seat of the President's followup car, who heard a sound like a firecracker as the motorcade proceeded down Elm Street. At that moment, Agent Bennett stated: "I looked at the back of the President. I heard another firecracker noise and saw that shot hit the President about four inches down from the right shoulder. A second shot followed immediately and hit the right rear of the President's head" (W-111).

The Report goes on to explain "Substantial weight may be given Bennett's observations" because "he recorded what he saw and heard at 5:30 P.M. November 22, 1963, on the airplane en route back to Washington" (W-111). According to Bennett, then, the first shot missed.

The Commission discussed other evidence to indicate the first shot did not miss. Then the Report goes completely awry. "If the first shot did not miss, there must be an explanation for Governor Connally's recollection that he was not hit by it. There was conceivably a delayed reaction between the time the bullet struck him and the time he realized that he was hit . . ." (W-112). Conceivably Governor Connally had a delayed reaction to realizing he was hit, but Abraham Zapruder's motion picture frames taken at the assassination scene did not register subjective findings. These frames recorded what actually happened and not what was subjectively felt. These films show, according to Governor Connally's own viewing, that the Governor's body reacted some 6-9 frames later than that of the President at frames 231 to 234 (W-112). The President's body showed reaction at frame 225 (W-112). According to photographer Phillip L. Willis, he "snapped a picture at a time which he also asserts was simultaneous with the first shot. Analysis of his photograph revealed that it was taken at approximately frame 210 of the Zapruder film which was the approximate time of the shot that probably hit the President . . ." (W-112). Therefore, according to Willis' photograph, the President was hit at frame 210 of the Zapruder film, or some 21 to 24 frames before Governor Connally's body seems to react. Some 1.04 to 1.31 seconds after the President's body reacted, Governor Connally indicates that he was hit.

If we are to assume that the Commission is correct in stating that the President's body was seen to react at Zapruder frame

225, and that he was hit at this point, then the Governor's body reacted from 3-9 frames later than when the President was hit. At 18.3 frames per second, this would be translated into the time period of 0.34-0.49 seconds. These films record that the Governor's body reacted 0.34-0.49 seconds after the President's body reacted. This interval is, as is the interval recorded by photographer Willis of 1.04 to 1.31, below the minimum firing time of 2.3 seconds necessary to operate the rifle. This 2.3 seconds was the top accomplishment of the Commission's marksmen, at stationary and not moving targets, which feat was only accomplished once and then never again approached by the Commission experts (W-193). Lt. Col. A.G. Folsom Jr., head, Records Branch, Personnel Department, Headquarters U.S. Marine Corps, evaluated Oswald's marine shooting ratings as indicating a fairly good shot'' (sharpshooter qualification) and as a ''rather poor shot'' (low marksman rating) (W-191). Naturally, both 0.34-0.49 and 1.04-1.31 second intervals represent time periods far above the maximum time of the bullet in transit from the President to the Governor.

Irrespective of Governor Connally's reaction time, the Zapruder films should show the Governor's body conforming to the simple law of physics which requires that every action have an equal reaction. If Governor Connally did not have any nervous system at all, his body would have had to react immediately when pierced with a rifle bullet from back to chest which projectile exited at the speed of 1500 feet per second (W-109). The Governor's body did not register any lurch when the first bullet struck the President. As a matter of fact, the Commission asks us to believe that the Governor executed a turn completely around to the right, and then partially to the left after he had been struck with at least one bullet in the back, through the right nipple, right wrist and left thigh.

The Governor's body did not react immediately after the President's body reacted. Therefore, he was not hit by the same bullet that hit the President. The Commission would have us believe that Governor Connally was wrong (W-112), his wife was wrong (W-112) the F.B.I.'s initial findings were wrong; all the eyewitnesses were wrong (none contradicted the Governor's recollection); the Zapruder films were wrong, and that there is no law of physics called action and reaction.[3] Governor Connally was not hit by the first bullet to hit President Kennedy. All of the above-mentioned evidence is against it.

See how weak the following testimony is in support of the Commission's proposition that the first bullet to hit the President also hit the Governor: "Dr. Frederick W. Light, Jr., the third of the wound ballistics experts . . . testified that the anatomical findings were insufficient for him to formulate a firm opinion as to whether the same bullet did or did not pass through the President's neck first before inflicting all the wounds on Governor Connally" (W-109). The Commission further states, "The alignment of the points of entry was only indicative and not conclusive that one bullet hit both men" (W-107).

If Governor Connally was not hit by the same first bullet to hit the President, then the Government's case is destroyed. The Government admits one shot missed (W-111). A separate shot removed the back of the President's head (W-199). This would constitute a minimum of four shots and would put the Government's theory that only three bullets were fired out of business. The explanation that the President and the Governor were first hit by different shots conforms to the "substantial majority of the witnesses who stated that the shots were not evenly spaced. Most witnesses recalled that the second and third shots were bunched together . . . " (W-115). Governor Connally said he was hit at a point corresponding to frames 231 to 234 of the Abraham Zapruder films (W-105). If, as the Commission states, the President was hit no later than at frame 225, then this would indicate two separate shots hitting close upon one another. Since they were fired within 6 to 9 frames of one another, or according to photographer Willis 21 to 24 frames of one another, this represents a time interval of from 0.34 to 1.31 seconds. This time gap is insufficient to allow firing from the same bolt-action rifle and therefore points to the existence of another marksman. Needless to say, the majority view of the spectators that the last

---

[3]Arlen Specter, Esq., Bar Association Meeting, October 22, 1964.

two shots were bunched, militates against a single carbine, bolt-action weapon doing all the firing. The time period between the first hit on the President and the final hit on him is not greater than 5.6 seconds according to the Commission's own findings. "As previously indicated, the time span between the shot entering the back of the President's neck and the bullet which shattered his skull was 4.8 to 5.6 seconds" (W-117). Therefore, 5.6 seconds being the longest time span, if there were two hits on the President and one separate hit on Connally, there could not have been any bunching of two shots since the once-accomplished 2.3 seconds minimum firing time could not permit bunching.

The Commission tries to have Connally nailed with the same bullet that struck the President. If logical fallacies were bullets, the job would have been done cleanly. Here is the reasoning: "The bullet that hit President Kennedy in the back and exited through his throat most likely could not have missed both the automobile and its occupants. Since it did not hit the automobile, Frazier testified that it probably struck Governor Connally" (W-105). But that argument assumes as proven that which the Commission had not proven, to wit, that no other marksman was firing from any vantage point other than the Book Depository Building. A shot from the tree and fence area above the grassy knoll on the north side of Elm Street would account for a shot passing through the President and not striking the ear in a flatter trajectory. This simple explanation which conforms to logic, geographical facts and trajectory is never considered by the Commission.

Additional evidence to the effect that there were more than three shots fired can be deduced from the testimony of the following: Royce G. Skelton who was on the railroad bridge "thought that there had been a total of four shots, either the third or fourth of which hit in the vicinity of the underpass" (W-116). Dallas Patrolman J.W. Foster, who was also on the Triple Underpass, testified that a shot hit the curb near a manhole cove in the vicinity of the underpass" (W-116). James T. Tague, as previously mentioned, was struck in the cheek by a missile" (W-116). These three witnesses could well be accurately recording separate shots missing their target. From all the above, I deduce that more than three shots were fired from more than one rifle.

In addition to the hard fact of the hitting of Tague, and the bullet strike in the curbing, we have in the Presidential limousine "the cracking of the windshield and the dent on the windshield chrome" (W-105). Where these hits came from is never explained satisfactorily by the Commission.

Finally, let us discourse briefly on the trajectory as revealed by the wounds. Assistant Professor of Surgery Robert N. McClelland, M.D. of Parkland Hospital stated that "cause of death was due to massive head and brain injury from a gunshot wound of the left temple" (W-527).

You will recall that Secret Service Agent Glen A. Bennett, stationed in the right rear seat of the President's followup car saw a "shot hit the President about four inches down from the right shoulder" (W-111). "An examination of the suit jacket worn by the President by F.B.I. Agent Frazier revealed a roughly circular hole approximately one-fourth of an inch in diameter on the rear of the coat, 5 $^3/_8$ inches below the top of the collar and 1 $^3/_4$ inches to the right of the center back seam of the coat" (W-92). "The shirt worn by the President contained a hole on the back side 5 $^3/_4$ inches below the top of the collar and 1 $^1/_8$ inches to the right of the middle of the back of the shirt" (W-92). "The tie had a nick on the side of the knot" (W-92). The Commission would have us believe that a trajectory of a bullet from the sixth story downward would hit the President four inches from the right shoulder, or 5 $^3/_4$ inches from the top of his shirt collar, and ranging upward emerge from his neck tie knot without having hit any bones. This proposed trajectory of down and then up fails to comport with a sixth-floor shot, and if possible at all, must have been fired from a lower level. Further they ask that this same bullet which exited flying upward after not hitting any bone in the President (W-88) then changed direction in mid-air and coursed downward striking the Governor in the back, chest, right wrist, and left thigh (W-92).

When I suggested to Arlen Specter, Esq. on the 22nd of October, 1964 that the Commission owes it to the public to enact the alleged performance of Oswald with a rifle on moving targets, he asked whether I would have them kill a man. The joke fell upon ears which detect no humor in murder. I insisted that the moving target could convey dummies. Mr. Specter then complained that the traffic conditions were terrible around the Book Depository Building. I explained to him that the conditions could be duplicated with a tower and an open field. To this he made no reply.

Having read the Report, I conclude that the evidence offered by the Commission indicates there was more than one rifleman firing on November 22, 1963. There were more than three shots. If Oswald was one of the gunmen, then with that gun, from that vantage point, in that timespan, suggested by the Commission, he could not have been alone in the performance of the terrible work that destroyed our President and wounded two other men.

A Philadelphia Lawyer Analyzes the Shots, Trajectories, and Wounds

by Vincent J. Salandria

Bullets inflicted certain wounds that killed President Kennedy on November 22nd, 1963. Since that time the Warren Commission has filed its report concerning them. (*Report of the President's Commission on the Assassination of President Kennedy*, United States Printing Office, Washington, D.C., 1964. References to this Report are designated by "W" followed by page number.) Chapter III of the report is entitled "The Shots From the Texas Book Depository" (W-61):

> In this chapter the Commission analyzes the evidence and sets forth its conclusions concerning the source, effect, number and timing of the shots that killed President Kennedy and wounded Governor Connally. (W-61)

The Commission's conclusions in this chapter are

> that the shots which killed President Kennedy and wounded Governor Connally were fired from the sixth-floor window at the southeast corner of the Texas School Book Depository Building. Two bullets probably caused all the wounds suffered by President Kennedy and Governor Connally. Since the preponderance of the evidence indicated that

Originally published in *Liberation*, IX, No. 10 (January 1965), 13-19.

> three shots were fired, the Commission concluded that one shot probably missed the Presidential limousine and its occupants, and that the three were fired in a time period ranging from approximately 4.8 to in excess of 7 seconds. (W-117)

If the reader will strip himself of all prejudice, we have work to do. Because of space limitations, we will concede *for the purposes of this article only,* that a gunman was firing a 6.5 mm. Carcano from the sixth floor at the southeast corner of the Depository Building. Our efforts will be to explore the Commission's conclusion that all the shots came from the Texas Book Depository Building, and that the assassination was the accomplishment of a single gunman.

In forming its conclusion, the Commission has relied, *inter alia*, upon "motion-picture films and still photographs taken at the time of the assassination" (W-61), especially the motion picture films of Mr. Abraham Zapruder. (Hereafter, when reference is made to a specific Zapruder frame, it will be done by a "Z" followed by a number.)

The Fatal Wound

First let us review the fatal wound of the dead President. For all its detailed appearance, the Commission's report on this wound is very incomplete.

The autopsy report prepared in the National Naval Medical Center at Bethesda, Maryland describes the following wound on the side of the President's head:

> There is a large irregular defect of the scalp and skull on the right involving chiefly the parietal bone but extending somewhat into the temporal and occipital regions. In this region there is an actual absence of scalp and bone producing a defect which measures approximately 13 cm. in greatest diameter. (W-540)

Dr. Robert N. McClelland of Parkland Hospital, in his statement prepared on November 22, 1963 at 4:45 P.M., said: "The cause of death was due to massive head and brain injury from a gunshot wound of the left temple" (W-526,527).

In support of Dr. McClelland's statement, which is not discussed by the Commission at all, I would like to bring forward a comment made by a very material witness who was never examined by the Commission. In the November 24th, 1963, *Philadelphia Sunday Bulletin* there is an article datelined Dallas, Nov. 23rd, 1963. In this article, on page 3, titled "How the Suspect was Subdued," Father Oscar L. Huber, pastor of Holy Trinity Catholic Church, described how he administered the last rites to the President:

> "The President was lying on a rubber tired table when I came in," Father Huber said. He was standing at his head. Father Huber said the President was covered by a white sheet which hid his face, but not his feet. "His feet were bare," said Father Huber . . . He said he wet his right thumb with holy oil and anointed a Cross over the President's forehead, noticing as he did, a "terrible wound" over his left eye.

As we write we notice that the advance Associated Press release of Jacqueline Kennedy's testimony before the Commission made reference to a gap in the transcript:

> At this point in the transcript appear the words "reference to wounds deleted." This is one of the very few omissions noted in the transcript. (*The Philadelphia Evening Bulletin*, Nov. 23rd, 1964)

We were told by J. Lee Rankin, the Commission's counsel, that classified material involving national security was withheld from the transcript volumes (*The Philadelphia Inquirer*, Nov. 20, 1964). What possible connection can the wounds inflicted on the President by a lone assassin have with national security — unless they are not the wounds described by the Commission in its report?

At this point, we will discuss the films to cast light on the crucial question of whether Governor Connally was struck with the same bullet which first hit the President.

The Commission concluded, "Two bullets probably caused all the wounds suffered by President Kennedy and Governor Connally" (W-117), and "one shot passed through the President's neck and then most probably passed through the Governor's body" (W-111). According to Special Agent Robert A. Frazier, Governor Connally was hit no later than "at some point in between frames [Z] 235 and 240" (W-106). President Kennedy was finally hit, according to the Commission, at frame 313 (W-108). Therefore, the Commission, in weaving one shot through the President and the Governor, had to conclude that the first shot, and not the second shot to hit the President, hit the Governor. If the reader does not accept the Commission's finding that the first shot that hit the President also hit the Governor, the reader parts company with the Commission on the lone assassin concept. The Commission found that "three shots were fired, . . . one shot probably missed the car and its occupants. The evidence is inconclusive as to whether it was the first, second, or third shot which missed" (W-111). If we agree with the Commission's findings that one shot missed and that the last shot to hit the President did not hit the Governor then only one shot is left. This shot must be passed through both the President and the Governor, or the Commission runs out of rifle ammunition.

Let us not be driven off course by the Commission's assertion:

> It is possible that the assassin carried an empty shell in the rifle and fired only two shots, with the witnesses hearing multiple noises made by the same shot . . . three empty cartridges were found . . .
> (W-110, 111)

This speculation conforms to none of the evidence. Analysis of the shot evidence will clearly show that the Commission's problem is quite the opposite of that which it suggests. The facts indicate that the shots fired at the assassination site were more than three and could not have been less than three.

Only if the first shot struck both the President and the Governor can the Commission rationally contend that no more than three shots were fired. Therefore the Commission's case must stand or fall with the validity or invalidity of this inference.

The Zapruder films indicate a definite reaction of the President to a hit in the neck region at frame 225 (W-112). Governor Connally's body shows no reaction to any hit at this frame (W-103). The Governor has repeatedly stated in the Report (W-112) and for the press and television, that he was not hit by the first shot that hit the President. Mrs. Connally corroborates her husband's testimony, stating:

> that after the first shot she turned and saw the President's hands moving toward his throat, as seen in the films at frame 225. However, Mrs. Connally further stated that she thought her husband was hit immediately thereafter by the second bullet. (W-112)

Of the many eyewitnesses to the assassination, not one lends the slightest credibility to the Commission's inference that the first bullet to strike the President struck the Governor. The report is devoid of testimony to this effect. No newspaper or magazine account of the assassination (and I have read hundreds) ever suggests a witness who saw it that way.

As the objective evidence continued to mount against the Commission on this critical point of the double hit, the Commission tried to retreat into subjectivity:

> If the first shot did not miss, there must be an explanation for Governor Connally's recollection that he was not hit by it. There was conceivably a delayed reaction between the time the bullet struck him and the time he realized he was hit . . .
> (W-112)

But the Zapruder films are more objective than the Commission and the Governor's nervous system. If the Governor were a sack of gelatine which could "realize" nothing, that sack would have probably lurched forward when pierced through from behind by a rifle bullet which exited at a speed of 1,776 feet per second (W-95). High school physics tells us that the law of action and reaction requires every action to have an equal and opposite reaction. The thrust of this bullet through the body of the Governor was not recorded by the Zapruder films. The pictures are excellent evidence that the first bullet to hit the President did not hit the Governor.

Now we turn to plane geometry and the trajectories of the shots. For this purpose, we start with the holes in the clothing of the President:

> An examination of the suit jacket worn by the President by F.B.I. Agent Frazier revealed a roughly circular hole approximately one-fourth of an inch in diameter on the rear of the coat, 5 3/8 inches below the top of the collar and 1 3/4 inches to the right of the center back seam of the coat. (W-92)

> The shirt worn by the President contained a hole on the back side 5 3/4 inches below the top of the collar and 1 1/8 inches to the right of the middle of the back of the shirt. (W-92)

Strange Inferences

At the time the first bullet impacted upon the President, Governor Connally, according to the Commission, was seated in a position which placed him in front of the President (W-106). The first shot to hit the President was designated by the Commission as having hit the Governor at any place between Z frames 207 through 225 (W-106). During these frames the angle from a rifle in the sixth floor window of the Depository Building was roughly from 21° to 20° (W-102, 103).

One would expect such a shot with a downward trajectory from the sixth floor, hitting the President 5 3/4 inches below the coat collar and not hitting any bone, (W-88) (the autopsy report describes the bullet entering "the upper right posterior thorax" [W-541]) would continue its path downward at a roughly 20° angle and emerge from the abdominal area. Instead, this remarkable bullet *turned upward.* It then exited from the President, who was sitting perfectly erect (W-102, 103), and tore through the left portion of his tie knot (W-91).

One would certainly, once accepting this unusual and highly improbable course of the bullet, have to concede that it would fly harmlessly over the Governor's head heading for the sky. But the Commission asks us to believe that this strange bullet *changed direction in mid-air.* No bullet ever has, unless spent. But this bullet was far from spent, for it had an entrance velocity after passing through the President of 1,858 feet per second (W-95).

In mid-air, the Commission *turned this bullet downward* into the back of the Governor, who was sitting erect with his back to the President (W-103). Then this extraordinary missile pierced the back of the Governor and emerged from his right nipple.

The United States Army ballistics experts, Drs. Olivier and Arthur J. Dziemian, "concluded that it was probable that the same bullet passed through the President's neck and then inflicted all the wounds on the Governor" (W-107-09). But the Commission is forced to conclude that: "The alignment of the points of entry was only indicative and not conclusive that one bullet hit both men" (W-107). As I see the alignment of the points of entry, they indicate conclusively that the same bullet could not have hit both men.

Dr. Frederick W. Light, Jr., the third U.S. Army ballistics expert,

> testified that the anatomical findings were insufficient for him to formulate a firm opinion as to whether the same bullet did or did not pass through the President's neck before inflicting all the wounds on Governor Connally. Based on the other circumstances, such as the relative positions

> of the President and the Governor in the automobile, Dr. Light concluded that it was probable that the same bullet traversed the President's neck and inflicted all the wounds on Governor Connally. (W-109)

Dr. Light has seen things "in the relative positions of the President and the Governor" which were not apparent to him in the anatomical findings and which were not even seen by the Commission which stated that: "The alignment of the points of entry was only indicative and not conclusive that one bullet hit both men."

An Extra Bullet

Failing to support through evidence and introspection the proposition that the same first shot which struck the President also struck the Governor, the Commission next tried its hand at logic:

> The bullet that hit President Kennedy in the back and exited through his throat most likely could not have missed both the automobile and its occupants. Since it did not hit the automobile, Frazier testified that it probably struck Governor Connally. (W-105)

This begs the question. Chapter III, entitled "The Shots from the Texas School Book Depository," did not prove that the shots originated exclusively from the Depository Building. We will show how the evidence of the Commission proves the contrary of the imputation.

A shot downward, into the erect back of the President, 5 ³⁄₄ inches from his collar top, and then up through the neck tie knot, describes a shot flying upward. It would indeed "have missed both the automobile and its occupants."

From our discussion thus far, I feel that the evidence of the Zapruder films, the testimony of Governor and Mrs. Connally, the impossible course or courses of the bullet described by the Commission, the demonstrative evidence of the bullet holes in the clothing of the President and the Governor, the contradictory ballistics testimony, the problem of the alignment of the President and the Governor, and the resort to logical fallacy on the part of the Commission spell out *at least one separate shot hitting the Governor after the President had been hit by a different bullet*. To conclude otherwise would be to grasp at not only the improbable but what photography, all the eyewitness testimony, logic, the laws of physics, and geometry tell us is impossible.

Once we conclude that a separate shot hit Governor Connally, we are confronted with an extra bullet, which puts the Commission theory of just three bullets from one gun into the limbo of historical myth. We must not forget that another man, James T. Tague, was wounded by one of those bullets, a fact to which we will return.

The Time Factor

Also there is the time difficulty:

> Examination of the Zapruder motion picture camera by the FBI established that 18.3 pictures or frames were taken each second, and therefore, the timing of certain events could be calculated by allowing 1/18.3 seconds for the action depicted from one frame to the next. (W-97)
>
> Tests of the assassin's rifle disclosed that at least 2.3 seconds were required between shots. (W-97)

Photographer, Phillip L. Willis, says he

> snapped a picture at a time which he also asserts was simultaneous with the first shot. Analysis of his photograph revealed that it was taken at approximately frame 210 of the Zapruder film

> which was the approximate time of the shot that probably hit the President . . . (W-112)

President Kennedy's body showed reaction at frame 225 (W-112). "Governor Connally viewed the film and testified that he was hit between frames 231 and 234" (W-106). According to Willis' photograph, the President was hit at frame 210 of the Z film. According to the Commission the President was clearly registering a hit at frame 225. We are now in a position to determine the time lapse between the hit on the President and the hit on the Governor by translating Z frames into units of time.

The fewest possible frames separating the hit of the President and the Governor is 6 (President hit at Z 225 and Connally hit at Z 231). The greatest possible frames separating the hit of the President and the Governor is 24 (President hit a Z 210 and the Governor hit at Z 234). To translate this into time is a simple operation of allowing 1/18.3 seconds for each frame. We get thereby a time span of 0.34 to 1.31 seconds separating the first hit on the President from the first hit on the Governor.

We know that the top accomplishment of the Commission's expert marksmen, firing the 6.5 mm. Carcano at stationary, not moving targets, was a minimum firing time of 2.3 seconds. The time span of the hits, 0.34 to 1.31 seconds, is below the minimum firing time. Therefore, we can safely infer that the photographic evidence indicates the existence of at least another gunman, not the alleged Carcano operator, who was firing at that time.

How does this inference stack up with the auditory clues of eyewitnesses? The Commission's testimony about the bunching of two shots helps disprove a finding that one gunman did the firing from a bolt-action rifle. Here is the Report:

> a substantial majority of the witnesses stated that the shots were not evenly spaced. Most witnesses recalled that the second and third shots were bunched together. (W-115)

From *The New York Times*, November 24th, 1964, page 30, we get the following testimony of Special Agent R. H. Kellerman of the Secret Service who was in the President's car. He stated he heard a "flurry of shots," which ". . . shells came in all together." He said ". . . it was like a double bang-bang, bang."

In answer to a question of Arlen Specter on behalf of the Commission as to whether he heard two shots in that flurry in addition to the head shot, he said: "Yes sir; yes sir; at least."

Now back to the Report:

> As previously indicated, the time span between the shot entering the back of the President' neck and the bullet which shattered his skull was 4.8 to 5.6 seconds. (W-117)

If 2.3 *seconds* is a *minimum firing time,* and the time span between the first and last hits on the President is *4.8 to 5.6 seconds,* then bunching of two shots by one rifleman is impossible. On this score, the Commission and the writer are in accord, for

> if the three shots were fired within a period of 4.8 to 5.6 seconds, the shots would have been evenly spaced. (W-193)

Therefore, if we conclude, as we must, that three separate hits were made, two on the President, and one on the Governor, then the Commission's findings leave the realm of credibility on another score. For in such a case states the Commission

> the gunman would have been shooting at very near the minimum allowable time to have fired the three shots within 4.8 to 5.6 seconds, although it was entirely possible for him to have done so. (W-117)

Possible? Among the Commission's experts, and they were top shots, who fired at stationary targets,

> one of the firers in the rapid fire test in firing his two series of three shots, hit the target twice within a span of 4.6 and 5.15 seconds. (W-194)

So, none of the Commission's top marksmen could score three hits on the stationary targets in the span of 4.8 to 5.6 seconds within which all the hits on the limousine's occupants occurred.

And the alleged assassin's ratings as a rifle shot never rose to any level capable of inspiring awe. We will take the word of the Commission's expert on this.

Based on the general Marine Corps ratings, Lt. Col. A. G. Folsom, Jr., head, Records Branch, Personnel Department, Headquarters U.S. Marine Corps, evaluated the sharpshooter qualifications as a "fairly good shot" and a low marksman rating as a "rather poor shot" (W-191).

As an additional problem, the alleged assassin was using a defective scope which caused accurately aimed shots to carry "high and to the right of the target" (W-194). The Commission, however, was quick to convert this disadvantage into an advantage by asserting: "Moreover, the defeat was one which would have assisted the assassin aiming at a target which was moving away" (W-194). It would be perhaps too hasty to assume that on the basis of this assertion, a new, defective design will be designed for rifle scopes which will direct shots "high and to the right of the target." So, we must conclude that the timing factor too weighs heavily against the Commission's inference that one assassin made all the hits on the President and Governor with a single, bolt-action carbine. The evidence indicates that the time separating the hits on the President and the Governor was under the minimum firing time, and much above the time required for any bullet to be in transit from the President to the Governor. No rifle expert could get three hits on stationary targets in the time span of the assassination shots. Our alleged assassin was at best only a "fairly good shot" and at worst "a rather poor shot." He operated a gun that had a faulty scope which directed shots "high and to the right."

Life's *Three Versions*

Now we must turn our attention to the head wound or wounds of the President once again. For this purpose I find the

October 2nd, 1964 issue of *Life* magazine invaluable. This issue contains excellent color reproductions of some of the Zapruder frames. I purchased three different copies — with surprising results. Each of the three copies differs in one important respect from the other two. The area of difference in each case is crucial in the determination of the direction of the final shot to hit the President. I will designate for expository purposes, the copies as "A," "B" and "C."

Copy "A" contains a caption for a picture designated no. 6. The picture appears on page 45 of this issue. The caption on page 42 reads as follows:

> 6. The assassin's shot struck the right rear portion of the President's skull, causing a massive wound and snapping of his head to one side.

What one sees on page 45 of copy "A" in frame "6" is a Zapruder picture, taking up half a page. In this picture a bullet is impacting on the President's head and causing a burst of red at the right parietal region of the skull. N.B. *Life's* caption for the picture states the result of the impact of the bullet from the back (Book Depository Building) is "a snapping of his head to one side." We must return to the law of action and reaction. A hit aimed from the back and above, on a car moving away from the source of the shot, hitting with such force that it carries away major parts of the skull (W-540), would not cause "a snapping of his head to one side." Rather such a hit on the head that is facing front, as the President's was, would have snapped the head forward and downward. *Life* erred, I guess.

Well, let us now shift our attention to my "B" copy of *Life.* On page 42 thereof there is a changed caption for picture "6" which appears on page 45. The caption reads as follows:

> 6. The direction from which shots came was established by the picture taken at instant bullet struck the rear of the President's head, and, passing through, caused the front part of his skull to explode forward.

But things still seem to be wrong in *Life*! For upon turning to the Zapruder frame marked "6" on page 45 of "B" copy, I see that *Life* has an entirely different no. 6. This picture appears to be a later one than that which appeared in copy "A." The shot in question has apparently done its work. Here, indeed, we see that the President is being driven over sideways and leftward by the fatal impact. He is falling into his wife's lap. This is strong evidence that the shot came not from the back, i.e., the Depository Building, but rather, the right side (north side of Elm Street), to wit, the elevated grassy knoll area.

Now, we must look at copy "C" of *Life*. This copy contains, on page 42, the caption identical to the caption found in copy "B." The frame designated no. 6 on page 45 of "C" is identical with the frame which appears in copy "A."

But the damage cannot be undone, because all three shots show on page 46, no. 7 (all identical now), the President being impelled to his left side by the hit shown impacting in no. 6 of page 45 in copies "A" and "C." Such a force had to originate on his right and not from his back. Since his head was bent slightly forward and facing front when this wound was inflicted, the force of a shot from the back which carried away so much bone of the skull would have caused him to fall towards the Governor in front of him.

Another Man Wounded

Is there any other evidence in the report to the effect that there was a gunman or gunmen on the grassy elevated knoll on the north side of Elm Street? Yes, there is. We will now examine it.

The Commission reviewed the testimony of the following persons who believed that the shots came from the grassy knoll: Frank E. Reilly, an electrician on the railroad bridge, stated that he heard three shots that seemed to come from the trees "on the north side of Elm Street at the corner up there" (W-76). Thomas J. Murphy said the two shots he heard "came from a spot just west of the Depository" (W-76). Lee E. Bowers. Jr. "and others saw a motorcycle officer dismount hurriedly and come running up the incline on the north side of Elm Street" (W-76). "Mrs. Jean L. Hill stated that after the firing stopped she saw a white man wearing a brown overcoat and a hat running west away from the Depository Building in the direction of the railroad tracks" (W-640). S. M. Holland heard "four shots which sounded as though they came from the north side of Elm Street where he saw a puff of smoke" (W-76).

Better evidence than the verbal testimony of the above witnesses is the wounding of James T. Tague off the assassination site. This incident is of tremendous importance in arriving at conclusions concerning the source of the assassination shots. So as not to run the risk of misinterpreting what the Commission has said on this occurrence, I will quote all of the Report's testimony on this vital matter:

> At a different location in Dealey Plaza, the evidence indicated that a bullet fragment did hit the street. James T. Tague, who got out of his car to watch the motorcade from a position between Commerce and Main Streets near the Triple Underpass, was hit on the cheek by an object during the shooting. Within a few minutes Tague reported this to Deputy Sheriff Eddy R. Walthers, who was examining the area to see if any bullets had struck the turf. Walthers immediately started to search where Tague had been standing and located a place on the south curb of Main Street where it appeared a bullet had hit the cement. According to Tague, "There was a mark quite obviously that was a bullet and it was very fresh." In Tague's opinion, it was the second shot which caused the mark, since he thinks he heard the third shot after he was hit in the face. This incident appears to have been recorded in the contemporaneous report of Dallas Patrolman L.L. Hill, who radioed in around 12:40 P.M.: "I have one guy that was possibly hit by a ricochet from the bullet off

> the concrete." Scientific examination of the mark on the south curb of Main Street by FBI agents disclosed metal smears which, "were spectrographically determined to be essentially lead with a trace of antimony." The mark on the curb could have originated from the lead core of a bullet but the absence of copper precluded the possibility that the mark on the curbing section was made by an unmutilated military full metal-jacketed bullet such as the bullet from Governor's Connally's stretcher. (W-116)

Here is a gold mine of material. Tague was between Commerce and Main Streets. The bullet or bullet fragment hit the South curbing of Main Street. From my view of the maps, diagrams, photographs, and after a personal inspection of the situs, at no point would Tague have been in the line of fire from the Depository Building to the Presidential limousine. He was some 1½ blocks from the Depository Building, about a block south of the limousine. But he was directly across from the grassy knoll on the north side of Elm Street. The simplest and therefore best explanation of the source of that bullet is the grassy knoll north of Elm Street. If this was the source of Tague's wound, then Tague was very much in the line of fire since the limousine was then between him and the knoll. The trajectory is consistent with an elevation beginning about 25 feet above street level (my estimate from personal inspection of the height of the grassy knoll) downward to the curbing and thence into his cheek. As between the Depository Building and the grassy knoll as the source of this shot, any speculation that it came from the Depository Building must be considered the more improbable of the two.

The Commission's conclusion that the fragment that hit Tague could not have been a whole bullet appears to be an overly hasty one. The F.B.I. experts disclosed metal smears which "were spectrographically determined to be essentially lead with a trace of antimony" (W-116). The Commission rightfully concludes that the bullet mark on the curbing, since it lacked copper, could not have been "an unmutilated military full metal-jacketed bullet such as the bullet from Governor Connally's stretcher" (W-116). This could have been a lead bullet without a metal jacket designed to inflict gaping wounds on the target by maximizing the area of damage. This could have been another type of bullet fired from another rifle. But the Commission never considered this possibility, despite supporting evidence in its Report. Let us look at this supporting evidence.

Dr. Alfred G. Olivier, chief of the Army Wound Ballistics Branch for 17 years, stated that from his long experience he did not believe that the type of head wound suffered by the President could have been inflicted by a copper jacketed bullet. But after a series of tests on a reconstructed human skull, he was persuaded that this case had an extraordinary aspect for which his 17 years of ballistics experience had not prepared him. Here is his testimony after the test result as furnished to him:

> It [the test result] disclosed that the type of head wounds that the President received could be done by this type of bullet. This surprised me very much, because this type of stable bullet I didn't think would cause a massive head wound, I thought it would go through making a small entrance and exit, but the bones of the skull are enough to deform the end of this bullet causing it to expend a lot of energy and blowing out the side of the skull or blowing out fragments of the skull. (W-87)

The evidence of the Report concerning the shots, trajectories, and wounds is convincing. It convinces me that this killing of one man and wounding of two could not have been the work of one man firing a bolt-action rifle from the Book Depository Building. The involvement of two or more people in the commission of this crime would point to a conspiracy — unless it turns out that they were, independently of one another, firing on the same target.

The Warren Report?

by Vincent J. Salandria

I. The President's Back and Neck Wounds

In this article we will analyze the Warren Commission's following crucial conclusion:

> President Kennedy was first struck by a bullet which entered at the back of his neck and exited through the lower front portion of his neck . . .[1]

Such is the conclusion of the Commission. It is our purpose to analyze the evidence which the governmental inquiry used to support this conclusion. We will delve into the source or *sources* of the shot or shots which inflicted the first wounds on the President. By examining these wounds we hope to shed light on the direction or *directions* from which the shots came. Such an exploration will, needless to say, provide valuable information on the question of the number of shots fired into the President. Our study will also help us decide the vantage point or *points* of the assassin or *assassins* on November 22nd, 1963.

First let us attend most carefully to the source or sources of the shot or shots which caused the wounds in question, i.e. the

---

Originally published in *Liberation*, X, No. 1 (March 1965), 14-33.

[1]*Report of the President's Commission on the Assassination of President Kennedy*, p. 19. United States Printing Office, Washington, D.C., 1964. References to this Report are designated by "W," followed by a page number.

back and neck wounds of the President. The reader will recall that the Commission concluded three shots were fired. It decided that all the shots were fired from "above and behind the Presidential limousine" (W-14). Our task can be simply defined as an analysis of the evidence offered by the Commission to determine whether such evidence supports the Commission's conclusions relative to the back and neck wounds of the President. All of the evidence discussed herein is derived from the Warren Report and its supporting notes of testimony and exhibits. Not a scrap of it comes from any outside source.

The first evidence of a back wound came from Secret Service Agent Glen A. Bennett, stationed at the time in the right rear seat of the President's followup car,

> who heard a sound like a firecracker as the motorcade proceeded down Elm Street. At that moment, Agent Bennett stated: ". . . I looked at the back of the President. I heard another firecracker noise and saw that shot hit the President about four inches down from the right shoulder. A second shot followed immediately and hit the right rear of the President's head." (W-111)

According to Bennett, the second shot hit "about four inches down from the right shoulder." His testimony indicated that the first bullet did one of two things: either missed, or hit the President at a point which Bennett did not or could not see from his position in the followup car.

His testimony gives rise to the following question: Could the President have been hit in the front of the neck by the first shot, directed from a rifle positioned in the front of the President, and then immediately thereafter struck in the back by a different missile, aimed from a weapon of an assassin posted in the Book Depository Building? Is there credible evidence to support an early hit on the President from the front? With the purpose of answering this inquiry, we must examine the wound in the President's neck.

The Neck Wound

The autopsy report was prepared at Bethesda Naval Hospital. It indicates a wound "in the low anterior cervical region" (W-541). This, in layman's terms, describes a wound in the front of the neck at the necktie knot. The Report concludes "that the bullet exited from the front portion of the President's neck that had been cut away by the tracheotomy" (W-88). Since we have adopted a view of healthy skepticism, there is no need for us to join in the Commission's conclusion that this wound was an "exit" wound. Rather, we will sift the evidence, and arrive at whatever independent conclusion the evidence directs us to.

The tracheotomy was prepared by Dr. Malcolm O. Perry of Parkland Hospital.[2] Dr. Perry described the neck wound as "a small wound in the lower anterior third in the midline of the neck, from which blood was exuding very slowly" (VI, H-9). Dr. Perry testified that he didn't know whether this wound was an entrance wound or an exit wound (VI, H-15). Dr. Charles James Carrico likewise described the President's throat wound as "fairly round, had no jagged edges" (III, H-362).

Dr. Charles Rufus Baxter of Parkland Hospital saw this neck wound and described it as follows:

> 4 to 5 mm. in widest diameter and was a spherical wound. (VI, H-42)
>
> Well, the wound was, I think, compatible with a gunshot wound. It did not appear to be a jagged wound such as one would expect with a very high velocity rifle bullet. We could not determine, or did not determine at that time whether this

---

[2]*Hearings Before the President's Commission on the Assassination of President Kennedy*, Vol. VI, p. 10. United States Printing Office Washington, D.C. 1964. References to the Hearing Notes and the Commission Exhibits are designated by the volume number, then an "H," followed by a page number.

> represented an entry or an exit wound. Judging from the caliber of the rifle that we later found or became acquainted with, this would more resemble a wound of entry. However, due to the density of the tissue of the neck and depending upon what a bullet of such calibre would pass through on the way to the neck, I think that the wound could well represent either exit or entry wound. (II, H-42)

Although Dr. Baxter stated that the wound "would more resemble a wound of entry," he was willing to say it "could well represent either exit or entry wound." Then Arlen Specter, assistant counsel to the Commission, put a lengthy hypothetical question to Dr. Baxter. This question was designed to elicit from the doctor information as to whether a wound through the back of the President which exited from the President's neck could have made a wound such as was found in the neck.

Dr. Baxter's answer did little to help support the Commission's ultimate conclusion that the neck wound was a wound of exit and not of entry:

> *Dr. Baxter.* Although it would be unusual for a high velocity missile of this type to cause a wound as you have described, the passage through tissue planes as you have described, the passage through tissue planes of this density could, have well resulted in the sequence which you outline; namely, that the anterior wound does represent a wound of exit. (VI, H-42)

But Mr. Specter knows too well that history is reluctant to regard as verity that which is "unusual." So Mr. Specter's anxiety about the judgment of history shows when he asks:

> *Mr. Specter.* What would be the considerations which, in your mind, would make it, as you characterized it, unlikely?
>
> *Dr. Baxter.* It would be unlikely because the

> damage that the bullet would create would be — first its speed would create a shock wave which would damage a larger number of tissues, as in its path, it would tend to strike, or usually would strike, tissues of greater density than this particular missile did and would then begin to tumble and would create larger jagged — the further it went, the more jagged would be the damage that it created; so that ordinarily there would have been a rather large wound of exit. (VI, H-42)

Mr. Specter had even more severe problems with Dr. Ronald Coy Jones of Parkland Hospital, whom he asked about the neck wounds:

> *Mr. Specter.* In this report, Dr. Jones, you state the following, "Previously described severe skull and brain injury was noted as well as a small hole in the anterior midline of the neck thought to be a bullet entrance wound." What led you to the thought that it was a bullet entrance wound, sir?
> *Dr. Jones.* The hole was very small and relatively clean cut, as you would see in a bullet that is entering rather than exiting from a patient. If this were an exit wound, you would think that it exited at a very low velocity to produce no more damage than this had done, and if this were a missile of high velocity, you would expect more of an explosive type of exit wound, with more tissue destruction than this appeared to have on superficial examination. (VI, H-55)

Even Mr. Specter could not find in this account much opportunity for turning this neck wound into an exit wound. So, in good prosecutor-like fashion, he prodded for the thin slant of Commission daylight in Dr. Jones's otherwise dark view of the Commission's suggestions:

> *Mr. Specter.* Would it be consistent, then, with an exit wound, but of low velocity, as you put it?
> *Dr. Jones.* Yes, of very low velocity to the point that you might think that this bullet barely made it through the soft tissues and just enough to drop out of the skin on the opposite side. (VI, H-55)

But the effort to get more government light into Dr. Jones's testimony only resulted in blowing the fuse and pitched the government case into darkness. For the kind of "low velocity" described by Dr. Jones would not support the Commission's estimate that the entrance velocity of the bullet that emerged from the President's neck was 1,776 feet per second. (W-95) This is the same bullet which allegedly pierced the President's throat and also caused Governor Connally's wounds.

Dr. Jones's testimony, despite all Specter's efforts, supports the inference that this wound in the President's neck was an entrance and not an exit wound. If the Commission is going to call this an exit wound, then Dr. Jones caused a short circuit on that aspect of the government case which requires us to believe that the same bullet coursed through Governor Connally, hitting the 5th rib, fracturing his right wrist and finally entering his left knee area. He reduced the velocity of the bullet emerging from President Kennedy nearly to zero, thus rendering it incapable of further harm.

The Commission sorely needed rifle ammunition. If it surrendered its contention that the same bullet which first hit the President also hit Governor Connally, it would have added one bullet to the case, and therefore would have destroyed the three-bullet-one-assassin theory. The reader will recall that one bullet or fragment was involved in the striking of a man, James T. Tague, 270 feet from where the President was finally hit in the head (W-116) (XX, H-2).

Dr. Jones's testimony punctured the government's case badly. In describing the wound as either an entry wound or the exit wound of a *spent* bullet, Dr. Jones has incapacitated the Commission's precious projectile. He rendered it impotent to perform the very heavy workload the Commission had designated for it, i.e., infliction of all wounds on Governor Connally in addition to the wounds in the back and neck of President Kennedy. Dr. Jones used up invaluable ammunition with his testimony, ammunition which the Commission had to economize if it was to retain any tenuous connection with reality.

With Parkland Hospital nurse, Margaret M. Henchliffe, Mr. Specter had no better luck:

> *Mr. Specter.* Did you see any wound on any other part of his body?
> *Miss Henchliffe.* Yes, in the neck.
> *Mr. Specter.* Will you describe it, please?
> *Miss Henchliffe.* It was just a little hole in the middle of his neck.
> *Mr. Specter.* About how big a hole was it?
> *Miss Henchliffe.* About as big around as the end of my little finger.
> *Mr. Specter.* Have you ever had any experience with bullet holes?
> *Miss Henchliffe.* Yes.
> *Mr. Specter.* And what did that appear to you to be?
> *Miss Henchliffe.* An entrance bullet hole — it looked to me like.
> *Mr. Specter.* Could it have been an exit bullet hole?
> *Miss Henchliffe.* I have never seen an exit bullet hole — I don't remember seeing one that looked like that. (VI, H-141)

The reader will recall that a tracheotomy (creation of an artificial breathing hole) was performed on the President by Dr. Perry of Parkland Hospital. For purposes of performing this tracheotomy, Dr. Perry employed the neck wound as an opening for the tracheotomy tube (VI, H-10). Therefore, by the time the Bethesda doctors saw the President's body and examined this neck wound, the wound had already been altered by the tracheotomy. Under the circumstances, it was necessary for the

Bethesda doctors to rely largely on the statements of the Parkland Hospital physicians concerning the nature and source of the neck wound of the President.

A fair reading of the Bethesda Hospital physicians' testimony relating to the throat wound would not dictate any definite conclusion concerning whether the throat wound was one of entry or exit. We suggest, however, that none of the Parkland Hospital witnesses had any difficulty seeing the wound in the front of the President's neck as an entry wound. If there was a preference expressed by the Parkland Hospital people, it was that the neck wound in the front of the President more resembled a wound of entrance.

Recapitulating, Dr. Rufus Baxter said that the neck wound was "unlikely" to be a wound of exit and "would more resemble a wound of entry" (VI, H-42). Dr. Jones stated: "The hole was very small and relatively clean cut, as you would see in a bullet that is entering rather than exiting from a patient" (VI, E-55). Nurse Henchliffe insisted: "An entrance bullet hole — it looked to me like. I have never seen an exit bullet hole — I don't remember seeing one that looked like that" (VI, H-141).

In addition, Secret Service Agent Glen A. Bennett, who had been stationed in the Presidential follow-up car, "heard a sound like a firecracker," then heard another shot and saw it hit the President's back and then saw a "hit on the right rear of the President's head" (W-111). Thus, his testimony is likewise compatible with the first shot entering the President's throat and a second and separate shot hitting him in the back. Bennett's failure to see the President react after the first shot is consistent with the President having been hit in the soft tissue in the front of the neck which impact would not have heen visible to Bennett.

Despite the utter failure of the above testimony to support the Commission's conclusion that the strike in the President's neck was an exit wound, the Commission concluded that it was:

> President Kennedy was first struck by a bullet which entered at the back of his neck and exited through the lower front portion of his neck . . . (W-19)

Clearly, on the basis of the testimony of Special Agent Glen A. Bennett and the Parkland Hospital group, the Commission *was not justified* in drawing such an inference.

The Back Wound

Here we must shift our attention backward. We will examine the Commission's inference concerning a bullet which allegedly entered the *back of his neck* and exited through the *lower front portion of his neck.* We urge the reader to keep his mind open on the question of whether the back hit we are about to discuss has an exit on the front of the neck or whether it has an exit at all. Nothing we have examined so far would prove the Commission's conclusion that this shot in the back of the President exited from the front.

At this point in the exposition, each reader will have in mind Bennett's oft-repeated testimony that he observed a missile "hit the President about four inches down from the right shoulder" (W-111). Special Agent Clinton L. Hill saw the President's body being worked on at the morgue in Bethesda during the course of the autopsy. He stated to the Commission that just before the body was placed into a casket "I saw an opening in the back, about six inches below the neckline to the right-hand side of the spinal column" (II, H-143).

Special Agent Roy H. Kellerman testified about his experience at Bethesda during the autopsy studies there.

> There were three gentlemen who were performing this autopsy. A Colonel Finck — during the examination of the President, from the hole that was in his shoulder, and with a probe, and we — were standing right alongside of him, he is probing inside the shoulder with his instrument and I said, "Colonel, where did it go?" He said, "There are no lanes for an outlet of this entry in this man's shoulder." (II, H-93)

If Colonel Finck was correct, if there were indeed no lanes of exit from such a wound, then that is the end of the Commission's theory that one assassin fired all the shots at the assassination site. Such a finding of no outlet would make the back wound a separate hit. It would make the front neck wound a separate hit. It would place one gunman in front of the President. It would add one bullet to the three shells found in the Depository Building, thereby making four, and thereby requiring another gunman to accomplish all the shooting in the maximum allowable time. But while Colonel Finck at the autopsy in Bethesda was making this judgment on the dreadful night of November 22nd, 1963, the United States Government was proclaiming to the world that one man and one man alone had performed all the gory work in Dealey Plaza. This conclusion, in the light of the opinions of the autopsy experts, was utterly out of joint with the facts apparent at that time. At best, it was premature.

All the above testimony of Special Agents Bennett, Hill, and Kellermann indicates a hit in the back of the President roughly four to six inches below the inferior neckline. Material supporting evidence was found in the clothing of the President. FBI Agent Robert A. Frazier testified about the President's clothing as follows:

> I found on the back of the shirt a hole, $5\frac{3}{4}$ inches below the top of the collar, and as you look at the back of the shirt $1\frac{1}{8}$ inch to the right of the mid-line of the shirt, which is this hole I am indicating. . . . [T]he coat hole is $5\frac{3}{8}$ inches below the top of the collar. The shirt hole is $5\frac{3}{4}$ inches, which could be accounted for by a portion of the collar sticking up above the coat about a half inch. (V, H-60)

The bullet which made these holes would have only originated from behind the President, who was sitting erect, facing front, in the Presidential limousine. Both the Commission and the writer are in perfect agreement here. It would seem, also, that there is no room for disagreement with respect to where the missile which impacted on the President's back entered. But, alas, on this score, the disagreement between the writer and the Commission is sharp and goes to the core of the case.

The writer concludes from the evidence of Special Agents Bennett, Kellerman, and Hill that there was a wound in the President's back some 4 to 6 inches down from the neck line. The writer feels that the missile hole 5 3/4 inches below the top of the shirt collar and 1 1/8 inches to the right of the midline of the shirt, dramatically supports the testimony of these Special Agents. The missile hole in the President's coat: 5 3/4 inches below the top of the collar corroborates their testimony in a solid and impressive way. The Commission, however, concluded otherwise. Despite all the above evidence, the Warren Commission found that the hit in the back of the President was *above* the wound at the necktie knot. "The autopsy disclosed that the bullet which entered the back of the President's neck hit no bony structure and proceeded in a slightly downward angle" (W-91). We submit that the Commission was in grievous and obvious error.

The Warren Commission had to recognize that a bullet in the back 5 3/4 inches below the top of the shirt which did not exit, would end the lone assassin theory. For, if this bullet did not exit, the front neck wound constitutes a separate entry from the front. To add one bullet is to add one gunman, who cannot have fired from the Texas Book Depository Building. One gunman cannot be in more than one place at the one time.

An attempt was made to refute the evidence of the three Special Agents who stuck to the truth as they had seen it. The Warren Commission, trying to rebut this impressive evidence, hit rocks which caused its integrity to founder forever on the shoals of self-contradictory exhibits and finally *fabrication and withholding evidence.* Having made these charges, we will proceed to prove each of them.

A Lapse of Liaison

The Warren Report on the question has the following to say about the back and neck wounds:

> In the early stages of the autopsy, the surgeons were unable to find a path into any large muscle in the back of the neck. At that time they did not know that there had been a bullet hole in the front of the President's neck when he arrived at Parkland Hospital because the tracheotomy incision had completely eliminated that evidence. While the autopsy was being performed, surgeons learned that a whole bullet had been found at Parkland Hospital on a stretcher which, at that time, was thought to be the stretcher occupied by the President. This led to speculation that the bullet might have penetrated a short distance into the back of the neck and then dropped out onto the stretcher as a result of the external heart massage.
>
> Further exploration during the autopsy disproved that theory. The surgeons determined that the bullet had passed between two large strap muscles and bruised them without leaving any channel, since the bullet merely passed between them. Commander Humes, who believed that a tracheotomy had been performed from his observations at the autopsy, talked by telephone with Dr. Perry early on the morning of November 23, and learned that his assumption was correct and that Dr. Perry had used the missile wound in the neck as the point to make the incision. This confirmed the Bethesda surgeons' conclusions that the bullet had exited from the front part of the neck. (W-88-89)

In the above dissertation, the Warren Report asks of the reader that he swallow the idea that the tracheotomy incision had "completely eliminated" the evidence of a bullet hole in the front of his neck. The Report begs the reader to believe that Commander Humes did not know what the Parkland Hospital doctors were telling all the world on the 22nd of November, i.e. that President Kennedy had suffered a wound in the front of the neck through which a tracheotomy was performed. They ask us to believe that the government pathologists at Bethesda undertook an autopsy on the evening of November 22nd, 1963 on the President without consulting with any doctor at Parkland Hospital in Dallas. We are asked to believe that Commander Humes talked with Dr. Perry of Parkland Hospital for the first time on November 23rd, 1963. Such an idea seems to fly in the face of common sense. Let us see whether it also flies in the face of the evidence.

Observe how Dr. Malcolm O. Perry of Parkland Hospital recollects the conversation he had with Commander Humes concerning the tracheotomy in question:

> *Mr. Specter.* Dr. Perry, did you have occasion to discuss your observations with Cmdr. James J. Humes of the Bethesda Naval Hospital?
> *Dr. Perry.* Yes, sir; I did.
> *Mr. Specter.* When did that conversation occur?
> *Dr. Perry.* My knowledge as to the exact accuracy of it is obviously in doubt. I was under the initial impression that I talked to him on Friday, but I understand it was on Saturday. I don't recall exactly when.
> *Mr. Specter.* Do you have an independent recollection at this moment as to whether it was on Friday or Saturday?
> *Dr. Perry.* No, sir; I have thought about it again and again and the events surrounding that weekend were very kaleidoscopic, and I talked with Dr. Humes on two occasions, separated by a very short interval of, I think it was, 30 minutes or an hour or so, it could have been a little longer.
> *Mr. Specter.* What was the medium of your conversation?
> *Dr. Perry.* Over the telephone.
> *Mr. Specter.* Did he identify himself to you as Dr. Humes of Bethesda?
> *Dr. Perry.* He did.
> *Mr. Specter.* Would you state as specifically as you

> can recollect the conversation that you first had with him?
>
> *Dr. Perry*. He advised me that he could not discuss with me the findings of necropsy, that he had a few questions he would like to clarify. The initial phone call was in relation to my doing a tracheotomy. Since I had made the incision directly through the wound in the neck, it made it difficult for them to ascertain the exact nature of this wound. Of course, that did not occur to me at the time. I did what appeared to me to be medically expedient. And when I informed him that there was a wound there and I suspected an underlying wound of the trachea and even perhaps of the great vessels. He advised me that he thought this action was correct and he said he could not relate to me any of the other findings. (III, H-380)

It is fairly clear that Commander Humes wasn't saying much during the course of the conversation with Dr. Perry. "He advised me that he could not discuss with me the findings of necropsy. . . . he could not relate to me any of the other findings." Commander Humes apparently construed his primary job as something other than full and open communication aimed at reaching the immediate truth with respect to the wounds. For if he had seen his task as ascertaining the truth directly, he must have recognized the need for interchange of information between himself and Dr. Perry, who had seen the President and supervised the treatment prior in time to Commander Humes.

Again, in a later deposition taken by the Commission's assistant counsel, Arlen Specter, Dr. Perry hardly confirmed the Commission's finding that the phone calls between Dr. Perry and Commander Humes occurred on Saturday, November 23rd and not on Friday, November 22nd:

> *Mr. Specter*. And will you relate the circumstances of the calls indicating first the time when they occurred.

Dr. Perry. Dr. Humes called me twice on Friday afternoon, separated by about 30-minute intervals, as I recall. The first one, I, somehow think I recall the first one must have been around 1500 hours, but I'm not real sure about that; I'm not positive of that at all, actually.
Mr. Specter. Could it have been Saturday morning?
Dr. Perry. Saturday morning — was it. It's possible. I remember talking with him twice. I was thinking it was shortly thereafter.
Mr. Specter. Well, the record will show.
Dr. Perry. Oh sure, it was Saturday morning — yes.
Mr. Specter. What made you change your view of that?
Dr. Perry. You mean Friday?
Mr. Specter. Did some specific recollection occur to you which changed your view from Friday to Saturday?
Dr. Perry. No, I was trying to place where I was at that time — Friday afternoon, and at that particular time when I thought that he called initially. I seem to remember it being Friday, for some reason. (VI, H-16)

Dr. W.K. Clark says that Dr. Perry, discussing a Saturday morning press conference, told him of having "talked to the Bethesda Naval Hospital on two occasions that morning and that he knew what the autopsy findings had shown" (VI, H-23). On two scores Dr. Clark therefore contradicts Dr. Perry: on the date of the calls and on whether Dr. Perry was told what the results of the autopsy were.

Well, the Commission concluded that the conversations between Commander Humes and Dr. Perry occurred on Saturday, November 23rd, 1963. If the Commission had decided otherwise, we would be left only with Commander Humes's initial consideration that the bullet in the back may have dropped out of the President:

> *Commander Humes.* I did not at that point have the information from Doctor Perry about the wound in the anterior neck, and while that was a possible explanation for the point of exit, we also had to consider the possibility that the missile in some rather inexplicable fashion had been stopped in its path through the President's body and, in fact, then had fallen from the body onto the stretcher. (II, H-367)

You will recall that Special Agents Kellerman and Hill described the autopsy while it was in progress. Colonel Finck told Roy H. Kellerman: "There are no lanes for an outlet of this entry in this man's shoulder" (II, E-93). Clinton L. Hill "saw an opening in the back, about 6 inches below the neckline to the right-hand side of the spinal column" (II, H-143). No small wonder it was that the idea did not immediately occur to the pathologists that this hit down in the President's back emerged high up in the front portion of his neck. Such unusual insights germinate in the human mind only after considerable time is devoted to the consideration of the possible existence of more plausible alternatives. In this case, apparently, there were no other alternatives available. That accursed shortage of ammunition which restricted the Commission to but three shots interposed itself again.

A Clash of Exhibits

The face sheet of the autopsy report which was prepared by Commander Humes is marked Commission Exhibit 397 (XVII, H-45) On this sheet there are two diagrams representing schematic drawings of a front view and a back view of the autopsy subject, identical in height, and in juxtaposition. Each figure extends the same distance up (heads being 3 3/4 inches from the top of the page) and the same distance down (feet extending 2 1/4 inches from the bottom of the page). In the front view, on the left, one sees the mark designating the hole in the front of

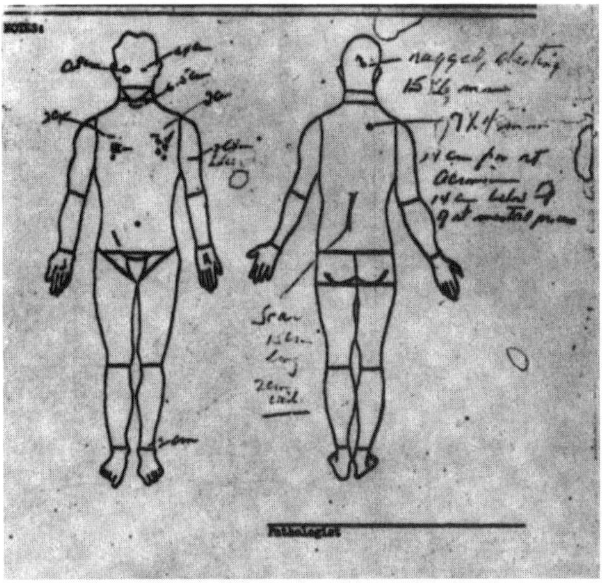

Commission Exhibit 397

the neck caused by the bullet wound and the tracheotomy. In the back view, on the right, one sees the back wound slightly to the right of the middle of the President's back and considerably below his collar. The back wound, as drawn, is 3/8 of an inch from the lower level of the collar line. The neck wound, in the front, as drawn, is 1/6 of an inch from the lower level of the collar. *Therefore, the back wound is definitely drawn lower than the front neck wound.*

Now, let us turn to Commission Exhibits 385 and 386 (XVI, H-977). These two exhibits represent drawings of the upper portion of the President's body. Commission Exhibit 385 shows a side view of the President. The hit in the back is now placed *high up on the neck.* This back entry point is drawn above the exit point in the front of the President's neck. On the rear view of Commission Exhibit 386, the back hit is again seen *high up on the neck* and now almost to the extreme right of the President's body.

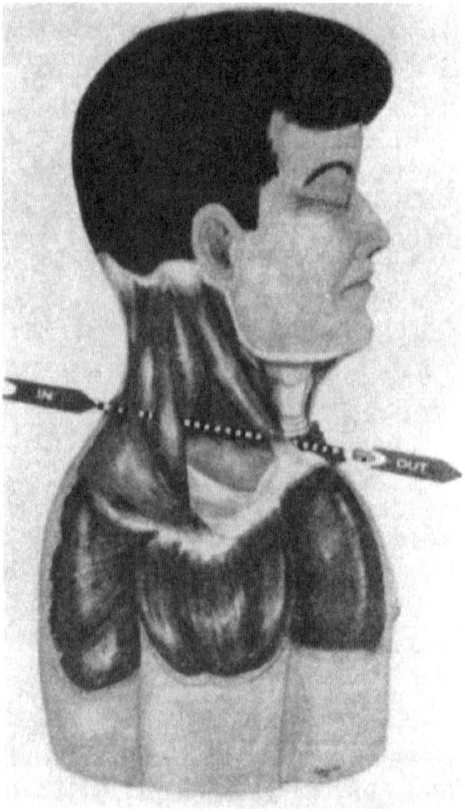

Commission Exhibit 385

These drawings are extraordinary in light of the following testimony relating to the President's suit coat:

> *Mr. Specter.* Would it be accurate to state that the hole which you have identified as being the point of entry is approximately 6 inches below the top of the collar, and 2 inches to the right of the middle seam of the coat?
> *Commander Humes.* That is approximately correct sir . . . (II, H-365)

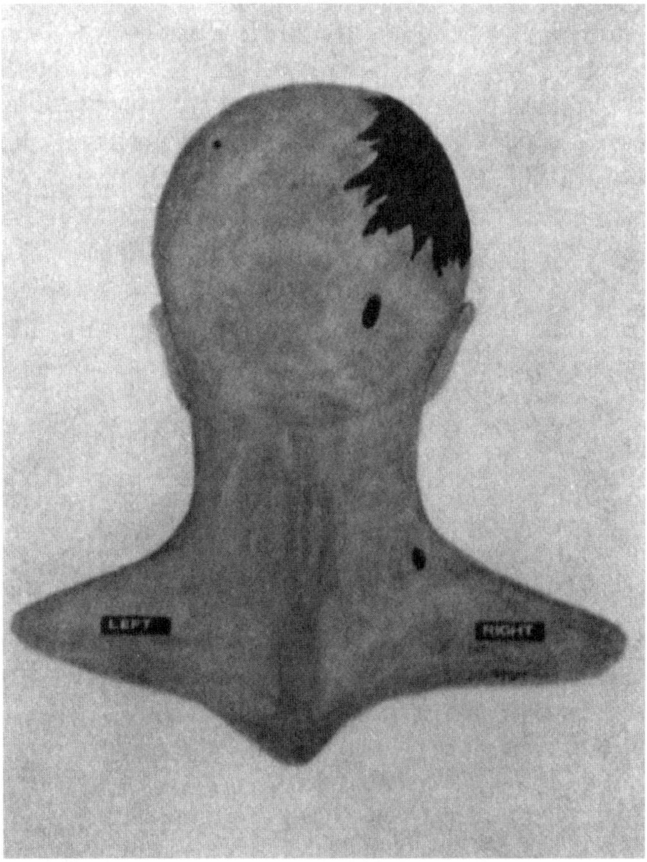

Commission Exhibit 386

But how did the President's suit coat get pierced 6 inches below the collar, when the bullet is supposed to have entered high up on the collar region so as to be above the necktie knot from which this bullet was supposed to have emerged? The explanation out of the context of an assassination would constitute "high" comedy. The bullet hole in the back of the President is simply lifted high and to the right on the President by the force of sheer nonsense. Here is the explanation:

> *Mr. Specter.* As to the muscular status of the President, what was it?

> *Commander Humes.* The President was extremely well-developed, an extremely well-developed, muscular young man with a very well-developed set of muscles in his thoraco and shoulder girdle.
> *Mr. Specter.* What effect would that have on the positioning of the shirt and coat with respect to the position of the neck in and above the seam?
> *Commander Humes.* I believe this would have a tendency to push the portions of the coat which show the defects here somewhat higher on the back of the President than on a man of less muscular development.
> *Mr. Specter.* Mr. Chief Justice, may it please the Commission, I would like to mark for identification Exhibit 396, which later proof will show is a picture of President Kennedy shortly before the first bullet struck him, and ask the doctor to take a look at that. Will you describe, Doctor Humes, the position of President Kennedy's right hand in that picture?
> *Commander Humes.* Yes. This exhibit, Commission Exhibit No. 396, allegedly taken just prior to the wounding of the late President, shows him with his hand raised, his elbow bent, apparently in saluting the crowd. I believe that this action —
> *Mr. Specter.* Which hand was that?
> *Commander Humes.* This was his right hand, sir. I believe that this action would further accentuate the elevation of the coat and the shirt with respect to the back of the President. (II, H-366)

Exhibit 396 shows President Kennedy gesturing to the crowd by lifting his right hand, no higher than his forehead, with elbow bent. I defy the most muscle-bound man in the world to cause the center part of his shirt to lift roughly six inches, and then climb up his neck. I defy him to do so, not by such a simple gesture, but rather I would instruct him to lift both hands high over his head and gesticulate wildly. Such gesticulation may perhaps displace the shirt and coat as much as an inch, but the Warren Commission syndrome, I urge, is utterly incapable of duplication. The shirt and coat of President Kennedy could not have been so displaced by such a simple gesture such as bending his right arm at the elbow and lifting his hand to forehead height. If you entertain any doubts with respect to this, the President's tailor should be consulted. He would be outraged by the suggestion.

Commission Exhibits 385 and 386 conform to nothing that we know from the testimony of the Special Agents who were present at the autopsy. These curious exhibits contradict the evidence found in the holes in the President's clothing. These strange works of an artist seem to erase a back wound six inches from the neck line and to give birth to a wound high up on the neck line. How were they arrived at, these strange twin children of the Commission?

> *Commander Humes.* When appraised of the necessity for our appearance before this Commission, we did not know whether or not the photographs which we had made would be available to the Commission. So to assist in making our testimony more understandable to the Commission members, we decided to have made drawings, schematic drawings of the situation as we saw it, as we recorded it and as we recall it. These drawings were made under my supervision and that of Dr. Boswell by Mr. Rydberg, whose initials are H.A. He is a hospital corpsman, second class, and a medical illustrator in our command at Naval Medical School.
>
> *Mr. Specter.* Did you provide him with the basic information from which those drawings were made?
>
> *Commander Humes.* Yes, sir.
>
> *Mr. Specter.* Distances, that sort of thing?
>
> *Commander Humes.* Yes, sir. We had made certain physical measurements of the wounds, and of their

> position on the body of the late President, and we provided those and supervised directly Mr. Rydberg in making these drawings.
>
> *Mr. Specter.* Have you checked the drawings subsequent to their preparation to verify their accuracy?
>
> *Commander Humes.* Yes, sir.
>
> *Mr. Specter.* And proportion?
>
> *Commander Humes.* I must state those drawings are in part schematic. The artist had but a brief period of some two days to prepare these. He had no photographs from which to work, and had to work under description, verbal description, of what we had observed.
>
> *Mr. Specter.* Would it be helpful to the artist in redefining the drawings, if that should become necessary, to have available to him the photographs or X-rays of the President?
>
> *Commander Humes.* If it were necessary to have them absolutely true to scale. I think it would be virtually impossible for him to do this without the photographs. (II, H-349-50)

So, therefore, Commander Humes, by his own admission, concedes that those two drawings of the artist are not "absolutely true to scale." He and the Commission concluded that it was not necessary to have them absolutely true to scale. But I trust that the United States Government will recognize at this time that it is indeed necessary to have them true to scale. This matter of where the bullet entered the back of the President is of essence to the case. The Commission's evidence on this point is hopelessly self-contradictory.

The Warren Commission was loaded with attorneys. Each one of them knew that *no criminal court in the land would have admitted those drawings as evidence without having first required the production of the autopsy X-rays with the colored and black and white photographs of the body.* These drawings are, by admission of Commander Humes, inaccurate fabrications. Why did the

Commission not exclude them and *insist on the presentation of the X-rays and the photographs taken at Bethesda?*

The following is testimony relating to the absence of these crucial exhibits:

> *Commander Humes.* I do not believe, sir, that the availability of the X-rays would materially assist the Commission.
> *Mr. Specter.* How about the same question as to pictures?
> *Commander Humes.* The pictures would show more accurately and in more detail the character of the wounds as depicted particularly in 385 and 386 and in 388-A. They would also perhaps give the Commissioners a bett — better is not the best term, but a more graphic picture of the massive defect in 388.
> *Mr. Specter.* Going back for a moment, Doctor Humes.
> *The Chairman.* Before we get off that, may I ask you this, Commander: If we had the pictures here and you could look them over again and restate your opinion, would it cause you to change any of the testimony you have given here?
> *Commander Humes.* To the best of my recollection, Mr. Chief Justice, it would not. (II, H-371-72)

On November 24, 1963, Commander Humes signed the following certificate:

> I, James J. Humes, certify that I have destroyed by burning certain preliminary draft notes relating to Naval Medical School Autopsy Report A63-272 and have officially transmitted all other papers related to this report to higher authority. (XVII, H-48)

The destruction of these historically crucial notes is a tragedy. But fortunately, the reasons which prompted Commander Humes to destroy these original autopsy notes, and therefore deprived posterity of the freshest notes on the wounds, did not also prompt him to destroy the X-rays and photographs prepared at Bethesda. *He turned them over to the Secret Service* (II, H-372). He and the Commission did not see why these X-rays and photographs should be produced at the hearing. They happen to constitute the best extant evidence of the wounds. If the United States Government will not produce this vital data, we must conclude that their omission from the Warren Commission Hearing was purposeful.

They must now be produced for the scrutiny of non-governmentally connected scholars. Not to do so would be to place the Warren Commission under the dark cloud of failure in its obligation to the American public. We have a right to know. Justice Warren has frequently supported such a right in his judicial opinions. Produce the X-rays and photographs.

Summary

To summarize, we maintain that the evidence gathered by the Warren Commission certainly indicates the existence of one entry wound in the front of the President's neck and a separate wound in his back. To avoid this obvious conclusion the Warren Commission appears to have involved itself wittingly or unwittingly in fabrication and withholding of vital evidence.

II. The Wounds of Governor Connally

We dedicate this article to Governor John B. Connally, Jr., who possesses a hard core of fundamental honesty.

Our task here is to analyze the propositions set forth by the Commission as follows:

> Governor Connally was struck by a bullet which entered on the right side of his back and traveled

> downward through the right side of his chest, exiting below his right nipple. This bullet then passed through his right wrist and entered his left thigh where it caused a superficial wound. (W-19)
>
> Although it is not necessary to any essential findings of the Commission to determine just which shot hit Governor Connally, there is very persuasive evidence from the experts to indicate that the same bullet which pierced the President's throat also caused Governor Connally's wounds. However, Governor Connally's testimony and certain other facts have given rise to some difference of opinion as to this probability . . . (W-19)

We learn immediately that "Governor Connally's testimony and certain other facts have given rise to some difference of opinion as to this probability." Let us then try to pick up the trail of these "certain others facts."

The Busy Bullet

Since the Commission found that one bullet emerging from President Kennedy struck the governor, let us follow this bullet on the second half of its journey. The Commission decided that the tiny wound in the front of the President's neck was a wound of exit. They also proposed that this bullet entered the President's back, 5 3/4 inches below the top of the shirt collar and emerged in front from the left side of his necktie knot (V, H-60). Such a bullet was, therefore, headed upward, entering at a lower point than its exit.

We remind the reader that the Commission's ammunition supply totals three bullets. This limitation was self-imposed by virtue of the dogma that the murder was the act of a single assassin who was unable to fire more than three shots from a single bolt-action rifle in the given time. By turning the bullet downward in mid-air and thus having it strike the Governor, the

Commission conserved ammunition. If the missile had not made this mid-air turn and struck the Governor, the Commission would not have had enough bullets to explain all the hits at the assassination site.

In addition this same missile by performing the down and up movement in the President, explained away the suspected entry wound in the front of the President's neck. It also protected the Commission from the problem of a bullet in Kennedy's back which the autopsy experts initially thought had no channel of exit.

But in addition to the "V" trajectory, this missile's path is described as plummeting downward while in flight, slicing through several diverse parts of Governor Connally. If Connally's wounds could not be explained by the same missile, the Commission would have been caught in impossible arithmetic. So, the Commission finally described the bullet as weaving downward, inward and upward in the President and then turning in mid-air, coursing downward and leftward in the Governor.

If this bullet did not cause all the Governor's wounds, a minimum of two bullets would have been required to explain the back and front neck wounds of President Kennedy and all the wounds of Governor Connally. Such an expenditure would have left but one more bullet to impact on President Kennedy's head. At which juncture the Commission would have been out of ammunition to explain the other bullet hits in Dealey Plaza on that day.

The Commission, if it had not conserved ammunition, by finding that the first bullet to hit the President accounted for all the wounds on the Governor, would be left without missiles to explain the impacts on the windshield and chrome in the front of the Presidential limousine and a hit on James T. Tague some 270 feet away. These extra bullet strikes are inexplicable if all three bullets are used in the smiting of the limousine's occupants.

"It Is Not Conceivable"

Let us now leave the realm of Commission speculation and examine the evidence about the double hit. Governor Connally testified as follows:

> . . . we turned on Elm Street. We had just made the turn, well, when I heard what I thought was a shot. I heard this noise which I immediately took to be a rifle shot. I instinctively turned to my right because the sound appeared to come from over my right shoulder, so I turned to look back over my right shoulder, and I saw nothing unusual except just people in the crowd, but I did not catch the President in the corner of my eye, and I was interested because once I heard the shot in my own mind I identified it as a rifle shot, and I immediately — the only thought that crossed my mind was that this is an assassination attempt.
>
> So I looked, failing to see him, I was turning to look back over my left shoulder into the back seat, but I never got that far in my turn. I got about in the position I am in now, facing, looking a little bit to the left of center, and then I felt like someone had hit me in the back.
>
> . . . Mrs. Connally pulled me over to her lap. I reclined with my head in her lap, conscious all the time, and with my eyes open; and the, of course, the third shot sounded, and I heard the shot very clearly. I heard it hit him. (IV, H-132-33)

> . . . after I heard that shot, I had the time to turn to my right, and start to my left before I felt anything. It is not conceivable to me that I could have been hit by the first bullet . . . (IV, H-136)

So, Governor Connally believes that the Commission's conclusion is not only mistaken but "not conceivable."

Mrs. John B. Connally, Jr. offered testimony as follows:

> I heard a noise, and not being an expert rifleman, I was not aware that it was a rifle. I turned over my right shoulder and looked back, and saw the President as he had both hands at his neck.

> . . . Then very soon there was the second shot that hit John. As the first shot was hit, and I turned to look at the same time, I recall John saying, "Oh, no, no, no." Then there was a second shot, and it hit John, and as he recoiled to the right, just crumpled like a wounded animal to the right, he said, "My God, they are going to kill us all." (IV, H-147)

Mrs. Connally's statement conforms exactly to her husband's description. It signified havoc for the Commission on the question of a single bullet hitting the two statesmen. The testimony of the Governor and Mrs. Connally was corroborated by every eyewitness. No witness suggested that Kennedy and Connally were wounded by the same bullet.

A Logical Fallacy

Tracing back the basis on which the Commission came to its unsubstantiated conclusion, we find that this was the reasoning employed:

> The bullet that hit President Kennedy in the back and exited through his throat most likely could not have missed both the automobile and its occupants. Since it did not hit the automobile, Frazier testified that it probably struck Governor Connally. The relative positions of President Kennedy and Governor Connally at the same time when the President was struck in the neck confirm that the same bullet probably passed through both men. (W-105)

Once stripped of the sad support provided by begging the question, the inference collapses under the weight of eyewitness, photographic, ballistics, and anatomical evidence.

To justify the Commission's conclusion concerning a dual hit, we also have to assume that which the Commission's evidence did not prove, i.e., the absence of any other gunman at any other post. As a matter of fact, Harold Feldman has come across 51 eyewitnesses who indicated to the Commission that the shots came from the north side of Elm Street, to wit, the grassy knoll area. A shot from the knoll, hitting the President in the front of the neck, in a slightly downward but flatter trajectory than that of a shot fired from the Book Depository Building, could well have accounted for a bullet hitting the President and "not hitting the automobile." The Commission chose to ignore the mass of witnesses who heard shots from the knoll, smelled gunpowder, and saw smoke in the locale.

Without viewing the autopsy X-rays and photographs, we cannot share the conclusion that the bullet in Kennedy's back exited from his necktie knot. All the evidence of the Commission, except for the artist's creations (Exhibits 385, 386), is against this proposition. Therefore, we reject the conclusion that the Governor's mere presence in front of the President proves that he was hit by the same bullet. Nor was the Commission justified in so concluding without examining the photographic and X-ray evidence of the autopsy.

Commission vs. Mssrs. Zapruder and Newton

Better evidence is provided by the Abraham Zapruder motion picture taken of the assassination. This film, as published (XVIII, H-11-80), consists of 160 frames which ran through the Zapruder camera at a rate of 18.3 frames per second (W-97). Therefore: "the timing of certain events could be calculated by allowing 1/18.3 seconds for the action depicted from one frame to the next" (W-97). It was the Zapruder film which compressed the Commission tightly into the time span of 4.8 to 5.6 seconds within which all the hits on the occupants of the Presidential limousine were scored. "From the timing evidenced by the Zapruder film, there was an interval of from 4.8 to 5.6 seconds between the shot which struck President Kennedy's neck (between frames 210 to 225) and the shot which struck his head at frame 313 (W-115).

Let us examine the film to determine if it supports the testimony of the Governor, Mrs. Connally, and all the eyewitnesses, that the Governor was pierced by a separate shot or shots. The Commission found that the Zapruder film showed the President's body first reacting to a bullet-imposed force at frame 225.

Governor Connally continued to sit erect and face forward from Zapruder frame 225 through 235. At frame 235 he began to turn right, just as he maintained in his testimony. The reader recalls that at frame 225 or before, the Commission found that a bullet had pierced Connally's back, shattered his fifth rib, caused compound fractures of his wrist, and hit him in the left knee area (W-93). Despite the fact that a great deal of tissue and bone was struck, the Governor's body is supposed to have registered no reaction to the bullet which allegedly struck him by frame 225 or before. Rather the Governor is seen beginning his turn to the right at frame 235. On the other hand, President Kennedy's body immediately reacted to this bullet which, according to the Commission, struck no bone.

The Commission well knew from the film that Connally's body evidenced no reaction at the time that President Kennedy's body did. The Commission's explanation of the Governor's failure to react is a headlong retreat from objective data to subjective guessing. "There was conceivably a delayed reaction between the time the bullet struck him and the time he realized that he was hit" (W-112). But the Zapruder films recorded reality and not the Commission's speculations of what is conceivable.

Newton's third law of motion cannot be so glibly bypassed. This law states that every action has an equal and opposite reaction, the forces occurring in pairs. The force on Connally, the Commission urges, was at first a single force which resulted in a delayed reaction. Back pierced, rib shattered, wrist fractured, thigh punctured — and no immediate reaction? This is not possible. In short, Messrs. Zapruder and Newton worked great damage on the Commission's fiat that the same first bullet to hit the President caused all the wounds on the Governor.

Commission Exhibit 399 — The Bullet

The most concrete evidence on this subject is the exhibit bullet itself. With one categorical assertion the Commission tried to eliminate any doubts about this bullet. "All the evidence indicated that the bullet found on the Governor's stretcher could have caused all his wounds" (W-95).

This bullet weighed 158.6 grains (W-557). A whole bullet of this type weighs 160 to 161 grains (W-77). Except for a minute extrusion of metal from the rear, the bullet designated Commission Exhibit 399 (XVII, H-399) was intact.

The Commission decided that *all the evidence* indicated this bullet caused all the wounds on Connally. In so concluding, they evidently no longer recognize the testimony of Commander Humes. This is the same Dr. Humes on whom they relied so heavily for the drawings that took the place of the photographs and X-rays.

> *Mr. Specter*. Dr. Humes, under your opinion which you have just given us, what effect, if any would that have on whether this bullet, 399, could have been the one to lodge in Governor Connally's thigh?
> *Commander Humes*. I think that extremely unlikely. The reports, again Exhibit 392 from Parkland, tell of an entrance wound on the lower midthigh of the Governor, and X-rays taken there are described as showing metallic fragments in the bone, which apparently by this report were not removed and are still present in Governor Connally's thigh. I can't conceive of where they came from this missile. (II, H-376)

It would have been understandable had the Commission repudiated Commander Humes's testimony about the autopsy. His burning of initial autopsy notes, his failure to produce X-rays and photographs, his introduction of contradictory exhibits — these certainly impeached him as a witness.

However, in this instance, Commander Humes reasoned competently. Whereas the Commission accepted his autopsy meanderings as verity, they acted as if he had never expressed himself on the subject of the bullet. For if they had taken cognizance of his testimony, they could not have concluded that "all the evidence indicated that the bullet found on the Governor's stretcher could have caused all his wounds."

On this score Humes had wide support. Dr. Robert Roeder Shaw of Parkland Hospital said:

> *Mr. Specter.* What is your opinion as to whether bullet 399 could have inflicted all of the wounds on the Governor, then, without respect at this point to the wound of the President's neck?
> *Dr. Shaw.* I feel that there would be some difficulty in explaining all of the wounds as being inflicted by bullet Exhibit 399 without causing more in the way of loss of substance to the bullet or deformation of the bullet. (IV, H-114)
>
> *Dr. Shaw.* All right. As far as the wounds of the chest are concerned, I feel that this bullet could have inflicted those wounds. But the examination of the wrist both by X-ray and at the time of surgery showed some fragments of metal that make it difficult to believe that the same missile could have caused these two wounds. There seems to be more than three grains of metal missing as far as the — I mean in the wrist. (IV, H-113)

Dr. Charles F. Gregory of Parkland Hospital concluded as follows:

> *Dr. Gregory.* The wound of entrance is characteristic in my view of an irregular missile in this case, an irregular missile which has tipped itself off as being irregular by the nature of itself.
> *Mr. Dulles.* What do you mean by irregular?

> *Dr. Gregory*. I mean one that had been distorted. It is in some way angular, it has edges or sharp edges or something of this sort. It is not rounded or pointed in the fashion of an ordinary missile.
> (IV, H-124)

Commission Exhibit 399 was "rounded" and "pointed." Except for a slight irregularity caused when the bullet core extruded through the back, it was in all respects an intact, unmutilated bullet. It does not conform to the missile which Dr. Gregory stated would have caused the Governor's wrist wound. This is further proof that *all* the evidence did *not* show that Commission Exhibit 399 caused all the wounds on Governor Connally.

In further testimony, Dr. Gregory strikes another blow at the weaving-bullet theory.

> *Dr. Gregory*. I would believe that the missile in the Governor behaved as though it had never struck anything except him.
> *Mr. Specter*. Well, wouldn't you think it possible, bearing in mind that my last question only went as to whether the same bullet could have gone through President Kennedy and inflicted the wound on Governor Connally's chest, would you think it possible that the same missile could have gone through President Kennedy in the way I described and have inflicted all three of the wounds, that is, the entry and exit on the chest, the entry and exit on the wrist, and the entry into the thigh which you described.
> *Dr. Gregory*. I suspect it's possible, but I would say it would have to be a remarkably powerful missile to have done so. (VI, H-103)

So, Dr. Gregory thought that a separate shot hit Connally. Dr. George T. Shires of Parkland Hospital also thought so:

> *Mr. Specter.* Do you think it is possible that Governor Connally could have been struck by two bullets, one entering his back and emerging from his chest and the second going into his wrist?
> *Dr. Shires.* I'm sure it is possible, because missile sites are so variable, depending upon the size of the bullet, the speed at which it travels, whether it was tumbling or not. We have seen all kinds of combinations of entrance and exit wounds and it's just impossible to state with any certainty, looking at a given wound, what the missile was, so I am sure it is possible. (VI, H-110)

Mr. Specter then asked if it was possible for a bullet to slice through the President and then cause all the Governor's wounds.

> *Dr. Shires.* I assume that it would be possible. The main thing that would make me think that this was not the case is that he remembers so distinctly hearing a shot and having turned prior to the time he was hit, and in the position he must have been, particularly here in Figure 5, I think it's obvious that he did turn rather sharply to the right and this would make me think that it was a second shot, but this is purely conjecture, of course.
> (VI, H-11)

Dr. Shires was too modest. His conclusion was not "purely conjecture." Conjecture is guessing from incomplete or uncertain evidence. All the eyewitness evidence (including that of the victim), the Zapruder film, the intact bullet, the testimony of Bethesda's Dr. Humes, and Parkland's Drs. Shaw, Gregory and Shires solidly support the view that a separate bullet or bullets struck Governor Connally. It was the Commission that conjectured to draw a conclusion that one bullet struck Kennedy and Connally. This inference is contradicted by overwhelming evidence. Analysis of the Commission's evidence compels us to conclude that it was wrong in finding: "All the evidence indicated that the bullet found on the Governor's stretcher could have caused all his wounds" (W-95).

An alert reader must by now be curious as to how one bullet could have coursed through the President from the rear, and pierced Governor Connally, who was sitting erect, through the back, right nipple, right wrist and left knee area. The only logical explanation for this extreme right to left and 35° back to front, downward and across bullet trajectory (V, H-172) would be a hit delivered from the right, from the north side of Elm Street, i.e., the grassy knoll area. No single bullet fired from the back into the Governor, who was sitting erect, would be likely to have accomplished those wounds in different geometric planes.

Governor Connally described his being hit while "looking a little bit to the left of center, and then I felt someone had hit me in the back" (IV, H-133), If we assume a direction from the right side of Connally, while he is turning a little left of center, it is possible to place all his hits through the back, out the right nipple, through the right wrist, and into the left femur, in *one* geometric plane. For the Commission to have concluded that the Connally shot was delivered from the right, would have corroborated the 51 witnesses who thought that shots were fired from the grassy knoll, but such a finding would have abolished the lone-assassin concept.

Summary

The heavy weight of evidence requires us to conclude that the Commission was mistaken in its determination that Governor Connally was struck by the same first bullet or bullets which wounded the President. This evidence consists of the Governor's testimony, his wife's, that of all the eyewitnesses to the assassination, the Zapruder films, the ballistics evidence with respect to Commission Exhibit 399, and the anatomical findings indicating an irregular missile had punctured Governor Connally's wrist.

III. The Head Wounds of President Kennedy

> The complexity of these fractures and the fragments thus produced tax satisfactory verbal description and are better appreciated in photographs and roetgenograms which are prepared. (Autopsy Report, W-541)

This is perhaps the most significant statement concerning the wounds in the President's head. Commander James J. Humes, Director of Laboratories of the Naval Medical School at Bethesda, who supervised the autopsy, made the following comment in his testimony before the Commission:

> *Commander Humes.* I have noted in my report that a detailed description of the lines of these fractures and of the types of fragments that were thus made were very difficult of verbal description, and it was precisely for this reason that the photographs were made so one might appreciate more clearly how much damage had been done to the skull.
> *Mr. Specter.* Were the photographs made available then, Dr. Humes, when Exhibit 388 was prepared?
> *Commander Humes.* No, sir.
> *Mr. Specter.* All right. (II, H-351)

Still later in his testimony Commander Humes contradicts the autopsy report and his former testimony as follows:

> *Commander Humes.* I do not believe, sir, that the availability of the X-rays would materially assist the Commission. (II, H-371)

Whereas in the autopsy report Commander Humes confessed the wounds of the head "tax satisfactory description," he later admits that the artist who portrayed the wounds of the head in Exhibit 388 was only given verbal description to aid in the preparation of his drawings. He no longer believes that "the X-rays would materially assist the Commission."

It was the Commission's job, *inter alia*, to ascertain the nature of the head wounds. Commander Humes had the obligation to provide the X-rays and photographs of these wounds which "tax satisfactory description." Drawings based on verbal description were inadequate for the Commission's purpose. Mr. Specter and his Commission fellow lawyers are too experienced in law to accept the secondary evidence of the drawings in lieu of the best available evidence, to wit, the X-rays and photographs.

To discuss the head wounds of the President without the X-rays and photographs is to undertake this crucial work without the essential tools. Therefore, our comments relating to these wounds, must be considered tentative since the Commission's data are incomplete. If I do not mistake the quality of our people, their pressure on the United States Government in the exercise of their right and desire to know will ultimately compel the production of this evidence. The Government in turn must recognize that the production of this evidence is the *sine qua non* of credibility in this case.

Working under this handicap, we will be compelled to depart from the official case record to include three newspaper comments in our evidence. First, we will state the official version of the President's head wound:

> The detailed autopsy of President Kennedy performed on the night of November 22 at the Bethesda Naval Hospital led the three examining pathologists to conclude that the smaller hole in the rear of the President's skull was the point of entry and the large opening on the right side of his head was the wound of exit. . . . (W-86)

> Colonel Finck testified: "President Kennedy was, in my opinion, shot from the rear. The bullet entered in the back of the head and went out on the right side of his skull . . . he was shot from above and behind." (W-86)

Eyewitness Testimony of Right Side Entry?

Certainly one of the closest eyewitnesses was Mrs. John F. Kennedy. Since President Kennedy's head was pitched into her by the force of the bullet impact, and she held him for a while, it is probable that she saw her husband's head wounds. Unfortunately we cannot know what she testified to with respect to them. For in the midst of her testimony appears the cryptic note: "Reference to wounds deleted" (V, H-180).

Why these references were deleted is a mystery. J. Lee Rankin, the Commission's counsel, assured us that only classified material involving national security was withheld from the transcript volumes (*The Philadelphia Inquirer*, Nov. 20, 1964). As we have previously asked, what possible connection can the wounds inflicted on President Kennedy by a lone assassin have with national security? Only wounds indicative of a trajectory pointing to an assassin other than the "lone assassin" would have any possible significance for the most bloated concept of national security. Commission censorship compels us to turn from Mrs. Kennedy to other eyewitnesses for help concerning the President's head wounds.

Here again the Special Agents assigned to the protection of the President offer their trained observations. Special Agent Samuel A. Kinney was "the driver of the follow-up car" (XVII, H-730). He reported the head strike as follows:

> I saw one shot strike the President in the right side of the head. The President then fell to the seat to the left toward Mrs. Kennedy. (XVIII, H-731)

Special Agent Kinney observed a hit on the right. He describes the President as falling leftward after being hit on the right side of the head. This conforms to what is shown by the Zapruder films which follow frame 313 (head impact picture) (XVIII, H-70-80).

Seated in the left rear of the Presidential follow-up car was Special Agent George W. Hickey, who observed the following:

> I heard what appeared to be two shots and it seemed as if the right side of his head was hit and his hair flew forward. (XVIII. H-765)

These agents thought they saw a hit on the right side of the President's head. The evidence of the Zapruder film, which shows President Kennedy's body being driven to the left, provides an indication of the direction from which this death-dealing shot came. A body being propelled to the left by a shot is indicative that the shot was fired from the right. A hit from the right side (grassy knoll area), which is supported by the statements of 51 eyewitnesses in the Commission's compilation of the evidence, would satisfactorily account for the President being pushed over to the left.

At Parkland Hospital, Special Agent Hurchel Jacks saw the President's body. He said about the head wound: "it appeared that the bullet had struck above the right ear or near the temple" (XVIII, H-801). If there was a hit on the right side, delivered from the right, then the left side of the head would be the logical place to look for some exit point of the missile or any part of it.

A Left Temporal Wound?

We must examine the eyewitness testimony to determine if there is evidence of any outlet channel on the left portion of the President's head.

The New York Times of November 23, 1963 (page 5, columns 7 and 8) carried a story entitled "10 Feet from President." This story refers to Norman Similas, 34 years of age, from Willowdale, Toronto, Canada, who was 10 feet from the President when a bullet struck his head. He saw the following:

> I could see a hole in the President's left temple and his head and hair were bathed in blood.

A.P. Photographer, James P. Altgens, who took the famous picture of President Kennedy registering his first hit or hits, was on the south side of Elm Street, to the left of the President. He said:

> There was flesh particles that flew out of the side of his head in my direction from where I was standing, so much that it indicated to me that the shot came out of the left side of his head. (VII, H-518)

The fact that the head hit caused particles to fly southward indicates force having been applied from the north. This is evidence of a shot from the grassy knoll through the right parietal and out the left temporal region.

Altgens' testimony to the effect that flesh was blown out the left side of the President's head is supported by two Dallas motorcycle policemen who were riding to the left rear of the Presidential limousine.

Officer B.J. Martin in a deposition for the Commission, testified as follows:

> *Mr. Martin.* I was assigned to ride on the left-hand rear side of President Kennedy.
> *Mr. Ball.* And were you riding alone there, or was another officer riding with you?
> *Mr. Martin.* There was another officer riding with me, B.W. Hargis.
> *Mr. Ball.* He was parallel to you on another motorcycle?
> *Mr. Martin.* Yes, sir, we were.
> *Mr. Ball.* Two motorcycles abreast?
> *Mr. Martin.* Yes. . . .
> *Mr. Ball.* Was there any breeze that day?
> *Mr. Martin.* Yes, there was.
> *Mr. Ball.* From what direction?
> *Mr. Martin.* I believe it was blowing out of the south-west at that particular location. It seemed like we were going to turn into the wind as we turned off of Houston onto Elm.

Mr. Ball. The wind was in your face?
Mr. Martin. Yes; the best I can recall. (VI, H-289-291)

Officer Martin then told of hearing the shots, going to Parkland Hospital, and directing traffic there. While working traffic, Officer Martin made a gory discovery:

Mr. Ball. You had a white helmet on?
Mr. Martin. Yes.
Mr. Ball. Did you notice any stains on your helmet?
Mr. Martin. Yes, sir; during the process of working traffic there, I noticed that there were blood stains on the windshield on my motor and then I pulled off my helmet and I noticed there were blood stains on the left side of my helmet.
Mr. Ball. To give a more accurate description of the left side, could you tell us about where it started with reference to the forehead?
Mr. Martin. It was just to the left of what would be the center of my forehead — approximately halfway, about a quarter of the helmet had spots of blood on it.
Mr. Ball. And were there any other spots of any other material on the helmet there besides blood?
Mr. Martin. Yes, sir; there was other matter that looked like pieces of flesh.
Mr. Ball. What about your uniform?
Mr. Martin. There was blood and matter on my left shoulder of my uniform.
Mr. Ball. You pointed to a place in front of your shoulder, about the clavicle region?
Mr. Martin. Yes, sir.
Mr. Ball. On the front of your uniform and not on the side?
Mr. Martin. No, sir.
Mr. Ball. That would be left, was it?

> *Mr. Martin.* Yes, on the left side.
> *Mr. Ball.* And just below the level of the shoulder?
> *Mr. Martin.* Yes, sir.
> *Mr. Ball.* And what spots were there?
> *Mr. Martin.* They were blood spots and other matter.
> *Mr. Ball.* And what did you notice on your windshield?
> *Mr. Martin.* There was blood and other matter on my windshield and also on the motor. (VI, H-292)

Officer Martin, therefore, while riding his motorcycle to the left rear of the President was splattered with blood and material from the President's head while riding into a wind. This also supports a shot from the right of the President, through the right side and out the left side of the skull. We will now focus on the testimony of the other policeman, Bobby W. Hargis, who was riding his motorcycle abreast of Officer Martin.

> *Mr. Hargis.* I was at the left-hand side of the Presidential limousine.
> *Mr. Stern.* At what part of the President's car?
> *Mr. Hargis.* Well —
> *Mr. Stern.* Front, or rear?
> *Mr. Hargis.* Oh. Rear.
> *Mr. Stern.* Riding next to Mrs. Kennedy?
> *Mr. Hargis.* Right.

Mr. Hargis told of hearing two shots.

> *Mr. Stern.* Did something happen to you personally in connection with the shot you have just described?
> *Mr. Hargis.* You mean about the blood hitting me?
> *Mr. Stern.* Yes.
> *Mr. Hargis.* Yes, when President Kennedy straightened back up in the car the bullet hit him

> in the head, the one that killed him and it seemed like his head exploded, and I was splattered with blood and brain, and kind of a bloody water. It wasn't really blood . . . (VI, H-294)

So Officers Martin and Hargis, riding on the left rear of the Presidential limousine, had themselves and their vehicles splattered by blood, brains, and fluids flying from the head of the fatally struck President. It would be surprising indeed if a bullet fired from the rear, impacting on the right rear of the President's head and exiting from the right side of his read, had propelled material to the left and rear of the limousine. Not being familiar with the Dealey Plaza physics applicable to this unique Commission frame of reference, we imagine, for the time being, that a bullet striking from the rear on the right side would have sent flesh and blood flying out right front and not left rear.

The Left-Temporal Wound — A Parkland Hospital Illusion?

Once the Presidential limousine arrived at Parkland Hospital, a related mystery began to take shape immediately. On November 24th, 1963, *The Philadelphia Sunday Bulletin* carried on page 3 an article describing how Father Oscar L. Huber, pastor of the Holy Trinity Catholic Church of Dallas, administered the last rites to the President. The article reports that Father Huber:

> wet his right thumb with holy oil and anointed a Cross over the President's forehead, noticing as he did, a "terrible wound" over his left eye.

The report of Dr. Robert N. McClelland of Parkland Hospital, who attended the President, dated November 22nd, 1963 at 4:45 P.M., corresponds exactly to what Father Huber had seen:

> The cause of death was due to massive head and brain injury from a gunshot wound of the left temple. (W-526, 527)

Father Huber was not called as a witness. Nor was Dr. McClelland asked for an explanation of his designation of a wound in the left temple as the cause of death. Apparently the Commission was not concerned with how posterity would regard these two men for seeing a left temporal wound of a "terrible" or "massive" nature when no such wound was supposed to be present.

But, these two men were in good company. You will recall the Canadian, Norman Similas, had seen: "a hole in the President's left temple." A.P. photographer Altgens thought: "the shot came out of the left side of his head."

Still others join Father Huber, Dr. McClelland, and Messrs. Altgens and Similas in suffering from this curious visual disorder. Dr. Adolph Hartung Giesecke, Jr. of Parkland Hospital was no less subject to illusion on this score:

> *Mr. Specter.* What did you observe specifically as to the nature of the cranial wound?
> *Dr. Giesecke.* It seemed that from the vertex to the left ear, and from the browline to the occiput on the left-hand side of the head the cranium was entirely missing.
> *Mr. Specter.* Was that the left-hand side of the head, or the right-hand side of the head?
> *Dr. Giesecke.* I would say the left, but this is just my memory of it. (VI, H-74)

This is strange. Still stranger is the fact that Dr. Marion Jenkins of Parkland Hospital also made the identical report of a left-temporal wound:

> *Dr. Jenkins.* I don't know whether this is right or not, but I thought there was a wound on the left temporal area, right in the hairline and right above the zygomatic process.
> *Mr. Specter.* The autopsy report discloses no such development, Dr. Jenkins.
> *Dr. Jenkins.* Well, I was feeling for — I was palpating here for a pulse to see whether the closed

> chest cardiac massage was effective or not and this probably was some blood that had come from the other point and so I thought there was a wound there also. (VI, H-48)

In summary, on the question of the possible existence of a left-temporal wound. Dr. Jenkins "thought there was a wound there also."

Six people in all thought there was a wound in the left temporal area of the skull. If these six people were mistaken, the Government can prove them in error by producing the X-rays and photographs taken at the autopsy. These six witnesses are backed up by the evidence of the splattering of Officers Martin and Hargis who were to the left and rear of the Presidential limousine. All of the above points directly to a hit from the right and not from the rear of the President. The evidence against the Government theory that the bullet which struck President Kennedy in the head was delivered from the rear is considerable.

Let us now examine the evidence which the Commission offered to support its hypothesis.

A Small Hole in the Back of the President's Head?

The Report states the following: "the smaller hole in the rear of the President's skull was the point of entry" (W-86).

To prove the existence of such a small hole in the back of the President's head was essential to the lone-assassin theory. For the eyewitnesses at the scene testified to a hit on the right side of the skull of the President, while he was facing forward. Such a hit is most consistent with a bullet delivered from the north side of Elm Street, which position was not that of the alleged assassin.

All the Government's proof of this small wound in the back of the President's head amounts to the statements of the doctors who conducted the autopsy, Drs. Boswell Finck and Humes, whose report described a "small occipital wound" (W-541). In addition, Special Agent Roy H. Kellerman testified to the existence of a large wound on the right side of the head and another wound in diameter equal to his little finger near the end of the hairline.

Exactly where this wound was, according to Mr. Kellerman's testimony, we will never know because of Mr. Specter's confusing designation of the wound as follows:

> *Mr. Kellerman.* Entry into this man's head was right below that wound.
> *Mr. Specter.* Indicating the bottom of the hairline immediately to the right of the ear about the lower third of the ear?

To the right of the right ear represents a point off the head. Therefore, Mr. Specter has obliterated any possible support Mr. Kellerman was providing for the Government's contention that there was a small wound in the occipital region.

Only the three autopsy doctors mention this wound. Many are asked about it. No one else confirms its existence. Let us review the parade of witnesses among whom Mr. Specter fished for some support for the existence of this small wound. The fishing was poor, to say the least.

Dr. Ronald Coy Jones told Mr. Specter that he saw "what appeared to be an exit wound in the posterior portion of the skull" (VI, H-56). Dr. Jones was of no help. He saw an exit wound where the Commission wanted an entry wound.

Dr. Marion Thomas Jenkins told Mr. Specter plenty about a massive wound in the left temporal region, but he could cast little light on the wound which Mr. Specter sought to establish in the back of the skull:

> *Mr. Specter.* Did you observe any wounds immediately below the massive loss of skull which you have described?
> *Dr. Jenkins.* On the right side?
> *Mr. Specter.* Yes, sir.
> *Dr. Jenkins.* No . . . (VI, H-48)

Dr. Gene Colman Akin, a Parkland physician, was able to

advise Mr. Specter about damage in the right occipital-parietal portion of the skull. But what he told did not conform to the tiny, neat, little hole which the Government needed to support a hit from the rear. Said Dr. Akin:

> The back of the right occipital parietal portion of his head was shattered, with brain substance protruding.

So, off to Dr. Paul Conrad Peters went the hapless Mr. Specter:

> *Dr. Peters.* I noticed that there was a large defect in the occiput. It seemed to me that in the right occipital-parietal area that there was a large defect. There appeared to be bone loss and brain loss in the area.
> *Mr. Specter.* Did you notice any holes below the occiput, say, in this area below here?
> *Dr. Peters.* No. (VI, H-71)

Dr. Peters was willing to discuss a large hole in the occipital-parietal area with Mr. Specter. But small holes no.

Dr. Adolph Hartung Giesecke. Jr. was the next doctor to have his memory conjured by the pertinacious Mr. Specter. He told of a "very large cranial wound" on "the left-hand side of the head." This was absolutely of no help to Mr. Specter, who tried again:

> *Mr. Specter.* Did you observe any other wound or bullet hole below the large area of missing skull?
> *Dr. Giesecke.* No. . . . (VI, H-74)

Dr. Jackie Hansen Hunt, the anesthesiologist, did not see the wounds. Nor more useful to the government theory was Dr. Kenneth Everett Salyer:

> *Mr. Specter.* What did you observe with respect to the head wound?

> *Dr. Salyer.* I came in on the left side of him and noticed that his major wound seemed to be in his right temporal area, at least from the point of view that I could see him, and other than that — nothing other than he did have a gaping scalp wound — cranial wound.

Registered Nurse Diana Hamilton Bowron also failed Mr. Specter:

> *Mr. Specter.* You saw the condition of his what?
> *Miss Bowron.* The back of his head.
> *Mr. Specter.* And what was that condition?
> *Miss Bowron.* Well, it was very bad — you know.
> *Mr. Specter.* How many holes did you see?
> *Miss Bowron.* I just saw one large hole.
> *Mr. Specter.* Did you see a small bullet hole beneath that one large hole?
> *Miss Bowron.* No, sir. (VI, H-136)

Dr. Malcolm Oliver Perry can't help Mr. Specter either:

> *Mr. Specter.* What did you observe as to the President's head, specifically?
> *Dr. Perry.* I saw no injuries other than the one which I noted to you, which was a large avulsive injury to the right occipitoparietal area, but I did not do a minute examination of his head.
> *Mr. Specter.* Did you notice a bullet hole below the large avulsed area?
> *Dr. Perry.* No; I did not. (VI, H-11)

Can Dr. William Kemp Clark come to the aid of Mr. Specter? Here is his testimony:

> *Dr. Clark.* I then examined the wound in the back of the President's head. This was a large, gaping

> wound in the right posterior part, with cerebral and cerebellar tissue being damaged and exposed.
> (VI, H-21)

> *Mr. Specter.* Now, you described the massive wound at the top of the President's head, with the brain protruding; did you observe any other hole or wound on the President's head?
> *Dr. Clark.* No, sir; I did not. (VI, H-25)

Dr. Clark, did say, however, that the wound "could have easily been hidden in the blood and hair" (VI, H-25).

Mr. Specter went on to Dr. Robert Nelson McClelland. Dr. McClelland was free in his discussion of a large wound in the skull:

> *Dr. McClelland.* As I took the position at the head of the table . . . I could very closely examine the head wound, and I noted that the right posterior portion of the skull had been extremely blasted. It had been shattered, apparently, by the force of the shot so that the parietal bone was protruded up through the scalp and seemed to be fractured almost along its right posterior half, as well as some of the occipital bone being fractured in its lateral half, and this sprung open the bones that I mentioned in such a way that you could actually look down into the skull cavity itself and see that some of the cerebellar tissue had been blasted out. . . . (VI, H-33)

Well, Mr. Specter was looking for just a little hole in the occiput, and this is what he got:

> *Mr. Specter.* Did you observe any other wound on the back of the head?
> *Dr. McClelland.* No. (VI, H-33)

Dr. Charles Rufus Baxter represented another chance for Mr. Specter:

> *Dr. Baxter.* The only wound that I actually saw — Dr. Clark examined this above the manubrium of the sternum, the sternal notch. This wound was in temporal parietal plate of bone laid outward to the side and there was a large area, oh, I would say 6 by 8 or 10 cm. of lacerated brain oozing from this wound, part of which was on the table and made a rather massive blood loss mixed with it and around it.
> *Mr. Specter.* Did you notice any bullet hole below the large opening at the top of the head?
> *Dr. Baxter.* No; I personally did not. (VI, H-41-42)

With respect to his interrogation of the Parkland Hospital staff on the small posterior head wound, Mr. Specter scored zero. Drs. Jones, Jenkins, Akin, Peters, Giesecke, Hunt, Perry, Clark, McClelland, and Baxter said they saw no small wound in the back of the President's head. Registered Nurse Diana Bowron said no. None of the Parkland Hospital staff observed that alleged hole.

Special Agent William Robert Greer also rejected Specter's suggestion. He described a wound in the skull which was in the "upper right side" where "The skull was completely . . . gone":

> *Mr. Specter.* Did you observe any other opening or hole of any sort in the head itself?
> *Mr. Greer.* No, sir; I didn't. No other one.
> (II, H-128)

Special Agent Clinton J. Hill spoke of the following wound in the back of the head:

> *Mr. Hill.* The right rear portion of his head was missing. It was lying in the rear seat of the car. His brain was exposed. There was blood and bits

> of brain all over the entire rear portion of the car. Mrs. Kennedy was completely covered with blood. There was so much blood you could not tell if there had been any other wound or not, except for the one large gaping wound in the right rear portion of the head. (II, H-141)

So the Commission concluded, as it had to, in order to retain its single-assassin-in-the rear theory, that there was a small wound of entry in the occiput of the President's skull. It is easy to accept the existence of such a wound. All one requires for such is the willingness to place absolute faith in the Bethesda autopsy doctors, whose testimony offered by Commander Humes is so patently self-contradictory on other points that it would have been self-impeaching in any criminal or civil trial where the Court sought to have evidence weighed impartially.

Without the X-rays and photographs, in the face of such tremendous evidence against the existence of such a small hole in the back, the Warren Commission lost all semblance of fact-finding when it argued the existence of a small rear head wound. The evidence which was offered to it clearly weighed overwhelmingly in the direction of a large and not a small wound in the occipital-parietal area of the skull.

The Large Head Wound on the Right Side

The Warren Commission accepted as fact that: "the large opening in the right side of his head was the wound of exit" (W-86). We can agree with the Commission that there was a large wound in the "right side of his head." I think that the reader, after reading the above, will agree with the autopsy report with respect to this wound:

> The complexity of these fractures and the fractures thus produced tax satisfactory verbal description and are better appreciated in photographs and roetgenograms which are prepared. (W-541)

We await the X-rays and photographs for fuller discussion of this wound. But, presently, we will undertake to explore in a tentative fashion the question of whether this wound was an entry or exit wound. Special Agents Kinney and Hickey thought that this right parietal wound was the point at which the President was struck, i.e., "in the right side of the head."

Bethesda's doctors provided the Commission with testimony to the effect that this large wound had a smaller hole below it and "the smaller hole in the rear of the President's skull was the point of entry" (W-86). This smaller wound was not described by any of the people who scrutinized the President's head at Parkland. On the contrary, this "smaller" wound of "entry" in the back of the President's head was described by the Parkland people as follows: "an exit wound," "back . . . of his head was shattered . . . ," "large defect in the occiput," "one large hole," "large avulsive injury," and "a large, gaping wound."

Without a small entry wound, the Commission would have had to come up with another entry for the wound of the "right side of his skull." For the Commission to have concluded that the wound on the right side was a wound of entry would have been to destroy the lone assassin theory on two scores. Such an entry would have placed the assassin on the right side of the President and not behind him. Such an entry, which created a massive wound on entry, would have required bullets different from the copper jacketed military-style bullets alleged to have been used by the supposed assassin. Such a bullet has a very firm head and a high degree of stability.

The Government witnesses, by concluding that there was a small entry wound below the large wound, decided that a soft-nose bullet could not have caused this wound. Here is how Commander Humes reasoned:

> *Mr. Specter.* Do you have an opinion, Dr. Humes, as to whether there were dumdum bullets used specifically on this wound which struck point "A" of the head, on 388?
>
> *Commander Humes.* I believe these were not dumdum bullets, Mr. Specter. A dumdum bullet is

> a term that has been used to describe various missiles which have a common characteristic of fragmenting extensively upon striking.
> *Mr. Specter.* Would you characterize the resultant effect on this bullet as not extensive fragmenting?
> *Commander Humes.* Yes. Had this wound on point "A" on Exhibit 388 been inflicted by a dumdum bullet, I would anticipate that it would not have anything near the regular contour and outline it had. I also would anticipate that the skull would have been more extensively disrupted and not have, as was evident in this case, a defect which quite closely corresponded to the overlying skin defect because that type of a missile would fragment on contact and be much more disruptive at this point. (II, H-356)

Dr. Humes is able to argue that the bullet on the skull did not "fragment on contact," because he uses the "smaller hole" in the back of the head which no one at Parkland saw as the entry wound. If the Secret Service Agents Kinney and Jacks were correct in their conclusion that the right parietal region had been the point of entry, then the bullet did in fact "fragment on contact."

Commander Humes thought that a dumdum bullet would have been much more "disruptive." The reaction of Army Wound Ballistics Branch Chief Dr. Alfred G. Olivier, was opposite to Dr. Humes. He thought that the wounds of the skull were not consistent with what his prior 17 years of experience had told him about stable bullets.

> It [the test result] disclosed that the type of head wounds that the President received could be done by this type of bullet. This surprised me very much, because this type of stable bullet I didn't think would cause a massive head wound, I thought it would go though making a small entrance and exit. (W-87)

Lt. Col. Pierre A. Finck, Physician, U.S. Army, is something less than candid on the question of the type of bullet likely to have inflicted the head wounds:

> *Representative Ford.* From your numerous case studies, is it typical for a bullet, for a missile in this circumstance as shown in 386 to fragment to the degree that this one apparently did?
> *Colonel Finck.* Yes, it is quite common to find a wound of exit much larger than the wound of entrance for weapons commonly used.
> *Representative Ford.* But is it typical for the missile to fragment to the degree that this one did as shown in Exhibit 388?
> *Colonel Finck.* Yes; it is.
> *Representative Ford.* Is it typical to find only a limited number of fragments as you apparently did in this case?
> *Colonel Finck.* This depends to a great degree on the type of ammunition used. There are many types of bullets, jacketed, non-jacketed, pointed, hollow-noses hollow-points, flatnose, roundnose, all these different shapes will have a different influence on the pattern of the wound and the degree of fragmentation.
> *Representative Ford.* That is all. (II, H-384)

With respect to the amount of fragmentation of the missile, Secret Service Agent Roy H. Kellerman, who viewed the X-rays of the skull at Bethesda on November 22, 1963, has the following to say:

> *Mr. Specter.* Now, did you observe during the course of the autopsy, bullet fragments which you might describe as little stars?
> *Mr. Kellerman.* Yes, of the numerous X-rays that were taken mainly of the skull, the head. The reason for it was that through all the probing

> which these gentlemen were trying to pick up little pieces of evidence in the form of shell fragments, they were unable to locate any. From the X-rays when you placed the X-rays upon the light the whole head looked like a little mass of stars, there must have been 30, 40 lights where these pieces were so minute that they couldn't be reached. However, all through this series of X-rays this was the one that they found, through X-rays that was above the right eye, and they removed that.
>
> *Mr. Specter.* How big a piece was that above the right eye, would you say?
>
> *Mr. Kellerman.* The tip of a matchhead, a little larger. (II, H-100)

Mr. Kellerman's testimony indicated that the bullet which entered President Kennedy's head splintered into dust-like fragments. This is hardly what one would have expected from a copper-jacketed, stable bullet. The Government experts, saved by the small hole in the occipital region, were able to argue that the entry wound of the bullet was regular and small. If it were not for this unconfirmed wound, invisible to all the Parkland Hospital personnel, the large wound of the right parietal area of the skull would have been quite consistent with a frangible, soft-nose bullet, smashing on impact and thereby maximizing the area of damage on entry.

Summary

The Commission's findings have to be considered in themselves inconclusive, as based on insufficient and secondary evidence. There is some credible evidence of a right side *entry* in the President's head. Six people asserted there was a left-temporal wound, among whom were three doctors who had examined the President at Parkland. The existence or non-existence of the left temporal wound can only be settled by the Bethesda photographs. Testimony of the Bethesda doctors concerning the existence of a small entry wound in the back of the President's head can hardly be considered conclusive in light of the numerous medical experts of Parkland who uniformly deny seeing such a wound.

We cannot rule out the possible role of a dumdum bullet as having caused the wounds on President Kennedy's head. Whether such a bullet did inflict the fatal wounds on Kennedy is dependent upon whether the small hole in the occiput of the President did in fact exist and whether it was in fact a wound of entry. If the right-parietal wound was the wound of entry, this would indicate that the fatal bullet was fired from the right of the President and not the rear, and was a dumdum bullet, not a copper-jacketed military bullet of the type allegedly employed by a gunman stationed in the Texas School Book Depository Building. Definite conclusions concerning the head wounds must await the issuance of the crucial X-rays and negatives made at Bethesda.

The Bullet Holes in the President's Jacket and Shirt

by E. Martin Schotz

The simplest and perhaps most elegant proof of conspiracy which demolishes the Warren Report involves a correlation of what the Warren Commission claimed was the path of Commission exhibit #399, the "magic bullet," with the holes in the back of the President's jacket and shirt. Contradicting the Commission's claim that a bullet entered the back of the President's neck are the positions of two overlapping bullet holes, one five and three-eighths inches down from the collar line of the back of the President's suit jacket, the other five and three-quarters inches down from the collar of the back of the President's shirt. Graphic photographs of this evidence, reproduced below, appeared in the FBI's Supplemental Report to the Warren Commission of January 13, 1964. This Supplemental Report, as well as the initial FBI Summary Report of December 9, 1963, did not appear in the 26 volumes of Warren Commission exhibits.

Two encounters that defenders of the Warren Report had over this issue speak volumes.

Arlen Specter Really Doesn't Remember

Vincent Salandria very early alerted Gaeton Fonzi to the jacket and shirt issue, so that Fonzi was prepared to explore the issue when he held a taped interview with the former Warren Commission Counsel Arlen Specter, now Senator Arlen Specter, the author of the "magic bullet theory." In *The Last Investiga-*

Supplemental Report exhibit 59: the back of the President's suit jacket, showing position of bullet entrance hole.

tion, Fonzi reports the encounter which occurred about a year after Specter completed his work for the Commission.

At one point Fonzi asks Specter to explain how holes down in the back of the President's shirt and jacket could have been caused by a bullet entering the back of his neck:

> *Specter*: Well, that difference is accounted for because the President was waving his arm. (He got

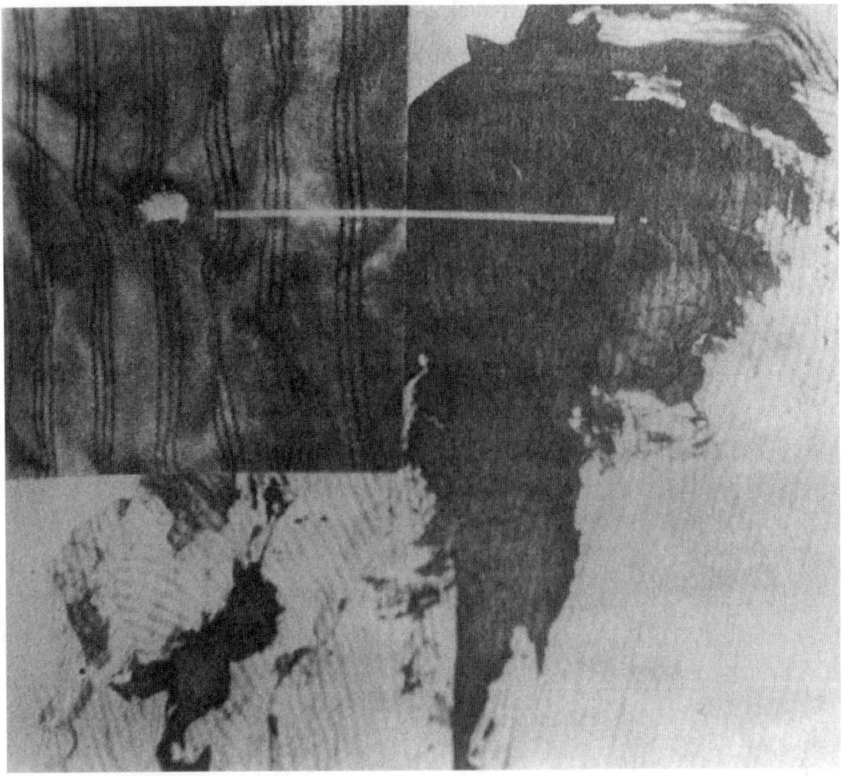

Supplemental Report exhibit 60: the back of the President's shirt, showing position of bullet entrance hole

up from his desk and attempted to demonstrate his explanation on me, pulling my arm up high over my head.) Wave your arm a few times, wave at the crowd. (He was standing behind me now, jabbing a finger into the base of my neck.) Well, see, if the bullet goes in here, the jacket gets hunched up. If you take this point right here and then you strip the coat down, it comes out at a lower point.
Fonzi: A lower point?
Specter: Well, not too much lower on your example, but the jacket rides up . . .
Fonzi: What about the shirt?
Specter: Same thing.

Was Specter saying there was no inconsistency between the Commission's location of the wound and the holes in the clothing?

Specter: No, not at all. That gave us a lot of concern. . . .
Fonzi: But where did it go in the back?
Specter: Well, the back hole, when the shirt is laid down, comes . . . aah . . . well, I forget exactly where it came, but it certainly wasn't higher, enough higher to . . . aah . . . understand the . . . aah . . . the angle of decline which . . .
Fonzi: Was the hole in the back of the shirt lower than the hole in the front of the neck of the shirt? (The President had had a throat wound made by a bullet that pierced his tie and made a hole in the front of the shirt at the throat.)
Specter: Well, I think, that . . . that if you took the shirt without allowing for it being pulled up, that it would either have been in line or somewhat lower.
Fonzi: Somewhat lower?
Specter: Perhaps, I . . . I don't want to say because I don't really remember. I got to take a look at that shirt.

I found it difficult to believe that Arlen Specter didn't take a very close look at that shirt — and that jacket — at the time of the investigation and that these factors didn't indelibly stick in his mind: Kennedy was one of the best-tailored presidents ever to occupy the White House, and if it is possible — but not probable — that he was wearing a suit jacket baggy enough to ride up five or six inches in the back when he waved his arm, it is inconceivable that a tightly buttoned shirt could have done the same thing.

And the Abraham Zapruder film shows Kennedy

> wasn't waving his hand higher than the level of his forehead before he was shot.
>
> After those interviews with Arlen Specter, my belief in . . . [the] Government would never be the same.

The Evening the Government Refused to Get Dressed

The problem of the position of the bullet holes in the jacket and shirt were also the source of consternation for another Warren Report defender, Professor Jacob Cohen, from Brandeis University, who found himself in the company of Vincent Salandria in a panel discussion/debate sponsored by the Universalist Unitarian Church in Cambridge, Massachusetts, in December of 1966.

In the midst of the discussion that evening, in which Cohen was attempting to defend the "single bullet theory," Salandria pulled out of his briefcase a shirt and jacket with holes positioned in the same location as they had been in Kennedy's jacket and shirt. Moving toward Cohen with the shirt and jacket, Salandria handed him the clothes and urged him to put the clothes on and demonstrate to the audience just how the government believed it was possible to get that shirt and jacket to ride up as they claimed it had.

Much to the amusement of the audience, Cohen responded by hurling the clothes back at Salandria. It seems the "government" preferred not to get dressed in its fallen emperor's clothes.

Appendix IV

Internal Data on the United States Government's Immediate Reaction to the Assassination

by E. Martin Schotz

The following appendix provides an analysis of important internal data concerning the U.S. government's immediate response to the Assassination. It includes two memoranda from Nicholas Katzenbach, then assistant to Attorney General Robert Kennedy, which document the fact that within three days of the assassination, the Justice Department had made the decision to cooperate in the cover-up. Also of interest are a series of letters which grew out of the revelation by Theodore H. White that on the flight back to Washington, President Johnson, aboard Air Force One, was informed that Oswald had been arrested and that there was no conspiracy. White confirmed this revelation, giving additional information, but Salandria met with a wall of resistance in his attempt to obtain a copy of the tape recorded communications between Air Force One and the White House on that flight.

Internal Data on the United States Government's Immediate Reaction to the Assassination

by E. Martin Schotz

In November of 1966, in the course of reading Theodore H. White's *The Making of the President, 1964*, Vincent Salandria came across an important revelation. On page 20 of this book Salandria learned that:

> There is a tape recording in the archives of the government which best recaptures the sound of the hours as it waited for leadership. It is a recording of all the conversations in the air, monitored by the Signal Corps Midwestern center "Liberty," between Air Force One in Dallas, the Cabinet plane over the Pacific, and the Joint Chiefs' Communications Center in Washington.

Then on page 48, Salandria found the following, concerning the flight back to Washington, D.C. from Dallas of the Presidential party aboard Air Force One, on November 22, 1963:

> On the flight the party learned that there was no conspiracy, learned of the identity of Oswald and his arrest; and the President's mind turned to the duties of consoling the stricken and guiding the quick.

On November 23, 1963, *The Dallas Morning News* had informed its readers that according to District Attorney Henry Wade:

> preliminary reports indicated more than one person was involved in the shooting . . . the electric chair is too good for the killers.

In Volume I, page 149 of the twenty-six volumes of Warren Commission exhibits, one learns from Marina Oswald's testimony that on Saturday, November 23rd, while waiting to see her husband:

> One of the men came by and said, "I am sorry that we are going to be delayed in letting you see Lee, . . . we have picked up another suspect."

And yet the White House had informed President Johnson and the other occupants of Air Force One, all of them witnesses to the hail of bullets which had poured down on Dealey Plaza, that as of the afternoon of the assassination there was to be no conspiracy and that Oswald was to be the lone assassin. If White's report were correct this would mean that federal officials in Washington were marrying the government to the cover-up of Oswald as the lone assassin virtually instantaneously. This could have occurred only if those federal officials had had foreknowledge that the evidence would implicate Oswald and that he would have "no confederates." An innocent government could not have reacted in such a fashion internally.

Salandria wrote immediately to White:

> Can you find time to advise in brief the source of the following information which appears on page 48 of your book?
>
> > On the flight the party learned that there was no conspiracy; learned of the identity of Oswald and his arrest; and the President's mind turned to the duties of

> consoling the stricken and guiding the quick.
>
> I would much appreciate you providing the source of this information and a designation of the nature of the Communication to Air Force One, i.e. whether it was commercial T.V., government radio or whatever.
>
> Please be advised that I have undertaken a very meticulous analysis of Warren Commission data and have written a number of articles on the subject. . . .
>
> Very truly yours,
> (signed)
> Vincent J. Salandria

White returned Salandria's letter, indicating awareness of Salandria's writings and penning at the bottom of the letter the following: "By government radio — all relays go through a big Signal Corps center in the Midwest — and the White House was in constant communications with the plane. (Signed) T. H. White."

Salandria wrote immediately to Dr. Robert Bahmer, Archivist of the United States, requesting access to the tape. But Bahmer replied:

> We have no knowledge of the existence or location of the tape recording mentioned by Mr. White, despite having made some efforts since the receipt of your letter to obtain some information about it.

Salandria next wrote to Pierre Salinger on December 3, 1966:

> In your fine work, *With Kennedy,* you make mention of radio communications with the White House and the cabinet plane over the Pacific on November 22, 1963 (pp. 22-25). You identify "Stranger" as Major Harold R. Patterson.

Theodore H. White, *The Making of the President, 1964*, also refers to these conversations but particularly related to those dialogues with the Presidential plane, Air Force One.

I have asked the National Archives for a copy of this tape. Dr. Bahmer, the excellent Archivist of the United States, cannot locate it, although Mr. White states on page 21 of his book: "There is a tape recording in the archives of the government." I enclose Dr. Bahmer's letter. Mr. White will not provide any further information.

Specifically what I am about is the verification of what Mr. White stated was on the tape, to wit: "On the flight the party learned that there was no conspiracy; learned of the identity of Oswald and his arrest; and the President's mind turned to the duties of consoling the stricken and guiding the quick." If such was said, before there was any evidence against Lee Harvey Oswald as the assassin, and while there was overwhelming evidence of a conspiracy, then the White House is in the interesting position of being the first to designate Oswald as the assassin and the first to have ruled out in the face of impressive evidence to the contrary, that there could have been a conspiracy.

Now, Mr. Salinger, let us face up to the plain fact that foreign intelligence services monitored that series of conversations and have long since broken the code. That tape is being denied only to the American public. . . . Will you render this service to civilian rule and democracy for which President Kennedy gave his life?

Respectfully yours,
(signed)
Vincent J. Salandria

Far from dismissing Salandria's letter, Salinger replied rather cordially on December 26, and indicated:

> The section of my book dealing with the conversations between the White House and the Cabinet plane were taken from a transcript of the tape of those conversations made by the White House Communication Agency. I have never either read or heard the tape to which Mr. White refers, i.e., the conversations with Air Force One. Since the tape with which I worked was provided by the White House Communication Agency, it would seem to me that the tape of the conversation to which you refer would emanate from the same source, if such a tape, in fact, exists.
>
> As to the conversation with the cabinet plane, the transcript of that conversation is in my personal files which have been turned over to the National Archives for placement in the Kennedy Library.
>
> I certainly have no objection to your seeing that transcript, although the National Archives will undoubtedly write and ask my permission since it is included in my personal papers.
>
> Sincerely yours,
> (signed)
> Pierre Salinger

Again Salandria wrote to Bahmer, this time requesting that Bahmer write to Salinger for authorization for Salandria to see the transcript to which Salinger referred. Again Bahmer replied:

> After receipt of your letter of December 28, a careful examination was made of the papers that Mr. Salinger has sent to us for storage. We have not, however, been able to find anything in the nature of a transcript of the tape recording that you are searching for.

I regret that our reply to your inquiries, therefore, must still be in the negative.

Salandria then wrote directly to the White House Communication Agency requesting access to the tape recording of communication between Air Force One and Washington and after a lengthy wait received the following:

January 2, 1968

Dear Mr. Salandria:

I have been asked to respond to your letter, addressed to the White House Communication Agency, concerning a tape recording to Air Force One, November 22, 1963.

Logs and tapes of the radio transmissions of military aircraft, including those of Air Force One, are kept for official use only. These tapes are not releasable, nor are they obtainable from commercial sources.

I am sorry my response cannot be more favorable.

Respectfully,
(signed)
James U. Cross
Armed Forces Aide
to the President

A tape and transcript to which White and Salinger respectively had had access had apparently disappeared. And despite the fact that at the time of their writings both individuals were private citizens and used access to the tape and transcript for commercial purposes, it appeared that where Salandria was concerned these materials were classified.

Could Theodore H. White have been mistaken? Has any other testimony surfaced which might corroborate White's report? In 1993 there appeared *"Let Us Begin Anew": An Oral*

History of the Kennedy Presidency, by Gerald S. and Deborah H. Strober, and on pages 450-51 one finds the following remarks by Assistant Secretary of State Robert Manning, who was aboard the Cabinet plane with Salinger:

> We took off from Honolulu in one of the presidential aircraft and were several hundred miles west of there. Several cabinet secretaries were with us, as was Pierre Salinger. I had been in the press, so I knew by the sound that there was a flash on the news ticker. I walked toward the communications area, and the sergeant had a piece of wire copy in his hand. He said, "The secretary [Rusk] will have to see this." It was a flash saying: Dallas. President Kennedy shot." Then a bulletin: "Perhaps shot fatally." we took it to Rusk and he asked me to bring the cabinet secretaries to his compartment.
>
> We immediately got on the phone with the White House Situation Room. They confirmed that something had happened and that the President had been rushed to the hospital. Rusk got on the public address system and told everybody we had some bad, unclear news: President Kennedy had been wounded, and we were going to turn back. Salinger got in touch with the White House and used his code name. He said, "This is Wayside. What word do you have on Lancer?" At the other end the fellow said, "Lancer is dead." Rusk then went back on the PA system and said, "I am sorry to have to bring you this grievous news, but President Kennedy has been killed. We now have a new president. May God bless our president and the United States of America."
>
> The news then came in that someone named Oswald who had been in the Soviet Union had done this.

Salandria's search for the elusive tape and transcript had proved futile. Years later the government would release what it claimed was the tape in question but with large gaps and sections missing. Nevertheless, Salandria persisted in his search for internal documentation of the premature identification of Oswald as the lone assassin and early foreclosure of an investigation by the government. Eventually as a result of the House Select Committee on Assassinations investigation, two memoranda surfaced which documented exactly this. The following is the full text of these memoranda written by Deputy Attorney General Nicholas Katzenbach. In reading these memoranda one must remember that Mr. Katzenbach was serving Attorney General Robert Kennedy. They therefore indicate that very early on the Kennedy forces were prepared to cooperate with the cover-up.

Memorandum for Mr. Moyers

It is important that all of the facts surrounding President Kennedy's assassination be made public in a way which will satisfy people in the United States and abroad that all the facts have been told and that a statement to this effect be made now.

1. The public must be satisfied that Oswald was the assassin; that he did not have confederates who are still at large; and that the evidence was such that he would have been convicted at trial.

2. Speculation about Oswald's motivation ought to be cut off, and we should have some basis for rebutting thought that this was a Communist conspiracy or (as the Iron Curtain press is saying) a right-wing conspiracy to blame it on the Communists. Unfortunately the facts on Oswald seem about too pat — too obvious (Marxist, Cuba, Russian wife, etc.). The Dallas police have put out statements on the Communist conspiracy theory, and it was they who were in charge when he was shot and thus silenced.

3. The matter has been handled thus far with neither dignity nor conviction. Facts have been mixed with rumor and speculation. We can scarcely let the world see us totally in the image of the Dallas police when our President is murdered.

I think this objective may be satisfied by making public as soon as possible a complete and thorough FBI report on Oswald and the assassination. This may run into the difficulty of pointing to inconsistencies between this report and statements by Dallas police officials. But the reputation of the Bureau is such that it may do the whole job.

The only other step would be the appointment of a Presidential Commission of unimpeachable personnel to review and examine the evidence and announce its conclusions. This has both advantages and disadvantages. I think it can await publication of the FBI report and public reaction to it here and abroad.

I think, however, that a statement that all the facts will be made public property in an orderly and responsible way should be made now. We need something to head off public speculation or Congressional hearings of the wrong sort.

Nicholas deB. Katzenbach
Deputy Attorney General[1]

* * * * * * * * * *

[1]Memorandum to Bill Moyers, Press Secretary to President Lyndon Johnson, from Deputy Attorney General Nicholas Katzenbach, written November 25, 1963, three days after the assassination of President Kennedy; rpt. from *Hearings Before the Select Committee on Assassinations of the United States House of Representatives*, 95th Congress, 2nd Session, Volume 3, pp. 566-67.

December 9, 1963

The Chief Justice
The Supreme Court
Washington, D.C.

Dear Mr. Chief Justice:

At the direction of President Johnson, I am transmitting herewith to you and the other members of the Commission copies of the report of the Federal Bureau of Investigation on the assassination of President Kennedy and on the subsequent shooting of Lee Harvey Oswald. You will note that in some aspects the Investigation is continuing and further information will be made available to the Commission as it develops. The Secret Service and the Department of State have also prepared reports with respect to the preparation made to guard the President and certain background information in the hands of the State Department with respect to Oswald. You will have these promptly.

The report is not a classified document since it does not contain defense information. However, we have been treating it as a highly classified document and I trust that you and the other members of the Commission will do likewise until such time as you determine to release matters contained within it. Within the Government it is being read by a very limited number of people on a "need to know" basis.

You will recall that at the time of announcing the Federal Bureau of Investigation investigation, and prior to the appointment of the Commission, President Johnson announced that the FBI report would be made public. I have, however, informed him of your request that this report not be released until the Commission has had time to review all of the facts and evaluate them. At the same time I am sure you are aware that there is such public speculation and rumor in this connection, which it would be desirable to allay as quickly as possible. For example, the latest Gallup poll shows that over half the American people believe that Oswald acted as part of a conspiracy in shooting President Kennedy, and there is considerable rumor in this country and abroad to the effect that Ruby acted as part of the same or a related conspiracy.

I think, therefore, the Commission should consider releasing — or allowing the Department of Justice to release — a short press statement which would briefly make the following points:

(1) The FBI report through scientific examination of evidence, testimony and intensive investigation, establishes beyond a reasonable doubt that Lee Harvey Oswald shot President Kennedy on November 22, 1963. The evidence includes ballistic tests, fingerprints and palm prints, clothing fibers and other technical data which places Oswald at the scene of the crime and establishes that he fired the shots which killed President Kennedy and wounded Governor Connally of Texas.

(2) The FBI has made an exhaustive investigation into whether Oswald may have conspired with or been assisted by any organization, group or person, foreign or domestic, in carrying out this dastardly act. In this regard, the FBI has questioned hundreds of persons and checked out numerous rumors and reports. To date this aspect of the investigation has been negative. No evidence has been uncovered indicating that any organization, group or person, including Dallas night club owner, Jack Ruby, was involved with Oswald

in the assassination of President Kennedy, or that the subsequent shooting of Oswald was part of a conspiracy.

I would be happy to discuss any of the matters contained in this letter or in the report with you or other members of the Commission at any time you should desire. I am, of course, always at your service.

Sincerely yours,
(signed)
Nicholas deB. Katzenbach
Deputy Attorney General[2]

---

[2]Letter to Chief Justice Earl Warren from Deputy Attorney General Nicholas Katzenbach, written twenty days after the assassination of President Kennedy; rpt. from *Hearings Before the Select Committee on Assassinations*, Volume 3, pp. 674-76.

Appendix V

Oswald and U.S. Intelligence

by Christopher Sharrett

The following is a compilation of biographical details on Lee Harvey Oswald which confirm his identity as an agent for U.S. intelligence services.

Oswald and U.S. Intelligence

by Christopher Sharrett

1. Oswald had relatives who had worked for the CIA.

2. Oswald had top secret security clearances while in the Marines, and was at one point stationed at Marine Air Control in the Atsugi Base in Japan. This was a top secret base, from which the CIA launched U-2 flights and performed other covert activities. For example, Oswald's unit was involved in a "top-secret" project, "Operation Strongback," a preparation for a coup against the government of Indonesia.

3. Oswald was later assigned to El Toro Air Station in California with security clearance to work on radar.

4. Oswald was assigned to study Russian at the special U.S. School of Languages at Monterey, a school which is used to train people selected to do work for the U.S. government.

5. While at El Toro, Oswald began expressing very openly pro-Russian and pro-communist views. Such expression did not trigger any concern on the part of his Marine superiors, and in no way affected his security clearances.

6. Oswald obtained a hardship discharge from the Marines within a week of applying for it. The reason given for the application turned out to be false.

7. Oswald had no visible means of income for his trip to Russia,

part of which could not have occurred by commercial transport because of its timing, but could have been accomplished by U.S. military transport.

8. On defecting to the Soviet Union, Oswald claimed that he intended to give away classified radar information to the Soviets.

9. No damage assessment was ever undertaken by U.S. intelligence services of the classified information Oswald was supposedly giving to the Russians.

10. Two and a half years after "defecting" to the Soviet Union, Oswald applied to return to the United States. At the time of Oswald's application, the U.S. Embassy in Moscow cabled the State Department about his request. Portions of the cable having to do with Oswald's identity were classified. On receiving his request the State Department ruled that for technical reasons, Oswald's relinquishing of his U.S. citizenship had not occurred. His return to the U.S. was approved and his travel and moving expenses for returning to the U.S. were funded by the U.S. government. Upon his return, Oswald was greeted not by police officials but by a representative of Traveler's Aid, who was also a prominent official of an ultra-rightist organization that enjoyed intelligence support.

11. His Russian-born wife was exempted from usual immigration quotas and the usual waiting period.

12. Our intelligence agencies never debriefed Oswald with regard to secrets he supposedly passed to the Russians.

13. No "Look-out Card" was ever filled out on Oswald, a standard procedure for a person who would have been considered a security risk, if his defection was legitimate. Although in the early 1960s the FBI published over a million names of potential subversives, Oswald's name wasn't included. Yet Oswald was sufficiently known to our intelligence sources that on June 3, 1960, J. Edgar Hoover wrote a memorandum to the State

Department about the fact that someone other than Oswald was using his name as an alias.

14. On his return to the U.S., Oswald created a public persona for himself as a leftist agitator, but in reality associated with a circle of people who are exclusively anti-communist, right wing activists closely linked to the FBI, the CIA, and U.S. Naval Intelligence, including David Ferrie, Clay Shaw, Guy Banister, George de Mohrenschildt, and Jack Ruby.

15. In New Orleans Oswald set up his own Fair Play For Cuba Committee without the authorization of the national headquarters of the organization which was based in New York City. Oswald was the only member of his committee and he used as an address the post office box of anti-Castro Cubans in New Orleans. Although he was ostensibly broke, he spent money on FPCC fliers and handbills, one batch of which lists the New Orleans FPCC office as located at 544 Camp Street, the headquarters of New Orleans anti-Castro, right-wing activism in the center of that city's U.S. government intelligence complex. Although broke, Oswald hired two men to help him distribute his handbills.

16. In New Orleans, in 1963, Oswald was granted a passport within twenty-four hours of its being requested.

17. In Texas, he and his family were befriended by members of a right-wing Russian emigré community. The husband of the family with which he lived had a security clearance at Bell Helicopter. His security clearance was not adversely affected by his close association with Oswald.

18. While some of Oswald's letters and other writings suggest a subliterate person, other writings, especially letters to leftist groups, suggest a sophisticated, literate person. Either Oswald's illiteracy was a pose or someone wrote letters for him.

19. Oswald was regularly monitored by federal agents. When arrested, Oswald had the name, address, and phone number of an

FBI agent in his possession. George de Mohrenschildt, Oswald's closest associate in Dallas, had ties to the CIA, and J. Walton Moore, a CIA agent, asked de Mohrenschildt to stay in contact with Oswald.

20. Both the FBI and Army Intelligence knew that Oswald used aliases. Army Intelligence in Texas knew Oswald's aliases and previous addresses, although the Pentagon "routinely" destroyed its files on Oswald. Dallas police officials told the Warren Commission that Oswald was an informant for both the FBI and CIA, information that the Commission termed a "dirty little rumor." Dallas officials years later retracted the information.

Sources of Information on Oswald

Garrison, Jim. *A Heritage of Stone*. New York: G.P. Putnam, 1970.

Meagher, Sylvia. *Accessories After the Fact: The Warren Commission, the Authorities and the Report*. New York: Bobbs-Merrill Company, Inc., 1967, pp. 210-19, 327-46.

Melanson, Philip H. *Spy Saga: Lee Harvey Oswald and U.S. Intelligence*. New York: Praeger, 1990.

Scott, Peter Dale. *Deep Politics and the Death of JFK*. Berkeley: University of California Press, 1993.

Scott, Peter Dale. *The Dallas Conspiracy*. Unpublished manuscript, 1970.

Weisberg, Harold. *Oswald in New Orleans: Case for Conspiracy with the CIA*. New York: Canyon Books, 1967.

Appendix VI

A "Political Translation" from Isaac Don Levine's *Mind of the Assassin*

by E. Martin Schotz

The following is a memorandum, prepared for the benefit of the committee of correspondents, which attempts to use a source which appeared four years before the President's assassination as a window on the process of cover-up. The method applied here is what one might call "political or ideological translation" as distinct from linguistic translation.

A "Political Translation" from Isaac Don Levine's *Mind of the Assassin*

by E. Martin Schotz

January 1, 1994

Re: *The Mind of the Assassin*, by Isaac Don Levine (New York: Farrar, Straus, and Cudahy, 1959).

This book by an associate of Allen Dulles is presented by the author as a study of Trotsky's assassination by Mercader, a study which Levine claims sheds light on the mind of assassins in general in the contemporary period. Documents from secret sessions of the Warren Commission reveal that Allen Dulles planned to use Levine to see to it that Marina Oswald would not testify that Lee Harvey Oswald was a U.S. government agent.[1]

The following quotations are of interest.

On the title page of the book, Levine quotes Camus: "In the twentieth century power wears the mask of tragedy." This as well as other references make clear that his book is intended to refer to a general modern phenomenon.

p. 143 — Re: Mercader. "[H]e had a strong tendency to tell much that was truthful about himself. Hence, his subsequent

---

[1]*Document Addendum to the Warren Report* (El Segundo, Ca.: Sightext Publications, 1968), p. 200.

statements to the police often involved a minimum of invention. All that was needed to bring out the truth in many of his accounts was to substitute the NKVD for the Fourth International."

p. 214 — "The key to Mercader, who typifies the modern political assassin, is to be found in the special character of the organization in which he has enlisted for life. The Soviet power is an amalgam of a temporal state and a political religion. It is in the nature of a military order in which the government authorities and the Communist Party priesthood are one supreme source of faith and strength. Mercader became an assassin both as a servant of that government and a missionary of its communist faith, and is beyond redemption."

p. 137 — Concerning Mercader's "confession note": "Experts would have recognized the letter as characteristic, both in style and content, of other known fabrications of the NKVD. However, this fact could not have been easily established had the assassin perished at the scene of the crime or escaped from it. Without being available for examination, the NKVD would have been enabled to make the Trotsky murder seem like an insoluble mystery. Yet the internal evidence that the letter was of NKVD manufacture was conclusive."

Since all understanding is to a significant degree projection, we are justified in asking whether Levine is talking about himself, Dulles, and the CIA as much as he is about the NKVD. In exploring the question I suggest we need only translate the following terms:

"Trotsky" into "Kennedy"
"Soviet" into "American"
"communist" into "anti-communist"
"NKVD" into "CIA"
"Mercader" into "Levine/Dulles/CIA"

> "Mercader's fabricated letter of confession" into "release of the U.S. mass media"

In this case we then get the following:

> Levine has a strong tendency to tell much that is truthful about himself and Dulles. . . . All that is needed to bring out the truth . . . is to substitute CIA for NKVD, etc. . . .
>
> The key to Dulles, who typifies the modern political assassin, is to be found in the special character of the organization in which he has enlisted for life. The American power is an amalgam of a temporal state and a political religion. It is in the nature of a military order in which the government authorities and the anti-communist party priesthood are one supreme source of faith and strength. Dulles became an assassin both as a servant of that government and as a missionary of its anti-communist faith, and is beyond redemption.
>
> Concerning the actions of the U.S. mass media surrounding the murder of Kennedy — Experts [such as Castro] recognized their releases as characteristic in style and content, of other known fabrications of the CIA. This fact could not be easily established because Oswald perished almost immediately and the others involved escaped from the scene. Without the "assassin" being available to be examined, the CIA was thus able to make the murder of Kennedy seem like an insoluble mystery. Yet the internal evidence that the press releases were of CIA manufacture is conclusive.

Appendix VII

The Nation and the Warren Report

The first item is an account of the public record of The Nation *magazine on the Warren Report. It can be compared with the memorandum by Fred Cook, which reveals the behind-the-scenes opposition he encountered from then-editor of* The Nation *Carey McWilliams. This public and private record of* The Nation *is relevant when one sees the way in which leading figures in the left/liberal community used the positions of such journals as* The Nation *and* I.F. Stone's Weekly *as a cover for their refusal to tackle the facts surrounding the President's murder. See also the section from* Addendum B, *by Ray Marcus, in Appendix VIII.*

A Summary of *The Nation*'s Editorial Policy from the Assassination to the Warren Report

by E. Martin Schotz

In its first public comment on the assassination of President Kennedy, the remarks of the editors of *The Nation* clearly reveal that they were aware of President Kennedy's important turn toward peace, as they quoted extensively from a speech the President delivered at the University of Maine on October 19, 1963. The following is the quotation from that editorial:

> While the road to peace is long and hard, and full of traps and pitfalls, there is no reason not to take each step that we can safely take. It is in our national self-interest to ban nuclear testing in the atmosphere so that all of our citizens can breathe more easily. It is in our national self-interest to sell surplus wheat in storage to feed Russians and Eastern Europeans who are willing to divert large portions of their limited foreign-exchange reserves away from the implements of war.
>
> It is in our national self-interest to keep weapons of mass destruction out of outer space, to maintain an emergency communications link with Moscow, and to substitute joint and peaceful exploration of the Antarctic and outer space for cold-war exploitation.
>
> No one of these small advances, nor all of

> them taken together, can be interpreted as meaning that the Soviets are abandoning their basic aims and ambitions. Nor should any future, less friendly Soviet action — whether it is a stoppage on the autobahn, or a veto in the U.N., or a spy in our midst, or new trouble elsewhere — cause us to regret the steps we have taken. Even if these steps themselves should be undone by the violations or renunciation of the test-ban treaty, for example, or by a decision to decline American wheat, there would still be no reason to regret the fact that this nation has made every responsible effort to improve relations.
>
> For without our making such an effort, we could not maintain the leadership and respect of the free world. Without our making such an effort, we could not convince our adversaries that war was not in their interests. And without our making such an effort, we could never, in case of war, satisfy our hearts and minds that we had done all that could be done to avoid the holocaust of endless death and destruction.

And then *The Nation* ends, "That he had brought us this far — and the polls would seem to show that he had struck a responsive chord — was the President's finest achievement."

This editorial was followed by one on the Warren Commission in the December 28, 1963 edition of *The Nation*. Based on what *The Nation* said at that point, its readers would have had every reason to believe that the magazine intended to take an independent critical stand in regard to the question of a conspiracy in the assassination. A quote from its editorial is as follows:

> *The Nation*, too, has been curious about the obvious discrepancies, inconsistencies, gaps, and unexplained aspects of the three murders [Kennedy, Tippit, and Oswald], but has resisted the temptation to enter [the process of speculation]

> . . . until an "official" version of the facts is available.
>
> . . . the public should maintain an alert, skeptical, wholly critical attitude, nor should public concern abate merely because the Warren Commission has set to work . . .
>
> The public is entitled to nothing less [than all the known facts] . . . For our part, we intend to make an independent assessment of whatever "official" report is eventually issued.

In the January 27, 1964 issue there appeared a most important article, "Oswald and the FBI," by Harold Feldman, and an accompanying editorial, "The Tasks of the Warren Commission." Here careful attention to detail is necessary because something strange began to happen.

The editorial accompanying the article stated:

> In this issue, Harold Feldman . . . suggests . . . that Oswald may have been an informant for the FBI. . . . Because the FBI has cautioned certain witnesses not to cooperate, it has been impossible . . . for the press . . . to verify the facts. . . . Mr. Feldman raises a question that calls for a finding by the Warren Commission. The article is published not to make a charge but to raise a question that, in fairness to the FBI and the public, requires a specific finding.

Given this editorial and the title which *The Nation* penned to Feldman's article, one would think that Feldman had simply raised a question of whether Oswald was somehow connected with the FBI. But if one carefully reads Feldman's article, it is clear that the author was going much further. Rather than restricting himself to a possible connection between Oswald and the FBI, Feldman had actually assembled a great deal of material that was appearing in the press and which linked Oswald to the

U.S. intelligence community in general and with the clear implication that the CIA might well be connected here. The following are some quotations from Feldman's article which indicate the breadth of the questions being raised beyond FBI involvement:

> If there is anything constant in Oswald's life, it is his need of money . . .
>
> . . . he was a pauper . . . But if there is another thing about Lee Oswald as certain as his indigence, it is that he was often capable of expenditures that would have cramped the purse of a suburban status seeker.
>
> After years of subsisting on a marine's pay from which he occasionally sent money to his mother, he undertakes a trip to Russia with a capital of $1600. . . . He borrows $435.71 from the United States Embassy in Moscow but, *mirable dictu,* he repays the loan between October, 1962 and January, 1963, during which time he was unemployed for several weeks and worked for a time as an unskilled developer of photostatic prints.
>
> A Miss Pauline Bates, public stenographer, whom Oswald paid for typing his notes for a book about Russia three days after his return, has said that "he hinted he had gone to the Soviet [Union] as a U.S. secret agent." He allegedly told her then that "when the State Department granted my visa, they stipulated they could not stand behind me in any way," an admonition suggestive of instruction, to an undercover man.
>
> . . . [he] goes to Mexico City for a week to get visas for a trip to Cuba and Russia that would have cost at least $1000. . . . After the murder of

> the President, the police find in his room, in addition to a wad of money, "several expensive cameras and rolls of film."
>
> For the Russian period, we have the unsupported assertion of *Pravda* that Oswald was an American spy who made numerous contacts with the American Embassy. This might indicate a CIA affiliation.

Returning to *The Nation*'s editorial referring to this article one searches in vain for any acknowledgment whatsoever that a question is being raised by Feldman about Oswald's potential connection to the CIA. Rather one finds the following:

> *The Nation* has been inundated with letters, manuscripts, and communications calling attention to this or that discrepancy or pointing to glaring omissions in the factual record. In the interval since November 22, certain key questions have been asked. Doubts have been raised, for example, about the rifle, the ammunition, the timing of the shots, the marksmanship involved, the role of the Dallas police, possible negligence in the precautions taken to guard the President, etc. The expression of these doubts should help the Warren Commission in its work.

The studious avoidance of any mention of Oswald's possible involvement with the CIA obviated the need for *The Nation* to address a very serious problem in regard to the make up of the Warren Commission, the problem that Allen Dulles, the former head of the CIA, whom Kennedy had fired from that position, was sitting right in the center of that investigative commission. It also obviated the need for *The Nation* to explain to its readers how the Commission was going to be able to investigate this angle of the case. Indeed, rather than dealing with this absolutely critical point, *The Nation* went off in a completely different direction and focused on how much stronger the integrity of the Warren Commission had become in recent weeks with the addition of various individuals such as J. Lee Rankin as counsel and Norman Redlich of New York University, and other establishment figures that *The Nation* characterized as "men of the highest integrity." Thus *The Nation* expressed that there was

> ample assurance that the Commission will ably discharge the extraordinary responsibilities which it has assumed.

Lest anyone think that *The Nation* was completely unmindful of concerns circulating about the CIA, it is interesting to note that in a completely unrelated editorial immediately following that on the Warren Commission and on the same page, *The Nation* editorialized on a recent press conference which the CIA held trying to brighten its image. In the course of this editorial *The Nation*'s editors noted in passing:

> The American public was gradually coming to the conclusion that the CIA was a self-perpetuating, ever-growing, tax-eating organization of spies, schemers and bunglers, with a few murderers thrown in.

From reading this, a trusting reader might not unreasonably have gotten the impression that one need not worry too much about an organization made up of a bunch of bungling schemers who have a few murderers hanging around.

In line with the way *The Nation* editorially deflected the thrust of Feldman's article is its subsequent coverage of the Warren Report.

On September 14, 1964, *The Nation* published a rather abstruse discussion by Maurice Rosenberg, Professor of Law at Columbia University, on the problem that the Warren Commission was asserting that it was merely a fact-finding body which was not interested in finding anyone guilty and at the same time fulfilling its charge of investigating who killed President

Kennedy. The Commission had refused Mark Lane's offer to serve as a kind of legal representative for Oswald on the commission, claiming this was not a judicial proceeding. Shortly thereafter the Commission decided to reverse itself and appointed another lawyer, Walter E. Craig, President of the American Bar Association and designee for the American federal district bench, as an "independent lawyer" to protect Oswald's interests.

On October 12, 1964, with the Warren Report now released, *The Nation* assured its readers that its previously promised critical evaluation of the "official" account was soon to appear in an article written by Herbert Packer, Professor of Law at Stanford University. And as if to imply that with Professor's Packer's forthcoming article all the questions about conspiracy would be laid to rest, *The Nation* at this point editorialized:

> Of the several major public issues raised by the Warren Commission . . . those relating to the role of the police and the media — Chapter V — should command top priority.

There then follows an editorial discussion in which *The Nation* laboriously discusses the role of the police and the media in the events surrounding Ruby's murder of Oswald. Again the attentive and trusting reader could well have inferred from all this that Mr. Packer's soon-to-appear article, *The Nation*'s promised careful scrutiny of the Warren Report, would not find the issue of Oswald's guilt or the issue of possible conspiracy to be major public issues any longer.

And sure enough, on November 2, 1964 *The Nation* renders its opinion:

> The Warren Commission
>
> At the time the Warren Commission was appointed, *The Nation* took the position that it would stoutly resist the temptation to enter the ranks of the rapidly expanding army of amateur "private eyes" and miscellaneous freelance James

Bonds who were even then busy as beavers mass-producing conspiracies among unnamed "oil millionaires" and offering each day a new theory of President Kennedy's assassination. We said then (December 28, 1963) that we would not add to the confusion and uncertainty — unless of course we were able to present some new and verifiable facts — nor would we draw any conclusions until an official version of the facts was available. At the same time we urged that public concern should not abate merely because the Warren Commission had been appointed, and advised that its work be kept under close scrutiny. We also said that we would make an independent assessment of the commission's report when it was issued (see article, Herbert L. Packer, p. 295).

We have had no occasion to regret these decisions. On January 27, we ran an article by Harold Feldman *raising certain questions about the FBI's interest in Oswald* [my emphasis]. In the same issue we devoted a second editorial to the Warren Commission, expressing our confidence in the staff and the commission and insisting, as we had done previously, that the Chief Justice's integrity in the matter was not to be questioned. *At the same time we pointed out that the questions raised about the role of the FBI were addressed to the commission and called for specific findings. The commission did not accept at face value assurances that Oswald had never been an informer for the FBI or any kind of agent for the CIA; it checked the personnel records of both agencies to verify these assurances. This is precisely the kind of specific finding that was needed and the only kind that would be acceptable to a deeply concerned world public* [my emphasis].

. . . In our view, then, the commission did its work well; the report is an admirable document, and the Chief Justice, his associates and the staff

> merit the praise they have received. The report should terminate the wilder speculations and more irresponsible rumor-mongering, but it will not do so. We have had occasion to experience, with more sadness than surprise, the depth and pervasiveness of the will to believe (notably among Left-of-Center groups) that the President's assassination was the result of a sinister conspiracy — the names of the conspirators to be filled in as need, fancy and bias dictate. Of course there are weaknesses and uncertainties in the report, and it may well be that facts still to be uncovered will throw fresh light on this or that aspect of the Dallas tragedy. But on the essential points, we share Mr. Packer's conclusions . . .

Turning to Mr. Packer's article on page 296, "A Measure of the Achievement," one finds that Mr. Packer wastes no time in getting to the point:

> The Warren Commission has admirably fulfilled its central objectives by producing an account of the circumstances under which President Kennedy was assassinated that is adequate to satisfy all reasonable doubts about the immediate essential facts. . . . If there are minor flaws . . . they are thrown into shadow by the conscientious and at times brilliant job that the commission has done. Only those who for whatever reasons of personal or political myopia cannot bring themselves to face reality will continue to think that the tragedy was proximately the work of more than one man . . .

It is not long, however, before even the most trusting reader is entitled to experience a sense of disquiet. For it turns out that Mr. Packer's critical review of the Warren Report's findings had been accomplished without Mr. Packer having available to him the evidence on which the commission based its conclusions.

Instead of carefully studying to what degree the commission's own evidence was consistent with its conclusions, Packer based his definitive statement exclusively on the Report, which the commission claimed to be a summary of its evidence.

To cite one example of the quality of Professor's Packer's critical review of the work of the commission one could take the first of five points which Packer refers to as the "minimal" case against Oswald. Here Professor Packer asserted that the commission proved:

> (1) *All of the wounds sustained by President Kennedy and by Governor Connally were inflicted by bullets fired from the rear and above.* This is demonstrated by the medical report on Governor Connally and the autopsy report on President Kennedy, as corroborated by (a) examination of the bullet holes in the President's clothing, which showed that the first shot that hit him entered his back and exited through the lower part of his neck; (b) the damage to the inside of the wind shield caused by a spent bullet fragment; (c) the absence of any damage that could have been caused by a bullet or bullets fired from the front.

Professor Packer's review of the critical physical evidence proceeds in a similar vein. This, then, is a measure of the quality of *The Nation*'s critical review.

That the Warren Report had virtually nothing to do with the commission's own evidence was obvious as soon as Salandria's articles appeared in *Liberation*. But then Mr. Salandria was not a member of the political establishment whose integrity the establishment would vouch for. He was merely an interested, independent critical citizen with a capacity to reason unencumbered by the phenomenon of "Crimestop."

Nor has *The Nation*'s editorial position ever wavered in the past thirty years. Presumably the editors of the distinguished left/liberal magazine understand what is at stake if one rejects its insistence that as citizens we not question the integrity of the Chief Justice of the United States.

The Truth is Too Terrible

by Fred J. Cook

Since so much has been written about the Kennedy assassination, I shall tell here only about my own involvement in efforts to bring about a thorough investigation. Early in December 1963 I went to Washington on a magazine assignment, and I learned from a number of sources that many veteran newsmen were as concerned as I about the lightning fast wrap-up of the case.

One of my contacts, who had been talking to a CBS news executive, told me that the executive was deeply disturbed and frustrated. His team in Dallas, he said, had uncovered leads that seemed to require further digging, but had run into the stone wall of network indifference. No one was pursuing obvious leads, and the official investigations seemed concerned with proving the official version without looking into any discrepancies.

Two of the best national reporters on the scene, Richard Dudman and Ronnie Dugger, had expressed doubts about the lone-assassin verdict. They were suspicious, for example, about the unbelievable speed with which the Dallas police had radioed an almost perfect description of Oswald just ten minutes after the lethal shots had been fired. Unless there was a setup, this seemed miraculous in the midst of so much turmoil and confusion.

Also while I was in Washington, a friend of mine who was working as an investigator for a Senate committee and had close

Originally published in Fred J. Cook, *Maverick: Fifty Years of Investigative Reporting*. New York: G.P. Putnam's Sons, 1984, pp. 273-282, 285-291. Reprinted by permission of the author.

ties to the National Rifle Association led me to stumble upon another unexplained angle:

The Mannlicher Carcano that Oswald allegedly used to kill the President was one of the crankiest rifles ever invented; its bolt action most peculiar (as I later found out the one time I handled it). The old World War I Springfield, with which I had had a passing association in ROTC in college, had a smooth bolt action — you pulled the bolt straight back to eject the spent cartridge, then slammed it straight forward to seat a new charge. With the Mannlicher Carcano, which had been the principal weapon of the Italian infantry, the bolt had a squirreling action that slowed its rate of fire and sometimes got stuck, to the frustration of the marksman. This was later established during test firing that the Warren Commission conducted. Although only championship marksmen were used, one of them, even after practicing with Oswald's rifle, became so entangled with the squirreling bolt action that he could not get a shot off at all during one round.

This squirreling bolt was not the only defect of the weapon: the ammunition was equally recalcitrant. Bullets tended to swerve and swoop instead of speeding unerringly to their target. When Italian resistance collapsed at the end of World War II, hundreds of thousands of these balky guns fell into American hands, and we had an immediate use for them if they could ever be made to work properly. Communist guerrillas were threatening to overrun Greece; the Greeks opposing them, whom we supported, needed arms. If the Mannlicher Carcano could be turned into an effective weapon, the vast numbers we had captured would be invaluable in the Greek civil war.

Nothing could be done about that awkward bolt action, but experts from the National Rifle Association and an Army ordnance team conducted extensive experiments at the Aberdeen proving grounds in Maryland. "And they came up with one of the most perfect bullets ever designed," my source said. "It could be fired from the Carcano, and it would go straight to its target every time. That had a lot to do with chasing those Communist guerrillas out of Greece."

And with the killing of our own president?

One skeptical marksman had written an article about his experiments with the Mannlicher Carcano. He had purchased a rifle just like Oswald's, had bought the right ammunition for it, and then on the firing range, he found that shot after shot turned out to be duds; hardly any went straight to the target. When I returned to New York, I visited several Lower Manhattan gunshops and asked about ammunition for the Mannlicher Carcano. All I could find was the old Italian-made ammunition, deteriorated from age and unreliable at best; none of the shops had the American-perfected cartridges.

Carey McWilliams [editor of *The Nation*] was not enthusiastic about the trend of my researches. He checked out the bullet angle with the district attorney's office in Dallas and was told (falsely, as it turned out) that Oswald had been using the original Italian-made ammunition. That was as far as Carey was willing to go just then.

President Johnson, the calculating political manipulator, had twisted the arm of Chief Justice Warren, persuading him to head a special commission to investigate the assassination. Norman Redlich, with whom Carey had been allied in civil-rights causes, was one of the senior counsels, as was Joseph A. Ball, whom Carey had known in California from law school days and for whom he had a great deal of respect.

"With Earl Warren heading the commission, this is going to be a thorough investigation," Carey told me. "Nothing is going to be covered up. Let's just wait until the commission has time to make its investigation and file its report."

I was still more skeptical and more impatient. FBI Director J. Edgar Hoover was using every stratagem at his disposal to determine what the verdict of the commission would be. In a memorandum to Carey on December 3, 1963, I spelled out my doubts about the kind of report that would be produced. I was especially disenchanted with the composition of the commission, all solid Establishment types who could be almost guaranteed to uphold the Establishment view. Gerald Ford had long been noted in Washington as a strong FBI partisan; and as for Allen Dulles, I wrote: "Naming Allen Dulles to the commission was about as suspect a thing as could be done." (Long after the commission's work was finished, it would be disclosed that Dulles sat there silently, not letting any of his fellow commissioners know that his CIA had already entered into partnership with the Mafia in plots intended to kill Fidel Castro, certainly a vital bit of information.)

As for Hoover, referring to articles that had appeared in the press, I wrote that "the old authoritative leak system at which the FBI is especially adept was used. Day after day we were treated to stories that contained only a smidgeon of new information in their leads — stories that went on to point out that the FBI report, whose details nobody was permitted to know, concluded definitely and positively that Oswald was the killer; that he acted alone; that there was no conspiracy. By the time the public is permitted to get a peep at the FBI details that justify this conclusion, the conclusion will have been so drummed into us, so thoroughly accepted, that it will be a bold man indeed — and where the hell does one find them today — who questions the details."

This turned out to be an uncannily accurate forecast, for once the Warren Commission got organized it found its case — a case it was expected to accept — had already been made by the FBI. Some members of the staff resented the way in which they had been boxed in. But Carey's faith in Earl Warren and the commission was unshakable. I could not move him. And since I had contracts for two major books that had to be finished not too many months down the road, I had to shelve my concern with the Kennedy assassination and get on with my work.

I have never seen an official report greeted with such universal praise as that accorded the Warren Commission's findings when they were made public on September 24, 1964. All the major television networks devoted special programs and analyses to the report; the next day the newspapers ran long columns detailing its findings, accompanied by special news analyses and editorials. The verdict was unanimous. The report answered all questions, left no room for doubt. Lee Harvey Oswald, alone and unaided, had assassinated the President of the United States.

The chorus of acclaim impressed me. I watched television program after program. I waded through the massive columns of

The New York Times — and even I was finally convinced. My earlier conviction that there must have been a conspiracy obviously had been wrong. The Warren Commission after months of investigation had found no trace of conspiracy, and all of the best news and editorial brains in the nation were hailing its conclusions. I accepted the verdict and turned to other things.

Two months later, left alone one evening with nothing else to do, I decided to take a closer look at the Report. I had purchased the Doubleday Edition, with an impressive foreword by the eminent attorney Louis Nizer. The television programs I had seen at the time the report was issued had left two vague, nagging questions in my mind.

The first stemmed from what I had heard in Washington the year before about the suspiciously fast description of the gunman. According to the report, these details had come apparently from Howard L. Brennan, a forty-five-year-old steamfitter, who had been sitting on a concrete retaining wall opposite the Texas School Book Depository at the corner of Elm and Houston Streets, where the presidential motorcade made a slow left-hand turn into Elm. Brennan told police that he had seen a man in the sixth-floor southeast window of the depository before the motorcade arrived and that he had seen him in the act of discharging his final shot.

The initial shot had been fired at 12:30 P.M.; the Dallas police description, according to the Warren Report, had apparently been based on Brennan's almost instantaneous account to police. Brennan had described the gunman as white, slender, about 165 pounds, 5 feet 10 inches tall, in his early thirties. Oswald was white, slender, about 150 pounds, 5 feet 9, twenty-four years old. It was a fantastic match. I wondered whether it was possible.

The sixth-floor window of the sniper's nest had been only partially open; the room behind it was dark, unlighted; cartons had been piled up behind the window as a screen, and one had been placed on the window ledge as a gun rest. Was it possible that, from 120 feet away, gazing up at what must have been a shadowy figure against this dark background, Brennan could have come up with a nearly letter-perfect description of Oswald?

I had doubted Brennan's ability and had tested my doubts. I walked around New York streets, looking up at lighted fifth- and sixth-floor windows in which men were working. Even in these circumstances, only a portion of a man's body would be visible; and I found I couldn't tell how tall the men were or what they looked like. Yet the commission had accepted Brennan's description, despite the physical difficulties involved. Brennan's accuracy was difficult to explain, unless Oswald had been pointed out to Brennan in advance — but that is something we will never know.

Next, I turned my attention to a second question that had been nagging me. Texas Governor John Bowden Connally, Jr., who had been riding on the jump seat in front of the President, had been struck by a bullet that entered his back, passed downward through his chest, exiting below his right nipple, then passing through his right wrist, which had been in his lap, and finally inflicting a wound in his left thigh. The Warren Commission had concluded that the first shot fired by the sniper had entered "the base of the back of his [the President's] neck, had passed through his neck and had continued downward," wounding Connally. In other words, both the President and Connally had been wounded by this same bullet.

Connally told a clear, cogent, convincing story. He said he had been familiar with guns all his life, and he had instantly recognized the first shot as a rifle shot. He knew it had come from behind him; he had turned his head to the right in the direction of the book depository; then he had started to turn to his left, trying to get a look at the President, when he himself was hit and collapsed in his wife's arms. In shock, he never heard the final, fatal shot that tore off the top of the President's head, but he was positive that he had been wounded not by the first shot that had hit Kennedy but by a second, separate shot.

Connally's calm, step-by-step, explicit recital had the ring of complete truth. Why, then, I wondered, had the Warren Commission discounted this best possible eyewitness evidence? Why had it insisted so strongly that Governor Connally *had* to be mistaken? To answer these questions, I hunted in the report's index and went directly to the sections dealing with Connally and the commission's interpretation of the shot sequence. It took me perhaps an hour, and I found the Warren Commission Report — so wholly accepted — falling to pieces in my hands.

The key, I quickly discovered, was the film of the assassination taken as it was happening by amateur photographer Abraham Zapruder with his 8mm movie camera. Zapruder's camera took 18.3 frames a second; so, by numbering the frames, it could be determined just how many seconds elapsed between shots. The sequence seemed to show that the President could not have been hit before frame 210, when he disappeared momentarily behind a Stemmons Freeway sign. When he emerged into view again at frame 225, his hands were just beginning to jerk upward toward his throat, a movement that was completed by frame 227. Yet at this time, the film showed, Governor Connally was facing forward, face serene; it was simply impossible to believe that his whole body had already been furrowed by a nearly lethal bullet.

Connally showed no visible reaction until frames 231-34; expert witnesses before the Warren Commission held that he could not have been hit after frame 240. Now another factor, firing speed, had to be added to the equation. The commission had determined that the fastest trigger finger in the FBI could not get off shots from Oswald's Mannlicher Carcano in less than 2.3 seconds between shots. On the basis of no evidence whatsoever, the commission had rationalized that Oswald, no champion marksman, could match the fastest gun in the FBI, but even this did not solve its problems with the lone assassin thesis. Even assuming that the President had been hit at the earliest possible instant, at frame 210, there would have had to be another 42 frames before the lone gunman could have gotten off the second shot at frame 252. But the Zapruder film showed that Connally had been wounded much earlier, no later than frame 240 — and so not even the fastest gun in the FBI could have gotten another shot off by that time. The whole lone-assassin theory foundered on this time rock, and the only way of resurrecting it was to theorize, as the Warren Commission had, that the first shot that hit the President must also have wounded Governor Connally.

But this was theory; this was rationalization; this was not hard judgment based on solid facts as everyone had supposed. As soon as I found this flaw, I saw that the report throughout was a tissue of rationalizations in which the most credible testimony (as in the case of Connally) had been discarded because it did not fit the lone-assassin hypothesis, and the most suspect word was accepted as valid and ultimate truth because it did.

I felt the hair prickle on the back of my neck with excitement at this discovery, and I hurried upstairs to my typewriter to start writing a memorandum tearing at the guts of the Warren Report. And that was the beginning of my trouble.

Knowing that I was challenging a verdict that was considered almost as holy as the Bible, I spelled out the firing sequence and the evidence of the Zapruder film in great detail. My memorandum ran some seven pages. Once it was finished, I was confronted with the problem of what to do with it. I knew Carey McWilliam's views, but I also felt that *The Nation* was the only magazine with sufficient independence and nerve to print the kind of article I wanted to write. In hopes that my reasoned analysis would persuade Carey, I sent him the memorandum.

There followed three weeks of silence. Then Carey rejected the idea, telling me that he and others could find no flaw in my reasoning, but *The Nation* didn't want to criticize the Warren Report. I gathered that he was influenced by one overriding fear: if the assassination proved to be the work of a conspiracy, it might start another irresponsible witch-hunt comparable to that of the detested McCarthy era.

I didn't agree. The most credible evidence seemed to me to point to a conspiracy; and if conspirators could get away with murdering a president as popular as Kennedy, there was no guarantee that they would not repeat the deed any time a leading politician's program posed a threat to their interests. Still, everywhere I encountered opposition. My literary agent, Barthold Fles, shuddered when he read the memorandum. Like Carey, he could find no flaw in it, but he had difficulty believing it. "You may be right, Fred," he told me, "but I wish you wouldn't do this." I told him I felt I had to, and I wanted him to try for publication. Reluctantly, he raised the issue with Peter Bittner, then my editor at Macmillan. "Oh, my God," Bart reported Peter's saying, "Fred has exposed the CIA, the FBI, and the military-industrial complex. All he needs now is to attack the Warren Report!"

On the domestic front, I was also getting a lot of flak. Julia had never questioned my writing decisions, but she did now. "Why don't you just forget it?" she asked. "Kennedy is dead, and nothing can be done about it." I explained my fear that an evil, dangerous precedent might have been set. "Well, who are *you* to challenge the Warren Commission?" Exasperated, I snapped, "Well, God gave me a brain to reason with, and just plain common sense says they were wrong. It's like adding two and two and getting six. *It just doesn't make sense. Goddamn it!*"

We never agreed, and I continued to press Bart Fles. He showed the memorandum to *Esquire*, but *Esquire* had already assigned Dwight Macdonald to write an assassination feature — an article, as it turned out, that was filled with philosophical words adding up to nothing. *True* magazine had run articles on the controversy arising from Abraham Lincoln's assassination, so I'd hoped it would prove receptive for my story. *True* weighed my little bombshell for almost a month, but finally decided it wouldn't go ahead because, well, who knew what might happen by the time the magazine got out? An editor at *Playboy* had expressed some interest in my writing, so my suggestion went there. There was another month's delay, and back it came with an excuse similar to *True*'s. No one could find anything wrong with my analysis, but no one was going to publish an article based on it either.

I took the memorandum back from Bart and decided to see if I could do something with it on my own. Finally, in summer 1965, I sent it off to Edward J. Keating, then the editor of *Ramparts*. Silence. Then, about 10:30 on an August night, just as my wife and I were about to set out on a three-week vacation we'd planned for some time, the telephone rang. Keating had studied my memorandum, he said; he had shown it to others; everybody agreed the analysis was solid. Could I turn it into a blockbuster article for *Ramparts* for the December issue? There went our vacation.

Little did I know I was about to get the worst double-cross I have ever had from a publisher. *Ramparts* agreed in a letter to

Bart Fles to pay $1000 for my article. Keating sent me a number of sensible editorial suggestions, which I accepted. The December 1965 *Ramparts* did not include my piece. We queried. When January and February came and passed, we protested. Then in March 1966 *Ramparts* made the incredible claim that it had never agreed to publish the article in the first place — this despite the fact that I had in my files a flier the magazine had sent out in the fall soliciting new subscribers and promising it would have among its upcoming exposes "Fred J. Cook's massive re-evaluation of the Warren Commission Report on President Kennedy's assassination." Finally, in April, 1966, after holding the article in cold storage for six months, *Ramparts* made me a token payment of $500 and returned the manuscript.

After over a year of struggle, I was more angry and frustrated than I had ever been. In desperation, I sent the article off to Carey McWilliams. Though I knew his views, I hoped that once he saw the finished product he might have a change of heart. Another month-long silence ensued. Then I read in one of the gossip columns that Edward J. Epstein had written a book, *Inquest*, a critical look at the Warren Report that was about to be published. I called Carey's attention to the item, warned him that time was running out and that if he ever intended to do anything with my article, he had to get a move on. So finally he did. *The Nation* published the article in two installments, June 13 and June 20, 1966, more than a year and a half after I had first proposed it. The editors prefaced it with a disclaimer that this was just my view.

* * * * * * * * * * *

Soon after the publication of my Warren Commission articles, there came a series of strange events in startling succession. I reported on the first of these in a letter to Carey on July 13, 1966. Bart Fles had received a cablegram just the previous Friday from a Japanese magazine that wanted to purchase rights to my Warren Commission articles; the matter was "urgent," the cablegram said, and an immediate reply was necessary. We accepted the offer in a cablegram that same night.

The next day, Saturday, Fles received a second cablegram: the magazine had called the deal off without explanation of any kind. "I'd like to be able to read the State Department cables on that one," I wrote Carey.

Next a devious attack was made on me in my own favorite publication, *The Nation*. A concerned Carey telephoned me one afternoon, saying he had an article written by a professor who reported that the Warren Commission had never seen the X-rays and photographs taken of the President's body at the autopsy because the Kennedy family had prohibited the use of this basic evidence. Carey wanted to know if it was all right with me if he ran the piece. I said I had no objection; I certainly didn't have any exclusive rights to everything about the Warren Commission; and if he had a good legitimate article from someone else, he should run it.

When I saw the article in the July 11, 1966 issue of *The Nation*, I blew my stack at Carey for the first time ever. The legitimate point of the article that Carey had mentioned to me was there, buried deep in the body of the piece. The whole approach, the whole tone, however, was slanted to ridicule critics of the Warren Report. The article was filled with snide references to me and to Vincent Salandria, a Philadelphia lawyer for the American Civil Liberties Union and one of the first critics of the report, and it was speckled with lines like: "Has it come to this, then — the doctors' word against the word of Cook, Epstein, Salandria, et al.?"

The rapidity with which the attack had been made — only twenty-one days had elapsed after my second *Nation* article — indicated to me that it must have been hatched almost the instant my articles appeared, and I began to smell a rat. Why Carey hadn't caught the odor, why he hadn't exercised rudimentary editorial judgment, I'll never know; but I was so furious I wrote a reply and delivered an ultimatum: unless Carey printed my answer to the academic character word for word, I would never write again for *The Nation*. The author of the back-stabbing exercise that so infuriated me had announced that he was going to withdraw from the ivy halls, become a full-time free-lance writer, and produce a book that would silence all critics and vindicate the Warren Commission. In my reply, I pointed out that I knew how extremely difficult it was to make a living by free-lance writing. I didn't believe it could be done by someone who hadn't established a broad reputation in the field, and I was convinced that the man who had done the job on me must be privately financed by some government agency like the CIA.[1]

There never was a rebuttal to this accusation. A couple of reactions came from other sources: from Tom Katen, who had been a professor at Monmouth College, in West Long Branch, New Jersey, and Vince Salandria. Their feeling was that, once the report was exposed and the assassination issue raised, agencies were going to have to take out after *somebody*. They had both met the back-stabbing author of *The Nation* article and asked him why he had gone out of his way to take such vicious potshots at me. He told them that he had done it "for that very reason" — because he wanted to discredit me in my own forum.

Katen and Salandria also told me about the reaction of Allen Dulles during a tape-recorded session with students at a California university. The students had copies of *The Nation* exposé and asked Dulles about it. "*The Nation*?" Dulles exclaimed — and then he went off into a fit of hyena-like laughter. The students, grim-faced, began to press him about aspects of the assassination, and Dulles abruptly broke off the exchange, remarking that if they didn't have anything better to discuss, he was going to bed.

---

[1]It was just some kind of intuition. I did not know at the time, none of us did, that the CIA was financing and sponsoring the publication of somewhere in the neighborhood of 1000 books that were being brought out in the United States as if they were the products of independent scholarship. This activity — totally illegal since the CIA had been specifically barred in its charter from domestic activities — did not become public knowledge until the mid-1970s investigations of our intelligence agencies. Even then, the CIA refused to identify any of the writers, books, or publishers it had helped finance; and efforts since that time to obtain such vital information under Freedom of Information actions have been barred in the courts. The result is that we to not know to this day the full extent and insidiousness of the CIA's brainwashing endeavors.

Sometime later in that summer of 1966, I got a late-night telephone call from Vince Salandria. He was in Boston, where he had just had a debate with my *Nation* back-stabber. Salandria was excited. "Fred, I told him that you had accused him of being a CIA front — and he did not deny it. He did not deny it!"

After the debate, Salandria said, he and his opponent had a long, private bull-session. "He's a very disturbed person," Salandria told me, "and I wound up feeling sorry for him. He has a lot of conflicts within himself, and he finally admitted that he knows we are right, but he said: 'The truth is too terrible. The American people would never be able to stand it.' In the end, however, he said he was not going to write the book." And he never did.

I got another strong personal indication from inside the Warren Commission itself that there were those who thought the critics could be right. In late July, 1966, over a telephone hookup, I did battle with Burt W. Griffin, who had been an assistant counsel to the commission and is now a judge, on Harv Morgan's Cleveland "Contact" show.

Griffin did his best to defend the report. He ridiculed my conclusion that a shot, or shots, had come from the grassy knoll overlooking Dealey Plaza at the right front of the motorcade. There was some exceptionally hard evidence, as well as the wounding of a spectator by a bullet splinter, to indicate shots had come from this direction. Griffin insisted that the first shot that hit the President had followed the downward trajectory necessary to wound Governor Connally. I told him what an expert pathologist had told me, and he conceded that if the one-shot, multiple-wound theory was invalid, the commission's whole lone-assassin case had to fall by the wayside.

Interestingly, it seemed to me, he admitted that there might have been too much haste in closing out the conspiracy angle. Warren had been impatient, he said; the commission was being pressured to get out a fast report; proof of conspiracy wasn't easy; and if anything had been overlooked, Griffin thought it was due to this impatience.

We discussed the very real possibility that Oswald had been an FBI informer. A Dallas deputy sheriff had told a reporter that he knew this was so; the Warren Commission had been thrown into a flap by what Warren called "this very disturbing" rumor — but the whole matter had been dropped on J. Edgar Hoover's word that Oswald hadn't been on the FBI payroll. Harv Morgan asked Griffin the direct question: Did he think Oswald was connected with the FBI? Griffin replied that he thought no one was ever going to know. I asked him if this wasn't a pretty horrible admission: here we had a very popular president assassinated — and we weren't going to be permitted to know about such an important link if it existed? "I am just stating a fact of life," Griffin said. He added that he was certain that if anyone from any of our great federal agencies had been involved, the record would have been covered up so thoroughly that no one could ever find out.

After the radio program was over, Griffin asked to speak to me personally. "I admire what you people are trying to do," he told me, "but I have to tell you that you're not going to get anywhere." He thought, he said, that the critics were performing "a public service" because he hoped that if anything like this happened again — and he prayed it wouldn't — "it certainly never ought to be investigated in this way."

Harv Morgan was as surprised as I was. "Fred, did you hear that?" he exclaimed after Griffin had gone. "My God, did you hear *that*!"

I wrote some additional, minor articles about the assassination and the Warren Report during the next few years, and in 1968 I joined the Committee to Investigate Assassinations formed by Bernard Fensterwald, Jr., a Washington attorney who had served as a counsel to different Senate committees. I had met Bud when he was chief counsel for Senator Edward Long, of Missouri, in an investigation into official invasions of privacy, an inquiry that was aborted after some of the federal agencies being investigated leaked stories to the press about the senator's receipt of legal fees from his private law firm, which was connected with the Teamsters.

Leaving government service, Fensterwald decided to devote his time to probing assassinations — not just that of President Kennedy, but also the 1968 slayings of Dr. Martin Luther King, Jr., and Robert F. Kennedy. The "lone-gunman" solutions of each had raised just as many questions as the assassination of the President. Bud's convictions stemmed in part from a personal encounter with the rabid Radical Right in Dallas. As the principal aide and speechwriter for Senator Estes Kefauver, he had accompanied Kefauver to Dallas during the 1960 presidential campaign. Kefauver had made a rousing speech in support of John F. Kennedy's candidacy. Afterward, a high police spokesman told Bud, "You know we have some pretty fanatical people here, and I think it would be a good idea if you and the senator didn't stay in town overnight, but left right away."

Bud had relayed the warning to Kefauver, who inquired, "Do we have enough bourbon?" Bud assured him the liquor cabinet was well-stocked, and Kefauver agreed to the change of plans, saying, "All right, then, let's go."

Fensterwald's hope in forming the committee was that it would be able to keep the assassination issue alive, help to mold public opinion, and bring enough pressure on public officials to force a genuinely thorough investigation, and several members of the committee worked extremely hard toward this end. I remember especially Mary Ferrell, of Dallas, a legal secretary and one-time secretary to a governor of Texas. She collected and analyzed every scrap of material pertaining to the President's assassination; she even had a separate air-conditioned room built on her home to house the collection, which remains probably the most thorough in the nation. Yet an orchestrated campaign was mounted in books and magazine articles to label all who questioned the validity of the Warren Report mere "scavengers" who were out to make a fast buck by preying on the trauma of the American people. No propaganda campaign was ever more vicious or more untrue; some of those engaged in the research spent thousands of dollars of their own money, almost bankrupting themselves in the process.

Yet the door of the media remained firmly closed. *The New York Times*, with one of the best journalistic staffs in the nation, ran a month-long investigation into the bona fides of the Warren Report. When it was all over, the *Times* deep-sixed the whole project. The paper's attitude became obvious in 1971 when its op-ed page included an essay by David W. Belin, one of the Warren

Commission counsels, upholding all the findings of the report — and, at the same time, it refused to print a responding letter from Fensterwald. The op-ed page is supposed to be a free forum in which opposing points of view can be discussed — but not where the Warren Report was concerned.

One of Fensterwald's arguments merited attention. He pointed out that Police Chief Jesse Curry, who had been in charge of the Dallas force when the President was assassinated, had developed serious doubts about the validity of the Oswald case. He had described these in a small book, *JFK Assassination File*, in which he had disclosed that scientific tests had not shown what they would have to have shown if Oswald had fired a rifle: after such a firing, powder residues are left on the cheek of the gunman. These may be detected by analysis of a paraffin cast. The FBI had made such a test of the side of Oswald's face, but had failed to find any residues. The Bureau had argued ambiguously that such tests were not always infallible — so the Warren Commission had disregarded the evidence. There was, however, a more sophisticated and infallible test: neutron activation analysis. The FBI, as Fensterwald pointed out, had performed this test — and had failed to find any trace of residues that would show Oswald had fired a rifle. This negative finding, which seemed, as Fensterwald wrote, to show that "Oswald did not fire a rifle on November 22," was what had shaken the faith of Police Chief Curry in the Warren Commission verdict. But it did not make any difference to the *Times*.

The efforts of the committee continued for years. Gradually, I devoted less and less time to it, mainly because I had a free-lance living to make and couldn't make it if I didn't stick to the typewriter. Finally, in 1976, partly as a result of the committee's efforts, a Congressional committee was appointed to investigate the assassinations of President Kennedy and Dr. King. Unfortunately, the probe became snarled at the outset with personality conflicts, and it never did get itself on the track. The internal wrangling gave dubious members of Congress the only excuse they needed to scrimp on funds and cut the inquiry short. However, through acoustic tests the committee did establish that a fourth shot had been fired from the grassy knoll overlooking

Dealey Plaza, as I and many other critics of the Warren Report had contended.

The findings of the Congressional committee were forwarded to the Department of Justice for further action; but, if the experience of the past is any criterion, they can be expected to rest in peace in Justice — forever.

Appendix VIII

The Work of Ray Marcus: Excerpts from *Addendum B*

The following are excerpts from Ray Marcus, Addendum B: Addendum to the HSCA, The Zapruder Film, and the Single Bullet Theory, *1995, self-published. Although Marcus, a member of Salandria's committee of correspondents, is identified earlier in footnotes, those earlier passages hardly do justice to his enormous contributions to our knowledge with regard to the Kennedy assassination. In addition to* The Bastard Bullet, *he also authored a brilliant booklet on the separate hit on Connally which analyzes the Zapruder film minutely and demonstrates beyond doubt that Connally was hit by a separate shot. This booklet was originally prepared for the House Select Committee on Assassinations.*

Over the years Marcus has conducted extensive correspondence on the case and, as the material below will show, he possesses a treasure of historically important information. Recently Marcus published Addendum B, *a compilation of data concerning the case and detailing his contact with various individuals in academia and the media in his effort to get the truth before the American public. He has graciously given permission to quote and reprint from his recent work.*

The Work of Ray Marcus: Excerpts from *Addendum B*

Truman's Warning

from pages 74-76:

On December 22, 1963, just thirty days after the assassination of JFK, there appeared in an early edition of the *Washington Post* a remarkable article. Its heading read "U.S. Should Hold CIA to Intelligence Role." Its content was a warning to the American people that the CIA must be brought under presidential control. Its author was Harry S. Truman. I submit without qualification that it is the least known important public policy statement by any president or former president in the twentieth century, and probably in the nation's entire history. Following are a few excerpts from the article datelined Independence, Missouri, December 21:

> I think it has become necessary to take another look at the purpose and operations of our Central Intelligence Agency — CIA . . .
>
> For some time I have been disturbed by the way the CIA has been diverted from its original assignment. It has become an operational and at times a policy-making arm of the Government. This has led to trouble and may have compounded our difficulties in several explosive areas.
>
> We have grown up as a nation, respected for our free institutions and for our ability to maintain a

> free and open society. There is something about the way the CIA has been functioning that is casting a shadow over our historic position and I feel that we need to correct it.

How can it be that a statement of such obvious significance by a widely respected former president is virtually unknown to the public? I first learned of it in 1966, while reading Roger Hilsman's 1964 book, *To Move a Nation*. He quotes extensively from it in his chapter titled "The Problem of the CIA." It appears on his page 63.

This surprised me, for I thought I had followed Truman's public statements quite carefully, and this one was completely unfamiliar to me. I was even more surprised when I checked the referenced chapter note and saw the date of publication, December 22, 1963, in *The Washington Post* — distributed by the North American Newspaper Alliance.

I then went to the UCLA library and located a copy there. According to my information, it was not carried in later editions that day, nor commented on editorially, nor picked up by any other major newspaper, nor mentioned on any national radio or TV broadcast. (At my urging, it was reprinted in full more than eleven years after its original publication date on the editorial page of the *Los Angeles Times*, January 24, 1975. There was no editorial comment, follow up, or letters-to-editor presented.)

It is not mentioned in any of the prominent biographies which have since appeared, including David McCullough's excellent study, *Truman*. I have no reason to believe the authors were aware of it.

Can this be accidental? Can editors of all major newspapers, magazines, and news broadcasts have really been unaware of its existence? Can such individuals looking at the Truman article really have thought, no, this is of insufficient importance or interest to reprint, editorialize on, or even mention? Such an idea seems preposterously naive. It is much more probable that the article was consciously suppressed by deliberate inattention, at decisive points of intervention. The pertinent question is — why? Standing alone, the vital significance of the article, written by the man who originally caused the CIA to be established, is almost too obvious to comment on. Here is former President Truman warning the nation, "There is something about the way the CIA has been functioning that is casting a shadow over our historic position and I feel that we need to correct it."

If we could know to absolute certainty — as clearly we cannot — that Truman had no hidden agenda in mind when writing his article, it still would stand as a statement of the first order of importance by any objective measure. But the timing of the article makes it potentially even more crucial and explosive, for it implicitly suggests that Truman may have been also warning us, as subtly as he dared under the circumstances, consistent with his view of the public interest, that elements of the CIA may have had a hand in the assassination. Consider: Truman's article appeared on December 22, just thirty days after JFK's murder. The country was still reeling in shock. Rumors were rampant about possible conspiracies, foreign and domestic. Truman was not a reckless or irresponsible man. It would at least border on irresponsibility for him to release his article for publication so soon after Kennedy's death unless he was trying to warn the public, implicitly and obliquely, since it must surely have occurred to him that his words might be misconstrued to mean just that.

This clearly is speculation — we can never know for sure unless private papers of the former president clarifying his intention eventually are revealed. But neither is there any objective factual basis for dismissing the thought; and it therefore must logically remain a reasonable possibility.

Whether or not Truman had the assassination in mind while accusing the CIA of exceeding its legal authority, it is unlikely in the extreme that the effective suppression of his article could have been anything but deliberate.

I.F. Stone

from pages 30-33:

I.F. Stone, author of numerous books, including *The Hidden History of the Korean War*, was most famous for a weekly he began publishing in 1953 with 5,300 subscribers and which grew to a circulation of 70,000. Although most of his important work was done in Washington, he was not viewed as part of the political or journalistic establishment. Instead of cozying up to important insiders, he based his work primarily on the study of newspapers and comments, employing his exceptionally keen and probing intellect to slice through the fog of official positions on national and international affairs so as to expose the underlying truth to his readers with characteristic brevity and clarity.

Stone was an independent leftist. Although . . . in earlier years he tended to minimize Moscow's misdeeds while maximizing Washington's . . . he was no friend of Communist dictators. He bitterly denounced the Soviet bloc after his trip to the Soviet Union in 1956 and wrote, "The worker is more exploited than in Western welfare states. This is not a good society, and it is not led by honest men."

I was a charter subscriber to the *Weekly*. Having earlier subscribed to George Seldes' *In Fact*, I found Stone's newsletter a worthy successor and looked forward to each issue. The *Weekly* undoubtedly reached a readership far more influential than its small circulation would indicate.

In the months following the assassination I eagerly awaited Stone's critical analysis. With his long demonstrated ability to demolish official falsehoods, I had little reason to doubt he would make mincemeat of the just released Warren Report, whose no-conspiracy conclusions had been leaked to the press and public for many months, and whose questionable veracity in many crucial instances had already been amply demonstrated.

Then came *I.F. Stone's Weekly* of October 5, 1964, headed "The Left and the Warren Report." It was a paean of praise for the Warren Commission and its conclusions. He said, "the Commission has done a first rate job on the level that does our country proud and is worthy of so tragic an event." He regarded the case against Lee Harvey Oswald as the lone killer as "conclusive."

[Of the Commission members, he was full of praise and said that although he had] criticized Allen W. Dulles constantly over the years. . . I would not impute to him or any other member of the Commission conduct so evil as to conspire with the secret services to protect the killers of a President." Of Chief Justice Earl Warren he said, "This is also to assume this man, whom the right hates for his decisions protecting Negroes and radicals, would be a party to a conspiracy to protect a cabal of rightist assassins. He said those who, by rejecting the official conclusions could believe otherwise, "belong in the booby hatch."

. . . I was shocked. I wrote a lengthy letter to Stone listing fifteen highly improbable separate sets of circumstances surrounding the case, *all* of which would nevertheless have to be true for the official conclusions to be true. I urged him to study the questions and reconsider his position. I received no response to my letter.

In September 1966, I was planning a trip to the east coast. From L.A. I phoned Stone at his home in Washington. I told him I had previously written to him about his position on the case and requested a meeting with him so that I could present to him some important evidence, primarily photographic. His answer was immediate, loud (very loud), and clear: "*I don't care about that asshole case!*," he bellowed and then hung up. The thought occurred to me that had he written in his *Weekly*, instead of the actual contents of his October 5, 1964 issue, that he didn't care about the case (with or without the expletive deleted), it would at least have had the virtue of being honest, and incapable of misleading his readers, despite being an uncharacteristic position for I.F. Stone to take on so vital a matter of national interest.

Three years later, in his March 24, 1969 issue, Stone expressed his belief that the killing of Martin Luther King was the result of a conspiracy. He said, "J. Edgar Hoover, who hated and once insulted King, should be challenged to explain on what basis he announced within 24 hours of the killing that there was no conspiracy. How could he possibly have known so quickly?" He called for pressure on the White House for a complete investigation "independent of the FBI and its Chief," adding that "The only virtue of the Memphis deal (Attorney Percy Foreman's arrangement in which he persuaded James Earl Ray to plead guilty, ostensibly in order to avoid the death penalty) was that it keeps Ray alive someday to tell the full story."

I again wrote to Stone, and suggested that Hoover (and Attorney General Ramsey Clark) knew within 24 hours that there was no conspiracy just as the federal establishment "knew" within five hours following JFK's murder that Oswald was the lone assassin. I again asked him to reconsider his position on the JFK case. . . . Again Stone did not deign to respond.

A.L. Wirin and the Liberal Establishment

from pages 34-40:

Late in November 1964 a number of critics and other interested parties gathered for a few days at the home of Maggie Field in Beverly Hills. Largely as a result of Mark Lane's powerful defense brief for Lee Oswald published a year earlier in the *National Guardian*, a left-wing weekly, Maggie Field, who was already working on the case by the evening of November 22, 1963, and who in the coming months and years was to acquire an encyclopedic knowledge of the twenty-six volumes, had written to Lane, as had I. I had arranged a number of speaking dates for him in Southern California, primarily on university campuses, for late November and early December. These lectures were very well attended by large and receptive audiences. The highlight of his scheduled appearances was to be a debate with Joseph Ball, senior counsel for the Warren Commission, to be held December 4, 1964. This was to be the first time a senior WC staffer had agreed to publicly debate Lane. We all realized the importance of this event. The meetings at Maggie Field's house were for the purpose of poring over the volumes, which had just been published, in order to assist Lane in preparation for his confrontation with Ball. I had arranged for this event with a community organization, Discussions Unlimited, which regularly sponsored lectures and debates on matters of public interest and whose left-wing orientation did not prevent it from featuring prominent speakers of widely ranging viewpoints.

Although Lane and those of us working with him would have preferred to have a one-on-one debate, at almost the last minute the sponsor acceded to Ball's demand that the format be enlarged by inviting two additional prominent participants, Herman Selvin, past president of the L.A. County Bar Association, and A. L. Wirin, chief counsel for the American Civil Liberties Union in Los Angeles. . . .

Tape recordings of the entire two-and-one-half-hour proceedings exist, and constitute a small but significant part of the history of this case.

On the night of December 4, the auditorium was filled early to its 2000-seat capacity, with an estimated 1000 people turned away. Lane made a clear and forceful opening against the Warren Report. Ball, in response, attempted to uphold the validity of the WC's physical and circumstantial case against Oswald. Selvin accused Lane of engaging in an old courtroom strategy: when neither the facts nor the law are on your side, attack the opposing lawyer. He then made a few remarks about physical evidence in general which clearly indicated he knew virtually nothing about the actual evidence in the case under discussion. But next to Lane's presentation, it was the statement of A.L. Wirin to which many in the audience were looking forward.

Abraham Lincoln Wirin was a highly respected — even revered — figure among liberal and progressive circles in California. His record as a strong and effective advocate for civil liberties and civil rights had gained him a national reputation. The record of the ACLU in connection with the assassination had until then been less than exemplary. On the evening of November 22, 1963, representatives of the Dallas chapter appeared at the police building to determine whether Oswald was being deprived of counsel. They were told by police officials that he had been informed of his rights and was free to seek an attorney. The ACLU representatives were discouraged from seeking to consult with Oswald himself, and failed to insist on doing so. Gregory Lee Olds, the president of the Dallas chapter, later reproached himself for not having insisted on seeing Oswald, and for so readily accepting official assurances.

Nevertheless, it was my hope and that of a significant part of the audience that A.L. Wirin by now had taken a careful look at the circumstances of the case, and was prepared to subject official behavior and the WC's conclusions to sharp scrutiny. Disillusion was not long in coming. Wirin quickly indicated he was not himself conversant with the facts of the case, but that he was relying on others whom he trusted; and since they accepted the Warren Report's conclusions, so did he.

Because his statement is an extremely important example of the kind of thinking then prevalent in left/liberal circles, I will present extensive excerpts as they appeared in the *LA Free Press*, December 11, 1964:

> I have learned that in many instances I too have had to rely upon the integrity and the good judgment of others. Now I consider Carey McWilliams and *The Nation* as an individual and a newspaper, respectively, whose judgment I respect. I do not consider Mr. McWilliams or *The Nation* a person or a newspaper which would participate in a fraud or which would condone it. Mr. McWilliams in *The Nation* expressed a view which has great weight with me.
>
> And *The Nation* said, ". . . in our view, the Commission did its work well, the report is an admirable document, and the Chief Justice, his associates, and the staff merit the praise they have received." Now that carries a lot of weight with me. . . .
>
> I have known all my life a man by the name of I.F. Stone. I'm sure Mr. Lane has known him. Mr. Stone is an observer in Washington and a reporter of the highest integrity. Politically, he is where I am, left of center, as is *The Nation*. . . . and where I continue to be. And I will differ with my friends who are left of center when they are grossly mistaken in their judgments as is Mr. Lane here tonight. Now Mr. Stone, who has defended the rights of the left, of the communists, and others, to fair treatment and freedom throughout his life, who is no apologist for any rightists, said: "I

> believe the Commission has done a first-rate job." Very rarely does Mr. Stone ever commend a governmental agency, very rarely. And very rarely do I. But "I believe the Commission has done a first rate job on the level that does our country proud, and is so worthy of so tragic an event," he said this. I don't know if I would go so far as this but he said, "I regard the case against Lee Harvey Oswald as the lone killer of the President as conclusive." Now I am reading this to you merely to say to you this carries a lot of weight with me. Because I respect Mr. Stone and I think Mr. Stone in making that conclusion does it in terms of integrity and high honor. . . .
>
> Now let me tell you what someone is reported in the *Los Angeles Times* to have said, and whom I disagree with. . . . I read this without being personal to Mr. Lane, I respect him. I think he's grossly mistaken, but he thinks I am probably more mistaken, so we'll pass that. But in any event let's see . . . If what I am about to read to you . . . doesn't sound pretty much like Mr. Lane: "The Warren Commission Report," according to this quote, "on Mr. Kennedy's murder does a remarkable job of crime analysis. But when it comes to telling why and who is responsible, then I feel it does not fulfill its function."
>
> Indeed, this is a more conservative criticism of the Warren Commission than we heard from Mr. Lane tonight. This is the criticism of Herbert Philbrick, a stool pigeon and a rightist. And that's what the rightists are saying about the Warren Commission.

When Wirin dropped his punch line about Philbrick, who had been a long-time FBI agent in the Communist Party, there was an audible gasp of astonishment from the audience. For such a man as A.L. Wirin, given the entire history of his public life, to make such a statement at any time, and particularly in the given circumstances, was nothing short of breathtaking. . . . Wirin went on to expound his political analysis of the assassination:

> Now, finally, the Commission says that men on the left, neither the Soviet Union nor Cuba, had anything to do with the assassination of President Kennedy. Now this statement by the Commission, a statement in which the entire Commission, including Mr. Dulles, joined, this statement, saving all of us here who are left-of-center from the venom of the rightists, this statement protects the rights of us all. Now, had the Commission been irresponsible it might have failed to say that which [would have] resulted in an intensification of the cold war, had the Commission not given this clearance, as it were, to many against whom the rightists were pointing the finger, we might have had, following the assassination of President Kennedy, a real unleashing of terror against persons on the left.
>
> So, from my point of view, the Commission, instead of perpetrating a fraud upon the American people, has rendered a service of major importance to the American people, particularly by protecting their rights from hysteria and hostility, the rights of Americans who are, as I say, on the left, or left-of-center . . .

Lane made an eloquent response to Wirin:

> I mean no disrespect to Mr. Selvin when I say that because his reputation did not precede him to the East, I did not know him. Therefore, I can not pretend to be surprised at his remarks, associating anyone who dares question the Warren Commission Report with the impeachment of Earl Warren movement.

The same disclaimer can not be made for Mr. Wirin, who is known to us in New York and is known throughout the nation. And I had never thought that the day would come when I would share a platform with Mr. Wirin and hear him read a statement from Herbert Philbrick and say, "If Mr. Philbrick said that and Mr. Lane said that, what does that make Mr. Lane?"

. . . Now I know that it is only because of the extreme pressure of this establishment which Mr. Wirin so well emphasized in quoting Carey McWilliams, or I.F. Stone, that this unusual statement was made by Mr. Wirin. I know that he would not make it ordinarily and I know that it does not reflect his thinking generally. I have too much respect for Mr. Wirin, for the organization with which he is associated, to believe that it represents his thinking. And I know that the day will come in America, as it came in France, 12 years after the conviction of Dreyfus. The whole liberal establishment said, guilty, guilty, guilty, for 12 years. Dreyfus was not guilty when the Minister of Justice said it. Dreyfus was not guilty when the liberals in the Parliament of France said it any more than he was guilty 12 years later when the French government had the courage and the honor to reverse its position.

And Oswald is not guilty now — any more guilty than he will be when the U.S. government has the courage and the honor to state that it was wrong.

[*Editor's note*: For further relevant information see Appendix VII, in which the editorial policy of *The Nation* in relation to the assassination and Fred Cook's memoir of his conflict with Carey McWilliams over the assassination is detailed.]

Arthur Schlesinger, Jr.

from page 64:

In the fall of 1967, I received a call in Los Angeles from a local TV talk show host, Stan Bohrman. I had met with him several times and he had become convinced that there had been a conspiracy. He told me that Arthur Schlesinger, the noted historian and Kennedy intimate, was to be a guest on his show that afternoon, and Bohrman wanted me to meet with him. He suggested that I bring my photo materials and that he would introduce us following the program. When I arrived I was ushered into a waiting area, and there I spread out some of the Zapruder and Moorman photos [photos which reveal a gunman on the grassy knoll] on the table. Bohrman came in to say that Schlesinger was having makeup removed and would be in shortly. He was, and Bohrman introduced us, telling Schlesinger of my purpose. Schlesinger glanced at the photos and immediately paled, turned away and said, "I can't look and I won't look." That was the end of our meeting.

Leading American Intellectuals of the Left

Five Professors

from pages 66-68:

By early 1969, I felt I had completed my own research in the specific areas in which I had chosen to concentrate. I had from the beginning attempted to bring the results of my work, as well as that of others I respected, to the attention of influential individuals in media and government with the hope of getting them actively involved. At that time I was in Boston on an extended business trip, and found myself with spare time over a period of weeks between negotiations. I had believed for some time that what the movement for a reopening of the Kennedy assassination lacked was serious participation by prominent figures of the New Left (although my own overall political orientation by that time was moving gradually away from the left). I knew that a number of such individuals were teaching at Boston area universities, and I decided to try to reach them.

I contacted Noam Chomsky of MIT, Howard Zinn of Boston University, Gar Alperovitz of Harvard, and a second Harvard professor whom I shall here call "Harold Seltzer." In each case I requested a meeting of no more than one hour. For such occasions, I had assembled a portfolio of evidence, primarily photographic, that I could present briefly but adequately in 30-60 minutes. I believed this evidence carried sufficient conviction to impress most intelligent and open-minded people; and that should it fail to do so, I was satisfied that I had given the effort my best shot. Each of the four agreed to meet with me at his university office.

I first met with Noam Chomsky. Soon after our discussions began, he asked his secretary to cancel his remaining appointments for the day. The scheduled one-hour meeting stretched to 3-4 hours. Chomsky showed great interest in the material. We mutually agreed to a follow-up session later in the week. Then I met with Gar Alperovitz. At the end of our one-hour meeting, he said he would take an active part in the effort if Chomsky would lead it. Next was Howard Zinn. Afterwards he told me he had learned more in one hour than he had known previously about the case, but that he was concentrating his energy in the anti-war movement, and would probably not participate actively. The meeting with "Harold Seltzer" was the briefest. After 10-15 minutes, he said, "I don't give a shit who killed him — I hated the son-of-a-bitch."

When I phoned Chomsky to set up our second meeting, he asked if a colleague of his could also attend — Selwyn Bromberger, a professor of philosophy at MIT, whom Chomsky said had previously met me, and indeed he had. Eighteen months earlier, in July or August of 1967, while I was in Boston on a previous business trip, Bromberger came to the door of our rented house to solicit active support of "Vietnam Summer," the largest nationwide drive against the war yet mounted. (Martin Luther King had just a few months earlier openly joined the anti-war movement, and had promptly become the most prominent leader of the Vietnam Summer drive).

When I opened the door to Bromberger, he noticed the Kennedy photographic material with which I was working spread out on the dining room table. Curious, he asked me about it, which immediately led to a 1½-hour interruption of his door-to-door solicitation.

I welcomed Bromberger's attendance at the second Chomsky meeting, which again lasted much of an afternoon. The discussion ranged beyond evidentiary items to other aspects of the case. I told Chomsky of Alperovitz' offer to assist him if he decided to lead an effort to reopen. Chomsky indicated he was very interested, but would not decide before giving the matter much careful consideration. After the meeting, as they drove me back to my apartment, Bromberger expressed the view that, "If they are strong enough to kill the President, and strong enough to cover it up, then they are too strong to confront directly . . . if they feel sufficiently threatened, they may move to open totalitarian rule" ("they" was not further defined).

As we have seen from previous reactions by I.F. Stone, A.L. Wirin, and Carey McWilliams, this was similar to the fears expressed or implied by many leftist intellectuals among those who nevertheless professed faith in the Warren Report. From Bromberger, I was hearing it for the first time from someone who believed the report to be false.

I phoned Vince Salandria, of whom I had spoken to Chomsky, and asked him to send Chomsky his research and thinking. Salandria told me he was skeptical that Chomsky would actually get involved, based on his previous experiences with such left-oriented people. He reasoned that had they entertained any such intentions, they would have acted on them long before this. Nevertheless, he agree to send the material.

Upon returning to Los Angeles, I wrote a lengthy letter to Chomsky summing up my overview of the case to that time, and stating as cogently as I could the arguments for his active involvement.

He responded on April 18, 1969:

> Just a quick note. I got your long letter, and some material from Salandria. I'll read both carefully.

> But I won't be able to decide anything until I return from England, in mid-June. Right now things are simply too rushed, and I'm too harassed to give serious thought to anything. I'll be in touch with you then. I don't know what the odds are. I'm still open-minded (and I hope will remain so).

From the context of our previous meetings it was clear that what Chomsky "won't be able to decide" until he returned from England was not the question of whether or not there was a conspiracy — that he had given every indication of having already decided in the affirmative — but whether or not he wished to participate actively, even to assume a leading role, in the movement to reopen the case.

I never heard from him again, and Chomsky did not join such a movement. On the contrary, in recent years he has on a number of occasion gone on record attacking the critics' position and supporting the Warren Report.

[*Editor's note*: To be more accurate, what Chomsky has done of late is to claim agnosticism on the question of whether there was a conspiracy to kill President Kennedy, but has insisted that if there was a conspiracy, it was of no political significance, since there is no evidence of any shift in policy following the assassination. In addition to this Chomsky has played an important role in the orchestrated debate which has focused the significance of the murder of Kennedy around the issue of the escalation of U.S. involvement in the war in Vietnam. As discussed elsewhere in this volume, the function of this debate has been to divert public attention from Kennedy's important movement against the cold war, for peace, for rapprochement with the U.S.S.R., and toward normalization of relations with Cuba.]

The New York Times, *CBS, and the CIA*

from pages 61-63:

Fred Powledge

In Spring 1967, Fred Powledge was in New Orleans to assess the Garrison investigation on special assignment for the *New Republic*. During an interview, Garrison told him that "tremendous pressure from some sections of the Eastern press, especially those with connections with the administration . . ." was causing potentially important witnesses who had initially contacted his office to become reluctant to come forward.

Powledge writes (*New Republic*, June 17, 1967):

> I couldn't contradict that. I had known, since the assassination, that the most influential purveyors of news in the nation had gone out of their way to present the Warren Commission side of the story, and to ignore or downplay those who dissented. One organ of communication, I later learned, even sought the CIA's advice on how to treat a story about the investigation. This, if Garrison's allegations of CIA involvement are correct, is roughly comparable to a newspaper's asking "Bull" Connor how he would handle a story on the Birmingham Freedom Ride massacre, and then following his advice.

It is unfortunate, but not surprising, that Powledge did not name the "organ of communication" which felt it needed CIA guidance with its story about Garrison, but it was as a *New York Times* reporter that he wrote stories from Dallas and New Orleans immediately following the assassination. His statement brings to mind Carl Bernstein's revelations in his article in *Rolling Stone*, October 20, 1977, of long-standing CIA contacts and cooperation by top management of *The New York Times*. Powledge closes by saying:

> It was possible that the Central Intelligence Agency, given what little the public knows of its methods and philosophies, is covering up important information. It was possible (a certainty, in my mind) that the news media, in their haste to protect what they feel is the national security or to keep the nation from getting panicked, have tried so hard to believe the Warren report that they have overlooked their primary news function.

In checking Bernstein's *Rolling Stone* article, I realized again (not having read it in many years) how important it was, and how unremarked upon it had passed. In it he provides much detail about the major media's willing penetration by and cooperation with the CIA, naming many names in the process. One might have thought that Bernstein's great Watergate-generated celebrity would make his article difficult to ignore, but somehow the media largely managed it. Here is what he says about *The New York Times*:

> The Agency's relationship with the *Times* was by far its most valuable among newspapers, according to CIA officials. From 1950 to 1966, about ten CIA employees were provided *Times* cover under arrangements approved by the newspaper's late publisher, Arthur Hays Sulzberger. The cover arrangements were part of a general *Times* policy — set by Sulzberger — to provide assistance to the CIA whenever possible.

Sulzberger was especially close to Allen Dulles. "At that level of contact it was the mighty talking to the mighty," said a high-level CIA official who was present at some of the discussions. "There was an agreement in principle that, yes indeed, we would help each other. The question of cover came up on several occasions. It was agreed that the actual arrangements would be handled by subordinates. . . . The mighty didn't want to know the specifics; they wanted plausible deniability."

On CBS

CBS was unquestionably the CIA's most valuable broadcasting asset. CBS president William Paley and Allen Dulles enjoyed an easy working and social relationship. Over the years, the network provided cover for CIA employees, including at least one well-known foreign correspondent and several stringers. It supplied outtakes of newsfilm to the CIA, established a formal channel of communication between the Washington bureau chief and the Agency; gave the Agency access to the CBS newsfilm library; and allowed reports by CBS corespondents to the Washington and New York newsrooms to be routinely monitored by the CIA. Once a year during the 1950s and early 1960s, CBS correspondents joined the CIA hierarchy for private dinners and briefings.

The details of the CBS-CIA arrangements were worked out by subordinates of both Dulles and Paley. "The head of the company doesn't want to know the fine points, nor does the director," said the CIA official. "Both designate aides to work that out. It keeps them above the battle." Dr. Frank Stanton, for 25 years president of the network, was aware of the general arrangements Paley made with Dulles — including those for cover, according to CIA officials. (Stanton, in an interview last year, said he could not recall any cover arrangements.)

[*Editor's note*: Perhaps to complete the circle it should be noted that internal CIA memoranda reveal that it was Allen Dulles, then sitting on the Warren Commission, who met with a CIA administrator who had been sent by Deputy Director Richard Helms to discuss "certain questions which Mr. Dulles feels the Warren Commission may pose to CIA," including the rumor that Oswald was a CIA agent. Dulles counseled the CIA at the time on how the inquiry should be met. See Philip H. Melanson, *Spy Saga: Lee Harvey Oswald and U.S. Intelligence*. New York: Praeger, 1990, pp. 131-32.]

Appendix IX

The McCloy/Zorin Agreement

The following is a reproduction of an agreement initialed by a representative of President Kennedy, John McCloy, and a representative of Premier Nikita Khrushchev, Valerian Zorin. The agreement, informally known as the McCloy-Zorin Agreement, was initialed on September 20, 1961, and was subsequently endorsed by the United Nations General Assembly.

The McCloy/Zorin Agreement

The United States and the U.S.S.R. have agreed to recommend the following principles as the basis for future multilateral negotiations on disarmament and to call upon other states to cooperate in reaching an early agreement on general and complete disarmament in a peaceful world in accordance with these principles:

1. Secure Disarmament and Peaceful Settlement of Disputes . . . War No Longer

The goal of negotiations is to achieve agreement on a program which will ensure:

(a) That disarmament is general and complete and war is no longer an instrument for settling international problems, and
(b) That such disarmament is accompanied by the establishment of reliable procedures for the peaceful settlement of disputes and effective arrangements for the maintenance of peace in accordance with the principles of the Charter of the United Nations.

2. Retention of Non-Nuclear Forces for Domestic Order and a U.N. Peace Force

The program for general and complete disarmament shall ensure that States have at their disposal only such non-nuclear armaments, forces, facilities, and establishments as are agreed to be necessary to maintain internal order and protect the personal security of citizens; and that States shall support and provide manpower for a United Nations peace force.

3. All Military Forces, Bases, Stockpiles, Weapons, and Expenses to be Ended

To this end, the program for general and complete disarmament shall contain the necessary provisions, with respect to the military establishment of every nation, for:

(a) The disbanding of armed forces, the dismantling of military establishments, including bases, the cessation of the production of armaments as well as their liquidation or conversion to peaceful uses;
(b) The elimination of all stockpiles of nuclear, chemical, bacteriological, and other weapons of mass destruction, and the cessation of the production of such weapons;
(c) The elimination of all means of delivery of weapons of mass destruction;
(d) The abolition of organizations and institutions designed to organize the military effort of States, the cessation of military training, and the closing of all military training institutions; and
(e) The discontinuance of military expenditures.

4. Implementation by Timed Stages with Compliance and Verification Agreed to at Every Stage

The disarmament program should be implemented in an agreed sequence, by stages, until it is completed, with each measure and stage carried out within specified time-limits. Transition to a subsequent stage in the process of disarmament should take place upon a review of the implementation measures included in the preceding stage and upon a decision that all such measures have been implemented and verified and that any additional verification arrangements required for measures in the next stage are, when appropriate, ready to operate.

5. Equitable Balance at Every Stage So No Advantage to Anyone and Security for All

All measures of general and complete disarmament should be balanced so that at no stage of the implementation of the treaty could any State or group of States gain military advantage and that security is ensured equally for all.

6. Strict Control to Make Sure of Compliance by All Parties and Creation of an International Disarmament Organization with Inspectors having Unrestricted Access Everywhere Without Veto for Full Verification

All disarmament measures should be implemented from beginning to end under such strict and effective international control as would provide firm assurance that all parties are honoring their obligations. During and after the implementation of general and complete disarmament, the most thorough control should be exercised, the nature and extent of such control depending on the requirements for verification of the disarmament measures being carried out in each stage. To implement control over and inspection of disarmament, an international disarmament organization including all parties to the agreement should be created within the framework of the United Nations. This international disarmament organization and its inspectors should be assured unrestricted access without veto to all places, as necessary for the purpose of effective verification.

7. Disarmament Process Must be Accompanied by Measures to Maintain Peace and Security and a United Nations Peace Force Strong Enough to Deter or Suppress Any Threat or Use of Arms in Violation of the United Nations Charter

Progress in disarmament should be accompanied by measures to strengthen institutions for maintaining peace and the settlement of international disputes by peaceful means. During and after the implementation of the program of general and complete disarmament, there should be taken, in accordance with the principles of the United Nations Charter, the necessary measures to maintain international peace and security, including the obligation of States to place at the disposal of the United Nations agreed manpower necessary for an international peace force to be equipped with agreed types of armaments. Arrangements for the use of this force should ensure that the United Nations can effectively deter or suppress any threat or use of arms in violation of the purposes and principles of the United Nations.

8. States Should Seek Widest Agreement at Earliest Date While Continuing to Seek More Limited Agreements which Will Facilitate and Form Part of the Overall Program for Secured General and Complete Disarmament in a Peaceful World

States participating in the negotiations should seek to achieve and implement the widest possible agreement at the earliest possible date. Efforts should continue without interruption until agreement upon the total program has been achieved, and efforts to ensure early agreement on and implementation of measures of disarmament should be undertaken without prejudicing progress on agreement on the total program and in such a way that these measures would facilitate and form part of that program.

Appendix X

The Khrushchev-Castro Letter

The following excerpts are from a letter which appeared in The Cuban Missile Crisis, 1962: A National Security Archive Documents Reader, *ed. Laurence Chang and Peter Kornbluh. New York: The New Press, 1992, pp. 319-29. The context for this letter was a certain confusion and conflict which had arisen between Castro and Khrushchev over how the Soviets negotiated an end to the crisis and Communist China's effort to exploit this confusion. Castro eventually publicly acknowledged that his initial reaction toward the situation had been "immature," a result of a lack of experience, and that Khrushchev had been correct. Also included in this appendix is an analysis, excerpted from a letter to Vincent J. Salandria, of the Khrushchev-Castro letter's significance for understanding the motivation of the President's assassination.*

Letter to Fidel Castro January 31, 1963

by Nikita Khrushchev

Dear comrade Fidel Castro:

For some time I have been considering the idea of writing you this letter. Now, on my way to Moscow from Berlin, where I attended the Congress of Socialist Unity Party of Germany, I write to you. Our train is crossing the fields and forests of Soviet Byelorussia and it occurs to me how wonderful it would be if you could see, on a sunny day like this, the ground covered with snow and the forests silvery with frost.

Perhaps you, a southern man, have seen this only in paintings. It must surely be fairly difficult for you to imagine the ground carpeted with snow and the forests covered with white frost. It would be good if you could visit our country each season of the year; every one of them, spring, summer, fall, and winter, has its delights.

Cuba is a country of eternal summer. I remember that during our talk in New York, we reacted differently to the weather of that city. I was choking with heat, but you told me you felt chilly.

Nevertheless, all these thoughts about nature should not carry us away from the principal theme of this letter. The most important is the strong desire my comrades and I feel to see you and to talk, to talk with our hearts open. We have much to talk about. We hope that this meeting, this conversation, will not be delayed for long. We would like the meeting to take place as soon as possible.

Why? Well, because we have lived through a very important stage, one that represents a landmark in the historical development of Cuba, the Soviet Union, and the other socialist countries. For the first time since the end of the Second World War we have been close, very close, to war. Cuba has found itself at the center of the acute crisis in the Caribbean.

We understand that the extreme gravity of the crisis has now passed, but the danger of a confrontation has not yet ended. You understand this very well, and we fully share your worry and view the situation as you do.

But, what is most important today? Why do we need to meet and talk frankly?

The gravity of the crisis created by North American imperialism in the Caribbean has ended. But it seems to me that this crisis has left a mark, although barely visible, in the relations between our states — Cuba and the Soviet Union — and in our own personal relationship. Speaking frankly, these relations are not what they were before the crisis. I will not conceal the fact that this troubles and worries us. And it seems to me that the development of our relations will depend, in large part, on our meeting. . . . Correspondence is insufficient. Nothing can substitute for a personal conversation. It is precisely through such a talk that we can overcome more easily and quickly any misunderstanding of each other's positions. . . .

. . . During the Caribbean crisis, our viewpoints did not always coincide, we did not see the different stages of the crisis in the same way; it was clear that we viewed the ways to solve it differently. After our known statement, you even said publicly that during the development of the crisis there had emerged certain differences between the Soviet government and the Cuban government. You can understand that for us this was no cause for joy. Now the tensions have diminished; and now that we have entered into a new phase in the relations between Cuba and the Soviet Union, on one hand, and [between the Soviet Union and] the United States of North America, on the other, there are still gaps, which are difficult to assess, in our relations with Cuba.

That is why we want to meet — to even out, to close the gaps in our relations, whatever their extent; even if they are only small, we would try to smooth them out. In the relations between two socialist states there must be no rough edges; our relations must be truly fraternal.

Now that some time separates us from the acute stages of the crisis and we can proceed with a calm analysis of all its aspects, I shall permit myself, dear friend, to recall some events and examine the events that took place.

I would like to state frankly, so there is no doubt in your mind, why it is that we proposed to deploy our ballistic missiles in Cuba. I want to tell you this because even the representatives of certain socialist states are thinking in a rather curious way, distorting not only our initial steps but also those we took later, and obscuring their positions with vigorous revolutionary phrases regarding persistence in the face of common class enemies, and other Marxist slogans. Why then do they take the liberty to judge the steps of other governments when, as you know perfectly well, they didn't actually do anything to help Cuba when it faced mortal danger?

You may have observed that certain people and groups, and even the leaders of certain socialist countries, who limited themselves to observing the crisis, started to get agitated and to pontificate on the ways in which one should have acted during the crisis, criticizing those who carried the burden of the struggle. They say that we should have proceeded in this or that way, taken such-and-such a step, although they themselves took no steps and held themselves at the sidelines of the real struggle. We may rightly ask these critics why they, at the height of the crisis, did not take any step — verbal or material — that would have demonstrated their willingness to aid Cuba, to march with you if war broke out.

In those days, those critics gave no proof of any such willingness and limited themselves to insulting capitalism and imperialism. Were we to compete with them in this practice, we would win the contest easily: it is well known that the Russian language has an enormous number of insults.

In the first days of the revolution, we hurled prodigious vituperations against imperialism; but then we were the only socialist country; and our economic and military strength was weak. Today things are different: the Soviet Union is no longer the only socialist state, and there is a powerful socialist world system, the community of socialist states. This is why the Republic of Cuba is not alone. When it put itself under the banner of Marxism-Leninism, Cuba joined the community of socialist countries. We applauded it and we continue to do so — and not only with words.

Our country, which fought difficult battles to save the achievements of the October Revolution, repelled the intervention by fourteen states, and played a decisive role in the defeat of the Hitlerian war machine; our country, which went unrecognized by the United States for seventeen years and which other countries also did not recognize for a long time, has a very clear idea of the difficulties that confront the Cuban people, their leader, and his comrades in their efforts to defend the Cuban Revolution, to safeguard the right of the Cuban people to decide its own destiny when it has next to it a neighbor as strong, aggressive, and implacable as North American imperialism.

We were the first to know of the infinite vileness of the methods and ways of fighting of the enemy. When Churchill, who headed the crusade to strangle the October Revolution, was unable, with all his allies, to bring the Soviet nation to its knees through intervention, they turned to economic blockade. They were sure that we would lack the means, the strength, and the cadres needed to rebuild our shattered economy. They believed that Soviet Russia would disintegrate by itself, that hunger would smother it, that typhus would kill it, and that the experiment of building socialism would collapse.

But what happened? . . . Guided by the doctrine of Marxism-Leninism, communists have demonstrated their capacity to create material value on a new socialist base, as well as their capacity to develop culture, to elevate science to a level that is now the summit for all the states in the world. It is not by chance that after we launched our ships into space, the United States sent a delegation to our country to study our public education system, our preparation of engineers and of scientific personnel. That delegation developed a very high appreciation of our education system. In the Soviet Union we graduate three times as many engineers as did the United States, which is evidence of the intellectual development of society and of the way in which the peoples' knowledge has been extended. And the greater our knowledge, the earlier we will assure the final victory.

When the Cuban Revolution took place, its enemies were seized with panic. They saw that a socialist Cuba could be a guiding star, a magnet for all Latin American countries, for all peoples fighting for their independence and liberty. The peoples that have merely achieved their political liberation from the colonial yoke, but who have not yet managed to become the true proprietors of their countries, see in Cuba a model for the solution of their social problems.

This is why we are firmly convinced that the United States of North America will never resign itself to the existence of a socialist Cuba. We knew that they would do all they could to eliminate socialist Cuba and to maintain the capitalist system in all the countries of the western hemisphere. Precisely with this end in mind they went to the archives, and dusted off the Monroe Doctrine, which they had practically renounced.

. . . Today, the United States has reserved for itself the "right" to involve itself in the affairs of Europe, Asia, and the other continents, forming military alliances of imperialist countries to carry out a third world war. Nevertheless, it would hold the part of the Monroe Doctrine referring to the western hemisphere to remain in effect so as to suffocate liberating revolutions, to erect a barrier against socialism.

The leadership of the Soviet state — the presidium of the central committee and the government — often changed its views in looking for the most effective way to help Cuba. When the Yankees announced the economic blockade against Cuba, when they left it without fuel, without other materials and essential products, when the republic felt an acute need for prepared cadres and was running into enormous difficulties, we gave you, without hesitation, a fraternal helping hand to aid you in all areas.

The truth is that people who have lost their communist consciousness now accuse the Soviet Union of giving aid with mercantile goals in mind. But such accusations are motivated by ill will; the accusers have lost their common sense, the capacity to consider the question in a sensible way. We can take any dispute about this and present real facts that prove just how unfounded that accusation is.

I don't think that there is any proof lacking that, in aiding Cuba, we are not pursuing any self-serving ends. Only a madman would think that we are getting rich or profiting from it. In giving Cuba great material aid, we do it consciously because we are communists. We ourselves have suffered immense difficulties in our struggle for socialism, and we know from experience that it is not easy to create a new society. We have given aid to Cuba, and we will continue to give it. We are looking forward.

With the failure of its plans to strangle Cuba through the economic blockade and through the breaking of diplomatic relations, North American imperialism started to prepare armed invasion and, in 1961, unleashed its mercenaries against Cuba.

But North American imperialism underestimated the cohesion, the will to triumph, and the degree of organization of the Cuban people, its faithfulness to the ideas of liberty and independence, its trust in its leaders, its trust in you, dear Fidel. You defeated the enemy. All of us, all socialist countries, and all progressive men are proud of your glorious victory.

It was clear to us that the North Americans, having been defeated once, would not resign themselves to it, that they would change tactics and more or less repeat the invasion. However, it would be a much better prepared invasion, hence much more dangerous, since they would take into account the lessons from the first defeat. The North Americans themselves even spoke openly of this. For example, in their conversations with our representatives, they would frequently recall the events of 1956 in Hungary. They took them as an example of energetic measures, trying to find in them some justification for their measures against the Cuban Revolution. You, they told us, proceeded in this way in your own self-interest, because Hungary is close to your borders; but we also have the right to undertake such energetic measures against Cuba, which is close to our country. Naturally, our representatives emphatically rejected such "foundations" for a new invasion against Cuba.

Our party and our government saw that they were moving, in effect, toward an invasion. And you, Cuban comrades, as was shown in your statements, understood and felt the real danger of such an act of aggression, and you, exhorted the people to defend the revolutionary conquests.

We considered, and we still consider, that your slogan of "*Patria o Muerte*" [Fatherland or Death] was completely just, revolutionary. But, at the same time, we understood that it was impossible to restrain imperialism with only a heroic readiness to resist unto death. It was clear that the imperialists wanted to prepare the Cuban people for death, not for victory. And the imperialists of the United States disposed themselves of great forces to move on little Cuba, and Cuba naturally cannot confront such a war machine for long. How could one help Cuba in this situation? Some chose the path of revolutionary slogans. In the days of the crisis, they expressed their support for the Declaration of 1957 and the Declaration of 1958 of the eighty-one parties but, in fact, they did not lend any effective support, aside from protests and solidarity demonstrations with Cuba. These men, naturally, pronounced not a few just words on the heroism of the Cuban people, of its maximum leader, of his comrades in arms, of their intrepidness and readiness to die but not to surrender to the enemy. Yet, could aggression be contained by giving Cuba only that kind of help and insulting imperialism? You know very well that to proceed like that is not to take the primary, decisive measures.

We took another path. We decided to go to face the danger, to take measures that would place the imperialists of the United States in the dilemma of having to renounce the invasion of Cuba or to unleash thermonuclear war. To defend Cuba we proposed the installation of the missiles. If North American imperialism had unleashed the invasion, no protest of ours, no three-shift, three-week or even three-month demonstration would have stopped them. Only one thing could restrain them: the fear, the knowledge that if they began the invasion, the missiles would carry out their mission and the cities of North America would be left in ruins. We understood that placing such a weapon in Cuba was the most efficient way of defending it during that time.

We considered that Cuba needed the means that would make the United States renounce any armed invasion of the island.

We examined this question several times and we decided to propose the installation of the weapons, you know, serviced by our personnel. We started with the premise that the missiles would be in the hands of Soviet military units. We also want to stick to that system in the future. The aim was for our enemies to hold themselves to the same position, if only for a certain amount of time. It is clear that in the end, West Germany will also, probably, have such a weapon, but we are interested in pushing this into the future.

When this question was decided, we took into account that the imperialists could take advantage of such a step, to use it as a pretext to turn up the heat, to put the world on the brink of war, or even unleash war. And we took decisive steps on behalf of the defense of Cuba, on behalf of the whole socialist camp and of the proletarian solidarity of Marxist-Leninist parties. . . . We understood that our country could see itself dragged into a war in the Caribbean, which would have given the conflict a global character. . . .

These are not resolutions, they are not insults against imperialism, with which one cannot weaken it. As a Byelorussian proverb says: You can insult the master, but with that he only gets fatter. And so it is. You can insult imperialism as much as you like, but that won't make it wither, it won't make it weaker, nor will it diminish its insolence. Imperialism takes into account only real forces. It does not recognize anything else. That is why one can call it a paper tiger, dung, whatever you like; but if you do not let imperialism know that behind those words expressing our indignation there is a force, they will not be stopped by them nor will their insolence and aggressiveness be diminished.

We consider as a real force, in the first place, the economy, when the people are united around their leaders. Only with a firm economic base can you create the necessary weaponry.

We, the socialist countries, appreciate more than anything else the goodness of peace and dedicate all our forces to promote it. But we must never forget the existence of the imperialist camp and its aspirations to strangle the socialist countries. That is why we must observe the proper proportion of expenses, diversify the economy, which is also the fundamental base of military might; but we must do so without skimping on resources to create the most modern armed forces and the most modern equipment, which must be at a necessary level, even more, superior to our enemy's.

Without this, we cannot guarantee peaceful coexistence; without basing oneself on such real premises, it is impossible to safeguard peace worldwide.

Because of this, those who say that we are begging for peace are consciously distorting our position, or they simply do not understand what they're saying. As is said, only God knows what moves them: ill-will or incomprehension.

Some are now daring to slander us, claiming that in resolving the conflict in the Caribbean we guided ourselves exclusively by our own self-serving interests. That is the greatest offense against the Soviet people! . . .

Those who make such statements can only be men who, while calling themselves Marxist-Leninist, do not truly value that title. It is obvious, that while pursuing their own egotistical and adventurist ends, they dare to slander the Soviet Union — the first country to revolt, to build socialism, and to set an unyielding example in the face of the enemy in the fight against its own bourgeoisie and landowners, and a country that now gives the same unyielding example in the fight against imperialism. Doubtless, you know that the Soviet Union has extended, and extends, immense aid, even in weaponry, to peoples fighting for their liberation from imperialism. . . .

As you can see, dear comrade Fidel, I have gotten carried away and am now writing you a very long letter. You will understand, I hope, that I feel the need to do so. As we say among ourselves, among us Russians, one feels the desire to let off steam when talking to a comrade, to a friend, to a brother. Although we are carrying out this conversation at a distance, I'd like this letter to express my feelings. I hope that when you come to our country — and if you want to bring your comrades with you we would be happy — we will have more than one fraternal conversation.

I will not hide from you, it would be senseless to do so, that any imprudent step or even any roughness in our relations could today generate problems. . . . It is possible that under normal conditions, no one would attach any importance to this; but under the conditions that have now been created, I would say that serenity and self-control are necessary. You will understand, as is natural, that we, like you, have reason to be in a good mood. With you, we have stopped an aggressor poised to invade Cuba and, despite the mobilization it carried out, its concentration of immense forces, it did not dare to attack the isle of freedom. We cannot underestimate the aggressive imperialist forces that were ready to attack your republic. Those forces were superior to Cuba's, including our troops on your territory, who, comrade Fidel, would have fought shoulder-to-shoulder with your heroes and, had it been necessary, would have died with them for the cause of the revolution.

When Marshal Malinovsky was asked what Cuba could do to respond to an attack from the United States, he answered frankly, although it was very difficult for him to give this answer: "If we speak of the correlation of forces existing in the Caribbean, and we know what Cuba has at its disposal and we know our capacities there — he said — we could say that, with such a correlation of forces, it is impossible, unfortunately, to hold. And if hostilities start, it is very unlikely that Cuba will be able to resist for long because the forces are so unequal."

It may be that you do not agree with us. We too would have wished that the situation had been different. But, dear friend Fidel, you are a military man, I also spent almost the entire Second World War at the front and took part in the civil war: there is a real correlation of forces and it is impossible to escape it. . . .

But, why did the enemy — the North American aggressor — retreat, renounce the invasion? It is clear that they were not stopped just by the forces of Cuba, including the forty-two medium-range missiles we installed there. The principal thing that stopped North American imperialism was the powerful forces of the Soviet Union; they were deterred by the fact that an attack against Cuba would have meant a world war in which many countries would have been blown up. The United States of North America would have also suffered terrible damages.

As you will understand, we do not want to minimize in the slightest the important role played by the firm decision and willingness of the Cuban people to defend the conquests of the revolution.

This is what stopped the enemy — not the curses and insults against imperialism, not the resolutions. . . . I stress once again that the enemy can only be deterred by effective forces. . . . Even if he is confident of winning, he also has other calculations: he takes into account the colossal losses and understands that such losses, under actual conditions, would reduce his victory to nothing, and that his territories would be left a field strewn with corpses, and contaminated by radioactivity.

It's said that we cannot believe the enemy. We have always held, do hold, and always will hold this position.

It is clear to any Marxist-Leninist that North American imperialism will not renounce its plans to end the socialist regime in Cuba, to abolish the revolutionary order in your country, and to restore capitalism and reaction there. While there are two systems — the socialist one, which is edifying life on the basis of Marxist-Leninist doctrine, and the capitalist one — those systems will be antagonistic, and the struggle between them will not cease; it will not cease until one of the two achieves total victory.

We Marxist-Leninists are profoundly convinced of our victory. . . . Speaking frankly, at this time, there are few hopes of reaching a disarmament agreement.

This last observation does not mean, however, that we should renounce our efforts in the struggle for peace, or replace our slogan in the struggle for disarmament with one for the struggle for rearmament. With such an aim we would neither attract the masses nor be an attractive force for workers and for all friends of peace. If we put at the forefront not the struggle for disarmament but the struggle for the unleashing of war and for the destruction of capitalism through war, instead of through peaceful competition, we would practically be exhorting people to die. People go to their deaths when there is no other way out. Just that — when there is no other way out.

But we do have a way out! We are sure that we are right — and not only of our reason, but also of the possibilities for victory. These possibilities we have proven with the socialist construction in practice, with the very fact of our existence. Forty years ago, the Soviet Union ranked among the lowest of the European countries in terms of economic development; today we hold second place in the world, and by 1970, by what we see, we will be in first. We have also succeeded in making the words "peace" and "socialism" inseparable in the minds of all the peoples in the world.

Does that not encourage us? Should this incite us into adventure, into unleashing a thermonuclear world war? Why should we follow the principle of all or nothing? One acts in this way only when there is no way out. Desperation and pessimism are for imperialist circles. They are the ones who, having lost faith in winning the contest of peaceful competition, can take risks and unleash war; such aggressive forces exist.

But we do not need a world war to achieve the victory of the communist cause. We communists have better prospects; we hold firm convictions, and this certainty is based not in words, but in real facts.

In conditions of peace, socialism deploys to the fullest its forces and demonstrates its advantages in all fields, even in fields as decisive as the powerful growth of the economy, worker productivity, and the material and cultural level of the masses.

On the other hand, peaceful coexistence does not free capitalism from its insoluble contradictions — it contributes to sharpening the workers' class struggle, of the workers against the exploiters, and contributes to the rise of the national liberation movement.

You may have noticed that the strongest labor conflicts and the national liberation struggles of greatest scope have taken place over the past ten or fifteen years, that is to say, during the period of peaceful coexistence. Under the conditions of peaceful coexistence of nations with different social regimes, democratic revolutions, national liberation revolutions, and socialist revolutions are not only possible but certain, including, of course, the revolutions in Latin America, which Cuba precipitated. That is why we make all efforts to avoid the eruption of a thermonuclear world war. We are not interested in unleashing a war.

But we are ready to carry out a counterstrike. If imperialism tries to liquidate us with war, we can liquidate the imperialist forces and, in this way, end imperialism forever. It will be, as is written in the documents of our Party, in the Communist party program, and in the declaration of fraternal communist parties, the last war ever unleashed by imperialism. . . .

All of this I say from the heart. This is why we would very much like you to come to our country. We have been inviting you to come for some time, but in the recent past events have taken such a course that we ourselves advised you to delay your visit somewhat. Then we worried greatly that North American imperialism could profit from your absence and invade Cuba.

Now we believe — and we are sure of this — that the enemy will not try to take advantage of your absence from the country and your visit to Moscow to attack Cuba. There are, in spite of everything, commitments that the United States of North America has undertaken through the statements of their president. Obviously, one cannot trust them and take it as an absolute guarantee, but neither is it reasonable to ignore them totally. This declaration of the president of the United States is now a kind of international document, registered at the United Nations. The crisis in the area of the Caribbean Sea and the desire of North American imperialism to deploy armed forces in Cuba have become a world crisis. Now your relations with the United States of North America are not simply relations between only two countries, between Cuba and the United States; no, this matter is a global question now. However brazen, the aggressor will be forced to take this into account in some way.

Naturally, imperialism can change its tactics in its struggle to obtain its objectives. It will not renounce the objective it has set itself — fighting against socialism — and this should not surprise us, because we too speak openly of the global victory of socialism. We speak of peaceful coexistence and of the inevitable triumph of communism all over the globe. . . .

We want to reach this great objective in the conditions of peaceful competition. In the atmosphere of peaceful coexistence we are demonstrating the superiority of socialism compared to capitalism and, in this way, we attract more and more the peoples of the capitalist countries to the struggle within each country against the domination of capital — for its defeat, for the establishment of the dictatorship of the proletariat, and for the victory of peace, democracy, and socialism.

As has already been said, peaceful coexistence contributes to the development of the class struggle of the peoples of Latin America, Africa, and Asia, which also changes to a great degree the correlation of forces at the global level in favor of socialism. We have helped, and will help with all means, the peoples in their just struggle against imperialism.

Not long ago, Kennedy assembled all the counter-revolutionary crowd that you expelled from Cuba, along with other scum, and perorated before them, promising the participants of the invasion to return to Havana the banner they had given him, when another government is in power there. That does not discourage us in the least. You will surely recall that when I was in the United States I told them without evasion that capitalism would be buried. But I said that the gravedigger would be the North American working class. This class will bury North American imperialism on its own.

The Soviet Union does not exclude the possibility of furious action by North American imperialism. It would be stupid not to see the danger. But today, after the acute crisis in the area of the Caribbean Sea, there are reasons to believe that you have won a truce and that you will take advantage of it for peaceful construction. One must use this truce, above all, to expand the economy and agricultural production: this will allow you to improve the people's living standards. It is precisely this revolutionary example of Cuba's that the North American monopolists and imperialists most fear. That is why they want to strangle Cuba.

From this, it seems to us, important tasks can be derived today for the Republic of Cuba. One must concentrate efforts in the development of the economy and culture, in increasing the living standards of the masses. And we, comrade Fidel, are ready to cooperate with you. The Soviet Union is doing, and will do, everything possible to develop this cooperation. This cooperation requires us to give aid to your republic. In making its contribution to strengthening the economy of the Republic of Cuba and its might, the Soviet Union is in no way guided by any self-interested calculations. When we help to strengthen the economy and defense of Cuba, we consider it to be a contribution to the common cause of developing and strengthening revolutionary forces, of strengthening the unity of socialist countries. With joint efforts we open in the new continent the road to a new world, the world of socialism.

Revolutionary Cuba is a brilliant star in the western hemisphere. The more developed its economy and culture, and the higher the material well-being of the Cuban people, the brighter the light of the beacon that attracts the working class, the peasants, and the working intellectuals of Latin American, African, and Asians countries; they are encouraged by the struggle for liberty and for a better life.

These are, comrade Fidel, my sincere judgments.

Now I would like to tell you, comrade Fidel, what the best time, in our opinion, would be for you to come to the Soviet Union. From our point of view, the season of the year is of no great importance. But taking into account the tropical climate of Cuba, and remembering that you felt physically cold in New York, we must also take into account our Russian winter. . . . [I]t might be most convenient for you to come to our country at the beginning of spring, so that you could take part in the May Day festivities.

At another time you wanted to come to the Soviet Union precisely for the First of May, to watch our demonstration and parade. Because of this it would be good if you could come before the First of May so that you could get to know our cities, what we are building, our people. I would gladly travel with you through the country, and accompany you in your travels to certain cities. We could talk during those trips and then we could celebrate the First of May in Moscow, where you could see the parade and the demonstration. . . .

In a word, you choose the time that is most convenient for you. May Day with your participation would be an even more joyous holiday for Muscovites and for all the peoples of the Soviet Union. The popularity of your revolution, and your own personal popularity as leader of the Cuban Revolution, is very high among our peoples. The Soviets value you greatly and admire your revolutionary audacity. The Cuban Revolution has conquered the hearts of our people. You will feel this heat when you come to our country and meet with the people in any place: in the city, in the factory, the Kolkhoz and Sovkhoz, in every place you go.

I will not hide from you, comrade Fidel, that I myself had great desires to make a trip to Cuba. . . .

I thought that after ending this tension I could go see you in Cuba. But circumstances are such that, as far as I can see, I should not go. We have reached that conclusion because it could be falsely interpreted in your country and in other countries. Many will ask: Why is Khrushchev going to Cuba if comrade Mikoyan has just been there? Mikoyan's visit was interpreted in a twisted way in some countries, even in some socialist countries. And if, after this, Khrushchev shows up over there, they will say that obviously the relations between the Soviet Union and Cuba have become such that Khrushchev's visit was necessary.

Now, I reaffirm my great wishes to go to your country if you invite me. I'm sure that such a trip would be advantageous. But we will talk about that when you come to the Soviet Union, and together we can select the time of my visit to Cuba. . . .

Please accept, comrade Fidel, cordial communist greetings on behalf of my comrades and myself.

January 31, 1963 N. Khrushchev

Discussion of Khrushchev's Letter to Castro

by E. Martin Schotz

1/25/95

Dear Vince,

I have finally purchased Chang and Kornbluh, *The Cuban Missile Crisis, 1962: A National Security Archive Documents Reader*, and early this morning re-read *in toto* Khrushchev's long letter to Castro of January 31, 1963. I think this it is very important. For one thing it is apparent that Khrushchev is trying to clarify for Castro the emerging rift between the Soviets and the Chinese, and the significance of this rift for the struggle for socialism and peace. . . . Here there is a clear split in the socialist camp between the cautious Soviets who believe that the triumph of socialism hinges on peaceful co-existence and China which is advocating a militaristic warmongering line "against" the U.S. as well as the U.S.S.R. From Khrushchev's point of view, the Chinese position amounts to nothing more than slogans, slogans which verbally oppose imperialism, but objectively cause it no problem. The clear implication of the letter is that as far as the Soviets are concerned there is already at this point an emerging alliance between U.S. imperialism and Chinese communism.

What Castro said in his speech of 11/23/63 about the split in Washington parallels a split between the U.S.S.R. and China which Khrushchev is talking about . . . There are forces for war which wish to push the world along the lines of confrontation in order to selfishly achieve as much as possible with threats and weapons, and there are the forces of peaceful coexistence and moderation which are taking a different tack. On one side are the right wing in the U.S., including Dulles, Nixon, Kissinger, et al. . . . in alliance with the Chinese leadership including Mao. On the other side there are the Soviets and Kennedy and the more moderate side of imperialism which he represented. Khrushchev . . . cautions Castro not to be taken in by the Chinese, because the extreme "right" and the extreme "left" are destined to make common cause.

The other point to note is Khrushchev's view that the Cuban Missile Crisis was a watershed event which had changed the relations between the U.S. and U.S.S.R. and opened the way for the possibility of peaceful coexistence.

You can see from this the perilous balance of correlated forces which existed within the capitalist camp as well as within the socialist camp in 1963 and how the removal of Kennedy, the cancellation of his policy on Cuba, and the cancellation of movement on McCloy/Zorin had to bolster the emerging alliance of the Chinese leadership and the U.S. ultra-right, thus making the escalation of the Vietnam war inevitable.

And of course even today, the U.S. and China are still supporting Pol Pot. So you see what a devastating blow to the balance of forces and progress Kennedy's assassination was. Again, forget about the secret memos and secret presidential orders and Chomsky's nonsense about the internal record. It is not simply Kennedy as a personality that is at work here; it is Kennedy as a representative of certain forces within capitalism who are coming to recognize an interest in an alliance against a dangerous foe, the ultra-right of capitalism and the ultra-left of socialism. Kennedy was a representative of moderation who held the power to do something about it. And as Castro points out, with the removal of Kennedy the vacuum in civilian authority in Washington had to tip the balance to the ultra-right.

Appendix XI

Notes on the Dynamics of Public Denial in the Assassination

by E. Martin Schotz

The following notes are taken from letters by the author to the committee of correspondents which preceded the April 5th letter. They provide amplification of certain details of the analysis.

Notes on the Dynamics of Public Denial in the Assassination

by E. Martin Schotz

May 3, 1992
To Vincent Salandria:

On the Theory of a Black Star at the Center of Our Culture and Certain Psychological Implications

I imagine that at the moral center of our culture is a black star which absorbs all light which is thrown onto it. If you write something which impinges too closely to the center and send it to someone well-situated in the bureaucracy, you will rarely receive a reply. The existence of this black star is an essential element in the workings of our society; everyone relates to it in one way or another. When an individual accommodates this star, accepts it as morally valid, relinquishes the search for the truth, ceases to struggle against it, this process is reflected as a central moral blindness in the personality of the individual.

On the Psychological Process of Denial by Journalists When Confronted with Salandria's Work

By what psychological process could we conceive of competent journalists seriously investigating the murder of the President and yet denying to themselves and the public the obvious truth which Salandria's work established?

I think the process occurs as an automatic response beyond the awareness of the journalist. That the process goes on beyond the journalist's awareness makes it that much easier for him to engage in it.

Consider the following: A journalist is seriously looking into the President's murder. He starts talking to people and one way or another he turns up your articles [See Salandria's articles in *Liberation* in Appendix III]. He reads them. Now the immediate, inescapable conclusions of reading your articles are that: (1) there is no doubt there was a conspiracy; (2) the Warren Report is fraudulent; (3) the government of the United States is engaged in a criminal conspiracy after the fact to shield the assassins. There is one further conclusion, depending on the point in time this is happening. The journalistic establishment is by now more or less involved in the cover-up depending on how close to the release of the Report we are considering.

Let us limit ourselves to 1, 2, and 3. These are very powerful conclusions, which if accepted, would shatter the journalist's identification with the government. Remember what Fonzi said after that interview with Arlen Specter — that his faith was forever shaken in his government. These conclusions are very disturbing. To accept them is to suffer an intense sense of alienation, something akin to the profound sense of disturbance some people experience when first becoming aware of our government's actual policy toward nuclear weapons and the fallacies of nuclear deterrence. There is the sense that a system which one looked to for security and protection has turned against one. There is a sense of betrayal and danger, which is very painful. The more adult the person, the more formed the person's identity as contrasted with the typical adolescent, the more identified the person is with the system, the more disturbing will be these three conclusions.

What is the journalist likely to do under the threat of this experience? From psychotherapy we know the phenomenon of the person who has horribly disturbing obsessions, but despite them is able to function. How does the person do this? One of the ways this is accomplished is for the individual to keep the thoughts secret. Just as a dream tends to fade from memory if it is not written down or told to someone, so waking thoughts of a terrible nature which are not shared have only a partially conscious quality. Talking about such thoughts or writing them down stabilizes them by giving them existence beyond the internal psychology of the person. Once this occurs they cannot be so easily erased or forgotten.

So the journalist, having read your articles, is likely not to talk to anyone about them. If the journalist can keep from doing that, the experience which the articles created initially with time will begin to fade like a dream. The exact arguments and details will become blurred. Your proof that there was a conspiracy will be transmuted into your "theory" that there was a conspiracy — one theory among many competing theories.

What goes for not talking about your articles with anyone also applies to not writing about your articles. Having gone through the process of eliminating the very troubling experience with which your articles had threatened the journalist, there is now an understandable automatic tendency to avoid these articles when one sits down to write about the case. On a conscious level the journalist may just be thinking your articles were not that important: "There's nothing that different about Salandria's articles, so no need to quote them." On an unconscious level the mere thought of your articles sets off some dysphoric response which is likely to set in motion an avoidance reaction.

The journalist may well believe that there was a conspiracy. He may be very sympathetic to the critics and even to you. But he will only *believe* that there was a conspiracy; he will have avoided *knowing* that there was a conspiracy. And in that transmutation lies the transformation of a person who was on the verge of investigating the truth of the murder into an unwitting part of the cover-up.

What is true of the journalist holds true for the journalist's audience. They do not want a reporter who knows there was a conspiracy and explains it to them. Rather, the typical citizen is much more content to have a journalist who believes there was a conspiracy, but at the same time indicates there is doubt, room for debate, and thus one is not in a position to draw any firm conclusions and there is nothing to be done.

The "powers that be" can count on the fact that the more important the person or institution which commits a crime and the more serious the crime in regard to the system, the more central will be the threat of knowledge of the truth to the ordinary citizen, the more the psychological interest in uncertainty and confusion.

May 14, 1992
To Vincent Salandria:

The Battle of Belief Against Knowledge in the Struggle Over Oliver Stone's Film, JFK

Oliver Stone's *JFK* is a truly great film, and yet it is important to examine what happened to Stone in the period prior to its release and subsequently.

Prior to the film's release, indeed prior to even the final editing of the film, Stone was subjected to an unprecedented barrage of criticism in the media. He was called crazy and a drunk. The pressure was intense and Stone turned for advice to Frank Mankiewicz, an old Kennedy ally.

The advice apparently was that Stone should not insist that his film was the truth (which he knew it was), but that he should simply present it as his *interpretation*. Thus, with the release of the film Stone began referring to the film as his "myth." The instant he did that, the criticism was muted. He was invited to address Congress and call for the release of more information. Once again he became acceptable.

Stone knows this movie is not myth. It is a brilliant synthesis of twenty-five years of critical work by Garrison and independent citizens. It is completely factual except for the obviously created and condensed scenes. Beyond that, to call on the government to provide further information is to logically contradict the film's central thesis that the government was behind it. So Stone wound up being turned against his own film.

There is a very important lesson in this. There is no mystery in the JFK assassination today. And to pretend otherwise is to join the cover-up, something Stone has done in calling for the release of more information and referring to his film as "myth."

Stone was threatened with being completely blackballed by the media and left with no one to talk to. So he compromised. He traded his knowledge of the truth for belief and access.

What we have here is the way "the black star" organizes and perpetuates its tyranny of confusion, by threatening people with isolation and being labeled insane if they aren't willing to compromise.

March 25, 1993
To Vincent Salandria:

With Regard to Salandria's Correspondence with Chomsky

I think it may be helpful to examine carefully Chomsky's reply to you, taking him at his word.

In his letter to you he begins by saying he has "no opinion" on who killed JFK. He goes on to say his only interest is in whether there might have been a motive for a high level government conspiracy, and in attempting to answer this he examines the "record" seeking any talk of killing the President or any evidence that Kennedy might have differed from his high level advisors. He focuses on Vietnam as the center piece of the conspiracy theories, etc. He finds no evidence and finds it hard to imagine that he is reading a sanitized record, including conspiracy by "physicists and the medical profession." Then he ends up willing to accept the "low-level CIA conspiracy" theory as possible but of no consequence.

He has no opinion on who killed the President? No opinion? No opinion whatsoever? No opinion on whether Lee Harvey Oswald killed him? No opinion on whether the Warren investigation was a totally fraudulent process and whether the government of the United States and the media are in essence accessories after the fact in the murder of a President? Only someone profoundly uninterested in the murder of the President could honestly have no opinion on all this. So we must start off with that. At a very fundamental level Chomsky is not interested in this case.

Because he is uninterested in the case, he doesn't know the facts of the case. And Chomsky doesn't want to know, because Marcus spent hours with him years ago. We know that now because of the notes Marcus has in *Addendum B* and the letters they exchanged.

So Chomsky is conveniently ignorant of the physical evidence and passes over all this and wants to ask whether the CIA could have had a motive. The correct question is not whether there was a motive but what was the motive. Chomsky then goes to the record on Vietnam.

The Vietnam Diversion

It is significant that he focuses on Vietnam. He focuses on Vietnam because that is where Oliver Stone and our media now focus, a media which has all along been cooperating in the cover-up.

Why Vietnam? By focusing the assassination around Vietnam, one is permitted to argue, "We Americans really do have a wonderful country which has somehow gotten off track. Our democracy has been deformed by our military industrial complex as President Eisenhower warned, and it went out of control and killed a President and led us into Vietnam. And we the people have to get it back." Thus, the Vietnam War, Eisenhower's "military industrial complex," and the murder of JFK are torn out of the entire fabric of American foreign policy. The murder of Kennedy, the military industrial complex, and Vietnam are aberrations which are set against American democracy, as opposed to being seen as part and parcel of democracy as it is practiced in this country.

This is what Chomsky is reacting to. Fundamentally uninterested in the case, Chomsky reacts to Oliver Stone and the media hype. And understanding it from that point of view, you can see that wittingly or unwittingly Chomsky doesn't look at the murder of Kennedy but at an interpretation the public is being given of the murder, which is a subtle level of cover-up and distortion engendered by ideological bias.

The Centrality of Kennedy's Cuban Policy to the Motivation for the Assassination

If you want a central motivation for the assassination, you have to look at Kennedy's relations with Cuba and his rapprochement with Khrushchev. I think the Cuban Missile Crisis is the absolute center out of which the plot to kill Kennedy came.

As far as Chomsky not being able to find Kennedy fighting with top advisors, of course you, as an ardent "Chomskyist," are deluging him with public accounts from the time of the fight that was taking place. If Chomsky isn't looking at a sanitized record, where are the notes of the meeting where Dulles and his colleagues or the Joint Chiefs discussed the firing of Allen Dulles? Where are the records of their reactions to the test ban treaty, McCloy-Zorin, or the arms embargo Kennedy imposed on the Dominican Republic? Where are the minutes of the meeting at which our government leaders discussed the Katzenbach memoranda to Moyers and Warren? But most of all where are the notes of the meetings where Dulles and the Joint Chiefs and Angleton *et al.* reacted to the Cuban Missile Crisis, because here is where Kennedy stumbled into something and violated standard operating procedure for American foreign policy.

Standard U.S. operating procedure *vis-á-vis* the Third World is "we do what we want." And here you have Kennedy *negotiating* the withdrawal of missiles on a *quid pro quo* basis. Senator Stuart Symington, a former Air Force Secretary, was complaining on the Senate floor after the Bay of Pigs that the military was questioning the loyalty of the President in secret sessions before congressmen. Can you imagine what they were saying to themselves after the Cuban Missile Crisis?

Cuba has had the temerity to insist on its sovereignty. And this ninety miles off our shore. This is unheard of as far as the United States is concerned. This was the basis of the Cold War, that the Soviets throughout their history had loomed as a counterweight to the U.S. in the Third World. Indeed, once China started cooperating with us in the Third World we had no problem with them. But Cuba asserts for itself a right to send troops into Angola, a right to nuclear weapons just like us. And Kennedy's embargo of Cuba was an absolutely unjustifiable act, a gross violation of Cuban national sovereignty, typical of the U.S. when it comes to the rights of others. Kennedy's act was the height of irresponsibility, bringing us to the brink of using nuclear weapons. And he did this because the Cubans had the idea that they had the same international rights which we do.

But in the middle of this horror for which JFK was responsible, something totally unprecedented happened. He started dealing with Khrushchev. Behind the facade of "diktat" Kennedy *negotiated* the withdrawal of those missiles. And this was an act of treason to men like Allen Dulles and James Angleton or in this day and age an Elliot Abrams or Jeanne Kirkpatrick. This was a total violation of the U.S. policy of domination. With this act Kennedy demonstrated a weakness as far as people like Dulles were concerned, which made him unreliable and unacceptable. Not that Kennedy's actions were simply generated by moral concerns, but when it came down to it, there was a limit to the risk of nuclear annihilation that he was willing to run and in the process he had wound up negotiating with the Soviets.

This is not my personal view. This is the view of the two people in the world who were in the best positions to know, Fidel Castro and Nikita Khrushchev. Look at Khrushchev's letter after the Cuban Missile Crisis and the Castro speech on the assassination. You will see that the central distinction that Castro draws between the Kennedy people and the forces that were opposing them is that Kennedy had shown himself to be someone with whom the Cubans could deal. Let's not forget that William Attwood, as Kennedy's emissary, was secretly negotiating the recognition of Cuba in the U.N. at the time of the assassination.

This is very significant, because if the United States could have co-existed peacefully with Cuba, it could have done so with

Popular Unity in Chile, with Maurice Bishop, with Juan Bosch in the Dominican Republic. It could have peacefully co-existed with the Sandinista government in Nicaragua. Think about this and I think you will see what the implications were for a very different Latin and South America. But the United States has not been willing to peacefully co-exist with Cuba and is still not. And thirty years ago Dulles et al. were not about to live with a President who might be drifting in that direction, and we still don't have a President who is willing to speak of moving in that direction.

Thirty years later we have still not recognized Cuba and are violating international law by attempting to sow political chaos with our economic blockade. What seems so ironic is that one of Chomsky's great contributions is his withering documentation of the systematic and undeviating pattern of terror in U.S. foreign policy which is aimed at usurping rights of Third World people by any and all means necessary, and of the role of the U.S. media in selling this to the American people as a great humanitarian and democratic crusade.

Appendix XII

Two Dialogues

by E. Martin Schotz

The following are two dialogues which appeared in a closet drama, How Ronald Reagan Finally Saved the World, or As You Like It, So Long as You Save the World *(1984). The purpose of the dialogues was to investigate the logic of war and the logic of peace.*

Kennedy-Dulles Dialogue in Heaven: The Logic of War

by E. Martin Schotz

[The lights come up slowly; the location is the Colored House, Heaven. John Kennedy is sitting in a rocker reading a newspaper. Allen Dulles in panama hat and bermuda shorts enters suitcase in hand.]

DULLES: [friendly] Well, hello Jack.

KENNEDY: [jumps to his feet] You! You dare speak to me?

DULLES: Why Jack, what's the matter?

KENNEDY: Forget the pretense, do you think I don't know it was you who was behind my assassination?

DULLES: Oh, it's that, is it. Taking it personally, are you?

KENNEDY: You're incredible. Do you expect me to greet my assassin with open arms?

DULLES: Now hold on, Jack. It is one thing to say that I was behind your assassination. It's another thing to call me your assassin.

KENNEDY: And what would you call you?

DULLES: That's not the point, Jack. It's true I was behind your assassination, but who do you think was behind me?

KENNEDY: Who?

DULLES: Why the people, Jack, the American People.

KENNEDY: The *People*??

DULLES: Yes, and if the whole truth be told, who do you think was behind them?

KENNEDY: Tell me.

DULLES: You, Jack, none other than you.

KENNEDY: [laughs] You have nerve, Dulles. Isn't it strange that somehow I don't remember being in on the arrangements.

DULLES: No, it's not strange at all. It often happens that way.

KENNEDY: Well, since I missed my own participation, maybe you would like to let me in on it.

DULLES: Well, you see, as far as I'm concerned, you are as much to blame as anyone, if we want to start blaming people. Look here, you don't think you were killed out of any personal motive. We were all fond of you, I hope you realize that. It was simply a matter of politics. Yours versus the people's.

KENNEDY: The people's? Why, the people loved me.

DULLES: Yes, they loved you, Jack. But did they love your policies? You don't think there could have been a successful assassination without the assistance of the people? You don't think we could have returned America to her true Cold War traditions, if the people had really been in support of what you were doing. After all, we live in a democracy, Jack.

KENNEDY: A democracy you assaulted.

DULLES: A democracy I assaulted? Not at all, Jack. It was a democracy you assaulted. After all, did you not run on a platform of rebuilding our defenses and of a hard line against the Soviets and Cubans? Yes, it was on that basis that the people elected you. And what did you do with our public's trust? You *changed your mind.* Or to be more precise, you let the communists change your mind. [Now in an ironic tone] "To hell with Dulles, to hell with the CIA, to hell with those who had slaved for years to protect our system. To hell with what the people thought they were electing. I, Jack Kennedy, numero uno, I know what's best for them."

KENNEDY: And suppose I did know best?

DULLES: So what if you did, Jack. That's how the communists in Russia are always justifying what they do. They know what's best for *the people.* No, Jack, that's not our way. The people have the right to make mistakes and correct them.

KENNEDY: And suppose that mistake is blowing themselves and the rest of the world up. Is it necessary that *the people* have that right too?

DULLES: Yes, if they want it. Strange as it may seem, if we deprive them of that right, what will be the difference between us and the communists? Once you give up the principle that the people are leading the country, and let an elite with the power to manipulate the media lead the people, well, where will it end?

KENNEDY: Oh, I see, shooting the President is OK, but manipulating the media isn't.

DULLES: It's not a matter of being OK. None of us wanted to do what we had to do. I know it's hard not to get carried away by the way it happened. But try to look at it this way. Suppose you had had a stroke in Dealey Plaza that afternoon. Would the history of the United States really have been any different? We didn't take over the government, we just shot *you*. And the people realized that on the personal level it was a tragedy, but on the political level no serious damage had been done to our democracy and they supported our return to tradition. Even your family and advisers understood once it happened and helped us.

KENNEDY: *The people*, they didn't even understand my policies. How could they have fought your efforts to erase what I was doing?

DULLES: Precisely. And you had no business following policies that others didn't understand and support.

KENNEDY: This is ridiculous.

DULLES: You see, Jack, this was precisely the problem. This was the reason you had become a communist agent, Jack. Our system had ceased to make sense to you. You had stopped believing in our way.

KENNEDY: Do you mean you actually believe that I was a communist agent?

DULLES: I don't believe it. I know it. If and when the people decide they want peace with the Russians we will have it, but not before. That is the heart of our system, the free marketplace of ideas.

KENNEDY: Look Allen, I understand what you are *trying* to say but do you *realize* what this means? What you are saying is that if you're not free to commit suicide, you're not free.

DULLES: That fortunately or unfortunately, Jack, is the logic of our system, and only the people have the right to change the system. Freedom for us is liberty, free will, the absence of restraint. That is the system you took an oath to uphold, and that is the system that you betrayed.

KENNEDY: But what about the freedom that comes out of recognizing that something must be done? The freedom that is the product of knowledge which the people don't have and must be helped to see.

DULLES: That is the real difference between the communists and us, Jack. We believe that people are naturally born free and that no one has the right to restrain that natural God-given freedom. It is the communists who believe that without education, health care, a job, or what have you, you can't be free, that people have to be [sarcastic] *raised up so they can appreciate freedom.*

KENNEDY: In that respect do you think that their idea is so wrong?

DULLES: To tell you the truth, I don't know. But it's not for me to decide. I am simply a servant of our people.

KENNEDY: Allen, listen, I see what you are saying. Perhaps I did act rather rashly with you. I'm really sorry I didn't appreciate you more.

DULLES: [Putting his arm around Kennedy to comfort him.] It's all right, Jack. I understand. You were young and headstrong. It was natural for you to make such a mistake. Those Mickey Mouse civics classes we are all brought up on, which teach us the President is so important.

[KENNEDY and DULLES chuckle.]

KENNEDY: My family must have given you a lot of trouble?

DULLES: Not really.

KENNEDY: Not even Bobby?

DULLES: No, he took it better than I expected. Of course, Nick Katzenbach was a big help.

KENNEDY: [Embracing DULLES and then holding him at arm's length, smiling and looking DULLES straight in the eyes.] You forgive me . . . all the trouble I caused you, . . . the family, . . . everyone.

DULLES: Of course. [Dulles affectionately musses KENNEDY'S hair. They hug each other with vigor.]

Einstein-Sonrobe Dialogue: A Search for the Logic of Peace and the Unified Field Theory

by E. Martin Schotz

[Enter KING MALCOLM W.E.B. ALI SONROBE, a tall black man dressed as Othello with a golden cape. Despite his dress SONROBE's movement and manner of expression are unaffected, warm, and direct. He leans over EINSTEIN.]

EINSTEIN: My God, it is you.

SONROBE: Albert, how good to see you. How are you? [shaking EINSTEIN's hand with both of his.] It is a pleasure to be able to thank you in person for your public statements in my behalf.

EINSTEIN: Oh please, King, think nothing of it, but now I must ask your help. Is it true that you are the Greatest?

SONROBE: Albert, you know many people think that; but I fear that in doing so, they are mistaking me for the folk from which I have sprung.

EINSTEIN: I understand, for people make the same mistake with me. But nevertheless, the people judge you their greatest and that is good enough for me. Tell me, what is the plan that you use to win all your fights?

SONROBE: [laughing] It's quite an exaggeration to say I win *all* my fights. And as for a plan, Albert? Listen, if your car breaks down on the road, do you want a mechanic coming out with a plan or do you want him coming out with his tools? You need a lot more than plans to change things in this world. You've got to get your tools together, go to the scene of the trouble, analyze the problem on the spot, and settle things then and there.

EINSTEIN: Please, King, don't josh with me at such an important moment. I am trying to a find the law which will reveal the way everything in the universe is united and in so doing explain the motion of all bodies.

SONROBE: [laughs again] What sort of bodies do you have in mind, Albert?

EINSTEIN: All bodies.

SONROBE: What makes you think that all bodies obey one law? For as anyone can see, there are different types of bodies, with different types of motion, and these different types are moved by different kinds of forces.

EINSTEIN: No, you don't understand. I am not interested in how things appear. I am interested in the underlying motion of which everything else is a reflection.

SONROBE: No, Albert. It is you who don't understand. If you want to truly understand the motion of bodies you must understand overarching motions as well as underlying ones.

EINSTEIN: What is an overarching motion?

SONROBE: An overarching motion is a motion which overarches and dominates a motion which underlies.

EINSTEIN: That doesn't help me understand it, for you are simply defining one in terms of the other.

SONROBE: It is not I who is doing this but the motions themselves.

EINSTEIN: Well, then give me an example of an underlying motion and its overarching relative.

SONROBE: Take, for example, plants and animals. As a rule, which is to say almost always, animals run around and eat plants. Thus the law of the motion and development of animals stands in overarching relation to the law of motion and development of plants.

EINSTEIN: But still, King, are not these two forms of being, plants and animals, based on the same underlying laws?

SONROBE: Well, it is true that what underlies plants must also underlie animals. But still the motion of animals is guided by principles that are unknown to plants in themselves.

EINSTEIN: For example?

SONROBE: Animals struggle to survive and in this struggle have the capacity of self locomotion. Plants struggle to survive but their motion is limited to growing up. Thus animals can move themselves in relation to their natural conditions. They can go after what they want. They can adapt to nature in ways that are unknown to plants.

EINSTEIN: I am seeking the law which unifies all the forces in the universe.

SONROBE: I am seeking not only the laws of such a universe but that universe itself. I am convinced that such a universe must depend on Justice.

EINSTEIN: And what do you mean by Justice?

SONROBE: The people in command of their labor and enjoying together its fruits.

EINSTEIN: This is interesting, but we are drifting far afield from the question which I started out asking you. Would you say that my search for a unified field theory, my search for an understanding of the unity between gravity and the other forces of nature, that this search is foolish?

SONROBE: Well, that depends. What is your notion of gravity?

EINSTEIN: It is not my notion. It is everyone's notion. Gravity is the force of attraction between bodies. But you see I have discovered that what Newton and others thought of as an attractive force acting between bodies can just as properly be conceived of as the resistance of bodies to being accelerated.

SONROBE: In other words, from one point of view the force with which bodies are attracted to each other is from another point of view their resistance to a change in their form of action.

EINSTEIN: Hmm . . . resistance to a change in their form of motion . . . I guess you could say that.

SONROBE: Fine, go on.

EINSTEIN: Well, I am simply asking to understand the law in the universe which will explain the link between gravity and the other forces of nature.

SONROBE: But Albert, which gravity do you have in mind?

EINSTEIN: What do you mean "which gravity"? Gravity is a force which is the same throughout nature and depends only on the inertial mass of the body.

SONROBE: Here, Albert, I think you are forgetting something.

EINSTEIN: What do you mean?

SONROBE: We have agreed that gravity is the force with which bodies attract one another or the resistance they demonstrate to a change in their form of motion. I have no problem with this. But as we have already established, there are many different forms of motion in which matter exists, and as a result there are many different forms of resistance and many different forms of attraction. Thus there is not one gravity but many.

EINSTEIN: Huh . . . different forms of motion mean different gravities. Perhaps I need to understand better what you mean by a form of motion.

SONROBE: Well, for instance, let us take mechanics. Mechanics concerns itself with the movement of bodies from one place to another. Now some bodies are inanimate and so are only moved from outside while other move themselves and are called "alive."

EINSTEIN: Yes.

SONROBE: Well the problem of the displacement of inanimate bodies in space is not the same as the displacement of animate bodies in space.

SONROBE: Moving an opponent with a punch is a lot different from moving a punching bag.

EINSTEIN: OK, so we must differentiate between those bodies which do and do not move themselves.

SONROBE: Yes, and we must begin differentiating the variety of ways in which self-moving bodies move. For example, I have in mind the different ways plants animals and humans attract and are attracted or resist a change in their form of motion.

EINSTEIN: How would you differentiate animal motion from human motion?

SONROBE: With the emergence of human motion life ceases to be determined.

EINSTEIN: You mean you believe life depends on chance, that God plays dice with the universe?

SONROBE: [laughs] No, I don't believe that life hinges on chance. Of course God plays dice at times, but not as a rule with the universe. We all know it's mankind who is doing that at the moment.

EINSTEIN: All right, but if you do not believe life is a matter of chance then you must grant me that it is determined.

SONROBE: Well, if I grant you that life is determined, will you grant me that what is determining life is alive?

EINSTEIN: What do you mean "what is determining life is alive"?

SONROBE: I mean that not only is history determined, but determinism is historical, that new forces are growing up in our world constantly, that new overarching relations are forever emerging, and that these new relations subdue and negate the old ones.

EINSTEIN: Well, OK, I see no harm in believing that, but you said before that life had ceased to be determined.

SONROBE: That I did, for humans are those beings who, laboring on nature, transform her from something standing in opposition to them into something for them. We, humans, humanize nature and in the process create our own nature, rather than leaving it to some outside determining force.

EINSTEIN: So the overarching law of human motion is that human beings make themselves, that they are their own cause and are not determined from outside.

SONROBE: Not determined except for the historical limitations of any particular period.

EINSTEIN: So any person's particular historical period determines what he or she is free to cause.

SONROBE: Precisely.

EINSTEIN: At the moment I'm afraid that our historical limitations include the real possibility that mankind may not have a future.

SONROBE: Yes. It's a terrible irony.

EINSTEIN: What I've helped humans create! How stupid is this race to nuclear weaponry!

SONROBE: Stupid, Albert? No. Criminal, crazy, absurd, yes. But stupid, no.

EINSTEIN: You don't think it is stupid that mankind, faced with a choice of peace or nothing, wouldn't choose peace?

SONROBE: No, not at all, for peace is not something that can simply be chosen. It must be built, for it represents a whole change in our form of motion, and there is much resistance to it.

EINSTEIN: But tell me, King, if our future is not in the hands of chance and is not determined, what will determine it?

SONROBE: The question is not *what* will determine our future but *who* will determine it. Will our people continue to move with their traditional inertia or will they take the lead, and in so doing change themselves into a new force of attraction, a new human historical gravity worthy of its possibilities?

EINSTEIN: Do you see evidence of this new human gravity which can insure the future?

SONROBE: Yes, I see it everywhere in the people's movements. America doesn't know it yet but the people of Africa, Asia, and Latin America are on the move.

EINSTEIN: So you think human beings can build a form of gravity which can overarch the danger inherent in my formula, $E = mc^2$, the formula which reveals that the energy of the atom equals its mass times the speed of light squared?

SONROBE: Yes.

EINSTEIN: If only human energy could express itself as simply.

SONROBE: Well, it's not as simple but I do have a formula for what I've been saying.

EINSTEIN: Yes?

SONROBE: Yes, I call it the law of the masses energy: "When an idea seizes the masses it becomes a material force."

[EINSTEIN bursts into laughter]

SONROBE: What are you laughing about Albert?

[EINSTEIN and SONROBE are both laughing]

EINSTEIN: So you have no plan for your fights, eh? What about $E = mc^2$? That's a great plan for our fights. But of course mankind will need all its tools — its arts, its sciences, its religions, if it is to survive.

SONROBE: Yes!

EINSTEIN: How funny, and you think there is no guiding hand here? But now I see a problem. For before you said that peace depends on justice. But for me there must be peace or there will be no justice. For today the law of the atomic bomb stands before mankind, dominating everything.

SONROBE: And what is that law?

EINSTEIN: Without peace there will be no life, and without life there is no justice.

SONROBE: Perhaps that is your unified field theory, Albert. For what you are saying is that as we human beings look into the atom through human history we now see staring back at us the words: *As you do unto others, so will be done unto you.*

EINSTEIN: Not a bad formula, the human energy for peace as the masses in possession of the fruits of their labor, including Christ's gospel.

SONROBE: [smiling] I prefer to think of the human energy for peace as the struggle of masses for possession of the fruits of their labor, including Christ's gospel.

EINSTEIN: Yes.

SONROBE: You know, Albert, what you've just said has got me to thinking. Do you think it makes sense for me to continue going around killing Desdemonas?

EINSTEIN: Why not? Wasn't it you yourself who argued that however misguided your wrath, it was not a crime of passion but an assertion of the just wrath of one who has been betrayed?

SONROBE: It's true I said that. But times change and so must our plays. I am not sure we can afford today any misguided wrath, lest we purchase an untellable tragedy. No, Albert, today I want to arouse people with a different vision, to stir them up and help them look beyond Iago and Desdemona. I want them to see the farce of military superiority. I have a hunger to exchange this King's robe for simpler garb. But it's getting late and I must be off.

EINSTEIN: Can you not stay a bit longer?

SONROBE: I wish I could, but it's not possible. [SONROBE embraces him, and then takes his leave.]

Appendix XIII

With Hegemony and Intervention, There Can Be No Peace or Social Development

by Fidel Castro

The following remarks are from a speech at the final session of the United Nations Summit on Social Development, March, 1995. The text appeared in Granma International, *March 22, 1995, p. 3.*

With Hegemony and Intervention, There Can Be No Peace or Social Development

by Fidel Castro

Mr. President:
Your Excellencies:

"Life is built on a dream, and dreams are dreams," as Calderon de la Barca, the famous Spanish playwright, said some centuries ago.

Independent of the noble intentions of all those present, in a world where the rich get steadily richer and the poor get steadily poorer; where some countries receive lower and lower prices for their raw materials and basic products and others sell their manufactured items at increasingly higher prices; where the less fortunate countries' external debt is incessantly growing and has already reached the incredible figure of 1.5 trillion dollars; where interest rates rise arbitrarily from day to day; where the poorest areas have explosive population growth rates; where there is an increasing capital flight from the poor countries to the rich ones; where the brain drain constantly steals skills from where they are most needed; where women, indigenous peoples, black, and other ethnic groups suffer discrimination; and where chaos and anarchy rule under the blind and savage laws of the market, there can be no social development.

Where there is a lack of humanity, there can be no human rights. Where selfishness reigns, solidarity cannot exist. Where consumer societies and waste are established as models for a population already in excess of 5.7 billion human beings, environmental conservation and unpolluted and sustainable natural resources are impossibilities, as is viable social development.

Where the build-up of the arms race persists in spite of the end of the Cold War; where not one cent of what was previously squandered on arms has been dedicated to human progress; where military blocs are irrationally extended; where sophisticated arms are still being constructed and perfected, there can be no social development.

With hegemony and interventions of all types and under any pretext, which only happen in small countries and the Third World, without any respect for the sacrosanct right of every country to full independence and equality in international relations, there can be no peace or social development. This is a falsehood, a total deception.

Neoliberalism, the fashionable doctrine imposed on today's world, ruthlessly sacrifices the provision of health, education, culture, sports, social security, affordable housing, drinking water, and other basic populational needs in underdeveloped countries.

The fact that people live in poverty in the industrialized countries is simply a disgrace. The fact that unemployment cannot be reduced and that it actually grows in line with technological advances is proof of the irrationality of the dominant system. The unrestrained growth of drugs, xenophobia, and violence demonstrates its moral decadence.

Cuba, criminally blockaded because it does not share the ideas of its powerful neighbor to the north, and which lost 70 percent of its imported goods with the disappearance of the socialist camp and the Soviet Union, has not closed a single school, hospital, senior citizen's home, or day care center. In spite of being a poor country, we have the highest per capita totals of teachers, doctors, art teachers, and physical educational instructors in the world. Our infant mortality rate stands at under ten per 1000 live births. There is no illiteracy, and the life expectancy average is 75 years.

We have lived through an experience. We can talk about it. What those of us present here desire is possible, but more than promises, resolutions, and declarations are needed: we need the political will and we need justice, not only within individual countries, but among all countries. The world's wealth has to be better distributed among nations, and within nations, and genuine solidarity among the peoples of the world has to be established; only then can today's dreams become the realities of tomorrow.

Thank you very much.

References

Attwood, William. *The Reds and the Blacks: A Personal Adventure.* New York: Harper and Row, 1967.

Chang, Laurence and Peter Kornbluh, eds., *The Cuban Missile Crisis, 1962: A National Security Archive Documents Reader.* New York: The New Press, 1992.

Cook, Fred J. *Maverick, Fifty Years of Investigative Reporting.* New York: G.P. Putnam's Sons, 1984.

Cortàzar, Julio. *62 Model Kit.* New York: Pantheon Books, 1972.

Cousins, Norman. *The Improbable Triumvirate: John F. Kennedy, Pope John, Nikita Khrushchev.* New York: W.W. Norton, 1972.

Document Addendum to the Warren Report. El Segundo California: Sightest Publications, 1968.

Epstein, Edward J. *Inquest: The Warren Commission and the Establishment of Truth.* New York: Viking Press, 1966.

FBI Supplemental Report to the Warren Commission, January 13, 1964.

Fonzi, Gaeton. *The Last Investigation.* New York: Thunder's Mouth Press, 1993.

Galbraith, John Kenneth. *The Culture of Contentment.* New York: Houghton Mifflin, 1992.

Gorbachev, Mikhail. *Perestroika: New Thinking for Our Country and the World.* New York: Harper and Row, 1987.

Hearings Before the President's Commission on the Assassination of President Kennedy. 26 volumes. Washington, D.C.: United States Printing Office, 1964.

Hearings Before the Select Committee on Assassinations of the United States House of Representatives, 95 Congress, 2nd Session. Washington, D.C.: United State Printing Office.

Hilsman, Roger. *To Move A Nation.* Garden City, New York: Doubleday, 1964.

Kennan, George F. *The Nuclear Delusion: Soviet-American Relations in the Atomic Age.* New York: Pantheon Books, 1982.

Levine, Isaac Don. *The Mind of the Assassin.* New York: Farrar, Straus and Cudahy, 1959.

Mailer, Norman. *Oswald's Tale.* New York: Ballantine Books, 1996.

Mandela, Nelson. *Long Walk to Freedom.* Boston: Little, Brown, 1994.

Marcus, Raymond. *Addendum B: Addendum to the HSCA, The Zapruder Film, and the Single Bullet Theory.* Self-published, 1995. [For copies of this book, contact the author at 1224 Hi Point Street, Los Angeles, California 90035.]

Marcus, Raymond. *The Bastard Bullet.* Self-published, 1966. [For copies of this book, contact the author at 1224 Hi Point Street, Los Angeles, California 90035.]

Meagher, Sylvia. *Accessories After the Fact: The Warren Commission, the Authorities, and the Report.* New York: Bobbs-Merrill, 1967.

Melanson, Philip H. *Spy Saga: Lee Harvey Oswald and U.S. Intelligence.* New York: Praeger, 1990.

McCullough, David. *Truman*, New York: Simon and Schuster, 1982.

Morrissey, Michael. *Looking for the Enemy.* Self-published, 1993. [For copies of this book, contact the author at Am Ruesteberg 6, 34266 Niestetal, Germany.]

Orwell, George. *1984.* New York: Penguin Books, 1950.

Posner, Gerald. *Case Closed: Lee Harvey Oswald and the Assassination of JFK.* Garden City, New York: Doubleday, 1993.

Reeves, Richard. *President Kennedy: Profile of Power.* New York: Simon and Schuster, 1993.

Report of the President's Commission on the Assassination of President Kennedy. Washington, D.C.: United States Printing Office, 1964.

Salinger, Pierre. *With Kennedy*. New York: Doubleday, 1966.

Scott, Peter Dale. *The Dallas Conspiracy*. Unpublished manuscript, 1970.

Scott, Peter Dale. *Deep Politics and the Death of JFK*. Berkeley: University of California Press, 1993.

Stone, I.F. *In a Time of Torment: Our Most Distinguished Independent Journalist on the most Urgent Issues and Key Personalities of our Time: LBJ, the War in Vietnam, Fulbright, the Negro Revolution, the Kennedys, Malcolm X, the Left, Right, and Where Do We Go from Here.* New York: Random House, 1967.

Strober, Gerald S. and Deborah H. *"Let Us Begin Anew": An Oral History of the Kennedy Presidency.* New York: HarperCollins, 1993.

Weisberg, Harold. *Oswald in New Orleans: Case for Conspiracy with the CIA*. New York: Canyon Books, 1967.

White, Theodore H. *The Making of the President 1964.* New York: Atheneum, 1965.

Index